Kitchen & Bath Business Management

Financials ◆ Personnel ◆ Operations

Hank Darlington
With Ellen Cheever, CMKBD, ASID

NKBA
The Finest Professionals in the Kitchen & Bath Industry
National Kitchen & Bath Association℠

Professional Resource Library

About The National Kitchen & Bath Association

As the only non-profit trade association dedicated exclusively to the kitchen and bath industry, the National Kitchen & Bath Association (NKBA) is the leading source of information and education for all professionals in the field.

NKBA's mission is to enhance member success and excellence by promoting professionalism and ethical business practices, and by providing leadership and direction for the kitchen and bath industry.

A non-profit trade association with more than 25,000 members in North America and overseas, it has provided valuable resources for industry professionals for more than forty years. Its members are the finest professionals in the kitchen and bath industry.

NKBA has pioneered innovative industry research, developed effective business management tools, and set groundbreaking standards for safe, functional and comfortable design of kitchens and baths.

NKBA provides a unique, one-stop resource for professional reference materials, seminars and workshops, distance learning opportunities, marketing assistance, design competitions, consumer referrals, job and internship opportunities and opportunities for volunteer leadership activities.

Recognized as the kitchen and bath industry's education and information leader, NKBA provides development opportunities and continuing education for all levels of professionals. More than 100 courses, as well as a certification program with three internationally recognized levels, help kitchen and bath professionals raise the bar for excellence.

For students entering the industry, NKBA offers Supported and Endorsed Programs, which provide NKBA-approved curriculum at more than 47 learning institutions throughout North America.

NKBA helps members and other industry professionals stay on the cutting-edge of an ever-changing field through the Association's Kitchen/Bath Industry Show, one of the largest trade shows in the country.

NKBA offers membership in four different categories: Industry, Associate, Student and Honorary. Industry memberships are broken into eleven different industry segments. For more information, visit NKBA at www.nkba.org.

THANK YOU TO OUR SPONSORS

The National Kitchen & Bath Association recognizes with gratitude the following companies who generously helped to fund the creation of this industry resource.

PATRONS

www.americanwoodmark.com

www.kohler.com

BENEFACTORS

www.monogram.com

www.subzero.com

www.wolfappliance.com

CONTRIBUTOR

www.groheamerica.com

SUPPORTERS

www.nyloft.net

www.showhouse.moen.com

TOTO®

www.totousa.com

DONORS

Rev-A-Shelf | **Viking Range Corp.** | **Whirlpool Corp.**

This book is intended for professional use by residential kitchen and bath designers. The procedures and advice herein have been shown to be appropriate for the applications described; however, no warranty (expressed or implied) is intended or given. Moreover, the user of this book is cautioned to be familiar with and to adhere to all manufacturers' planning, installation and use/care instructions. In addition, the user is urged to become familiar with and adhere to all applicable local, state and federal building codes, licensing and legislation requirements governing the user's ability to perform all tasks associated with design and installation standards, and to collaborate with licensed practitioners who offer professional services in the technical areas of mechanical, electrical and load bearing design as required for regulatory approval, as well as health and safety regulations.

* Information about this book and other association programs
and publications may be obtained from the
National Kitchen & Bath Association
687 Willow Grove Street, Hackettstown, New Jersey 07840
Phone (800) 843-6522, Fax (908) 852-1695.

* ISBN 1-887127-55-0

* First Edition 2006

Top and bottom photo courtesy of Larry A. Falke Photography—Lake Forest, CA
Special thanks to Room Scapes—Laguna Niguel, CA

* Published on behalf of NKBA by: Fry Communications, Irvine, California

* Peer Reviewers:

Timothy Aden, CMKBD	Jim Krengel, CMKBD
Julia Beamish, Ph.D, CKE	Chris LaSpada, CPA
Leonard V. Casey	Elaine Lockard
Ellen Cheever, CMKBD, ASID	Phyllis Markussen, Ed.D, CKE, CBE
Hank Darlington	Chris J Murphy, CKD, CBD, CKBI
Dee David, CKD, CBD	David Newton, CMKBD
Peggy Deras, CKD, CID	Roberta Null, Ph.D
Kimball Derrick, CKD	Michael J Palkowitsch, CMKBD
Tim DiGuardi	Paul Pankow, CKBI
Kathleen Donohue, CMKBD	Jack Parks
Gretchen L. Edwards, CMKBD	Kathleen R. Parrott, Ph.D, CKE
JoAnn Emmel, Ph.D	Al Pattison,CMKBD
Jerry Germer	Les Petrie, CMKBD
Pietro A. Giorgi, Sr., CMKBD	Becky Sue Rajala, CKD
Tom Giorgi	Betty L. Ravnik, CKD, CBD
Jerome Hankins, CKD	Robert Schaefer
Spencer Hinkle, CKD	Klaudia Spivey, CMKBD
Max Isley, CMKBD	Kelly Stewart, CMKBD
Mark Karas, CMKBD	Tom Trzcinski, CMKBD
Martha Kerr, CMKBD	Stephanie Witt, CMKBD

TABLE OF CONTENTS

Introduction

THE GOAL OF THIS BOOK

It is a career dream for many professionals in the kitchen and bath business to own their own firm. More experienced business owners are on a continual quest to learn how to improve their earnings and performance. To help you reach these goals, this book, "Kitchen & Bath Business Management" has been written by Hank Darlington, Darlington Consulting and Ellen Cheever, CMKBD, ASID, Ellen Cheever & Associates, in collaboration with respected professionals in our industry.

This volume offers you a step-by-step management tool to be used to convert the novice business owner's entrepreneurial ideas into a successful business venture. It also provides many ideas for business improvement for more seasoned business owners and managers.

This book is not intended to take the place of a professional management team: business attorney, accountant, financial planner. Rather, the guidelines and insights within have been gathered and organized with the aim of sharing winning strategies for business management from people recognized as leaders in our field.

THE AUTHORS

The co-authors provide a balanced view of proper guidelines to manage a business.

Hank Darlington has over 40 years of experience as a business owner, professional manager, industry consultant, author and speaker. He founded, owned and managed a multi-branch kitchen and bath showroom on the West Coast for much of his career. Ellen Cheever has 35+ years as a design and marketing consultant in the industry and is recognized as a leading authority.

In addition to Hank and Ellen, the following experienced individuals have made key contributions to the text based on their areas of recognized expertise within the kitchen and bath industry.

* Leonard V. Casey – Strategy Acceleration
* James W. Krengel, CMKBD – Kitchens by Krengel
* Karla Krengel – www.Kitchens.com and Krengel Media
* David H. Newton, CMKBD – David Newton & Associates

In addition to these respected professionals, this volume quotes topical articles from major industry trade publications: *Kitchen & Bath Design News, Kitchen & Bath Business, Qualified Remodeler,* and *Remodeling.* These sources understand our industry.

Hank Darlington, Darlington Consulting

Hank Darlington has been active in the kitchen and bath industry for the majority of his career. Hank's experience stretches from a large wholesale plumbing distributor organization to an upscale, full-service (one-stop shopping) kitchen and bath showroom in Northern California with three locations.

Hank served as past president of the NKBA Northern California Chapter, on NKBA's Board of Directors and was a founding member of the Decorative Plumbing and Hardware Council. Hank was recognized for his industry contributions when he was inducted into the NKBA Hall of Fame in 2004.

As the author of four industry textbooks, Hank continues to contribute by presenting seminars for the National Kitchen & Bath Association, writing monthly articles for two national trade publications and by serving as a consultant to manufacturers, distributors and dealerships.

Ellen Cheever, CMKBD, ASID, Ellen Cheever & Associates

Ellen Cheever is an author and marketing specialist whose practical, yet innovative design solutions and professional writing/teaching helped shape the North American kitchen industry over the past 35 years. When working on residential kitchen projects, she collaborates with noted kitchen specialists throughout the United States, combining her design talents with the product specification expertise and skillful project management of trusted professionals within the client's community. In addition to her residential practice, the firm Ellen Cheever & Associates designs retail showroom spaces, major trade show exhibits and editorial sets.

A 1992 inductee of the National Kitchen & Bath Hall of Fame, Ellen was recognized as the Designer of Distinction for 2002 by the American Society of Interior Designers Pennsylvania East Chapter, and won 1st place honors in the 2004 KWC Kitchen Design Competition.

As the author of more than fifteen books and technical manuals covering the details of kitchen and bathroom planning standards, Ellen continues to write and speak about emerging design trends, ergonomic planning standards and winning business strategies within the kitchen design industry.

Leonard V. Casey, MBA, Strategic Acceleration

Educator, corporate executive, entrepreneur and global leader have all been used to describe Len Casey. After receiving his MBA and teaching at Florida Atlantic University, Len started a twenty-year career with the DuPont Company in 1972. While at DuPont, Len was responsible for such product groups as Teflon/Silverstone, Automotive and Corian. Because of these contributions at DuPont, he was awarded the DuPont Corporate Marketing Excellence award for both the Teflon and Corian businesses.

In the early 1990s, Len and a team of industry leaders purchased a respected upscale cabinet company and, for the next 8 years, he applied his business talent to growing the company into an industry leader. Today, he serves on the boards of several companies, using his experience of over thirty years to advise an array of domestic and international firms and supports a number of non-profit organizations to reach their organizational goals.

James W. Krengel, CMKBD, Kitchens by Krengel

Jim Krengel, CMKBD, began his career in 1966 at Kitchens by Krengel in St. Paul, Minnesota. Today, that design studio is in its third generation of ownership and Jim spends the majority of his time sharing his expertise through a series of professional seminars and via frequent contributions to industry publications.

During Jim's design career, he won numerous design awards, served as the Design Director of Maytag Kitchen Idea Center, and was a consultant to Wilsonart International as well as several other manufacturers. Jim helped form the Minnesota Chapter of NKBA and was National President from 1989-1990. The industry recognized Jim's contribution by inducting him into the NKBA Hall of Fame in 2003.

Jim is the author of two design books: *Kitchens: Lifestyle and Design* and *Bathrooms*. He served on the Advisory Board for Kasmar publications, and in collaboration with this respected book publisher, developed the first bathroom and kitchen CDs, each containing over 250 pages of ideas, articles and portfolios.

David H. Newton, CMKBD, David Newton & Associates

As a kitchen specialist in the kitchen and bath industry since the early 1970s, David Newton, CMKBD, was one of the first to expand into computer-generated programs, and to adopt the Deming Total Quality System to the kitchen and bath business.

David has been a respected training specialist and consultant in the kitchen and bath industry since the early 1980s. He served as the Director of Training for NKBA in the mid-1980s, and then expanded into his own consulting firm in the early 1990s.

As a member of the National Speakers Association and American Society for Training and Development, he is a regular contributor to NKBA's *PROFiles* publication and presents NKBA Professional Development Programs.

Karla Krengel, Kitchens.com and Krengel Media

Karla Krengel is a third generation kitchen and bath industry entrepreneur. She recently started Krengel Media, a publicity firm bridging the gap between kitchen designers and the media.

In addition to her "Internet Connections" column for *Kitchen & Bath Design News* Magazine, Karla is well recognized as the "face" of Kitchens.com, a website design firm begun by her brother Steve Krengel. The company creates websites for our industry as well as provides kitchen and bath design and product information to consumers. Prior to her work with Kitchens.com, Karla spent 9 years in television news, and holds a degree in communications.

Business Committee

A committee of seasoned Certified Kitchen and Bath Designers, as well as professionals with remodeling firms, set the table of contents, recommended the targeted reader profile, and reviewed the work of the authors.

The Business Committee included:

- Kimball Derrick, CKD, The Kitchen Design Studio

- Pietro Giorgi, Sr., CMKBD, Giorgi Kitchens & Designs

- Les Petrie, CMKBD, Mother Hubbard's Kitchens

- Kelly Stewart, CMKBD, Kitchens by Deane

- Tom Trzcinski, CMKBD, Kitchen & Bath Concepts

- Stephanie Witt, CMKBD, Kitchens by Stephanie

A PROFILE OF THE INTENDED READERS OF THIS BOOK

This volume is written for business owners, sales managers/directors and branch managers of kitchen and bath design firms (dealerships) which operate with a showroom, sell cabinets and counters and provide installation services—either with their own crew or through a network of qualified subcontractors. Where appropriate, comments are made for the independent kitchen designer whose business model does not include representing products or offering installation, but who can still benefit from the business information included.

This volume is particularly valuable to emerging business leaders—great salespeople who now are managing a sales force, for example, as well as individuals with experience in the kitchen industry who may have a career opportunity to manage a branch operation or a second showroom location for their organization. The material is also useful for companies in the midst of a succession plan with new family members who will become owners "learning the ropes" from the current company officers.

We have selected this business model focus because a dealership operating from a showroom is the most typical business model in our industry, and many people "grow" into business management positions.

THIS IS A REFERENCE BOOK

It is important to note that this book is a reference book—including material covering all aspects of business management for a new entrepreneur.

It is also valuable to existing companies who are interested in "refreshing" their business practices. Successful firms can benefit by evaluating their current business practices with an eye towards a better organized firm with a renewed focus on profitable projects.

THE BOOK'S BASIC PREMISE: SUCCESSFUL BUSINESSES ARE LED BY BALANCED MANAGEMENT

Lastly, this entire book is based on the premise that every business is made up of three parts: financial management, human resource management and marketing management.

The authors understand that there are always two parts of each business for the owner: those things one loves to do, and those things one must do. Most kitchen and bathroom firm owners are fairly strong in the marketing segment (design, sales, advertising, promotions), but are weak in —or, too often, reluctant to invest the time and effort to improve upon — financial management (budgets, financial statements, cash flow) and the human resource (people management) part of the business.

Studying high-profit businesses affirms that balance in all three areas is needed for success.

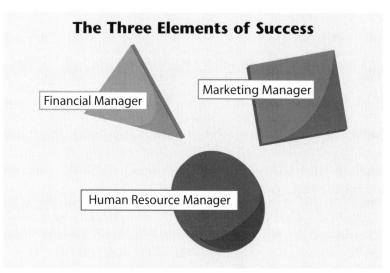

The Three Elements of Success

Financial Manager

Marketing Manager

Human Resource Manager

To help you identify specific areas of the text, sections focusing on financial management are designated with a diamond (▲); sections focusing on people management are highlighted with a circle (●); and marketing sections feature a square (■).

BUSINESS MANAGEMENT FORMS

Business management forms and checklists appear throughout this book. They are also on the CD "Forms for Managing People, Profits and Projects" which is included with this book. They have been formatted on the disk with space to include your own logo, and in an "unlocked" form so that you can reorganize and rewrite as you see fit. The forms and checklists can be printed and used as paper documents or integrated into your electronic management system.

Separately, the National Kitchen & Bath Association has recently updated its extensive Business Management Forms System, consisting of more than 20 forms available to members only. They provide systems for lead tracking, quotations, estimates, surveys, specifications, contracts, change orders, plus job progress, service, completion and follow-up. Select samples are included in an appendix at the end of this book. For more information on the NKBA Business Management Forms System, contact the Association.

IMPROVE YOUR "ROI" (RETURN ON INVESTMENT) – MAKE AN APPOINTMENT WITH YOURSELF

It is important to start a discussion of business management by recognizing the entire reason you are considering investing in your own business or have invested in an existing business: you are expecting a reasonable financial return on that investment. Accountants counsel you on the bottom line "ROI." Quite frankly, many individuals in our industry work hard during the year, develop excellent reputations and a strong repeat or referral business by satisfying their clients but, at the end of the day, have very little return to show on the investment they have made in their business.

Although conservative rate of returns vary with shifts in the economic marketplace—quite simply, you should make a before-tax profit on the money you have invested in your business equal to or greater than conservative returns found in the financial marketplace. Do not be satisfied with a 3% to 5% profit before taxes on your business endeavors—think about the money you have invested in your company and realize that this sum could be invested by your financial planner and reap a specific return for you. Demand of yourself that you spend the time to learn to manage your existing business better, or begin a new business venture managing your operations to enjoy an acceptable rate of return—and acceptable "ROI."

To plan properly or to initiate changes in your current business practices, begin by setting time aside to really study this material. Consider making an appointment with yourself to work on your weak areas.

To Find Balance
Make an appointment with yourself
to work on your weaker points

START BY SKETCHING OUT YOUR BUSINESS MODEL COMPONENT PARTS

A chart detailing the steps even the simplest of new construction/remodeling projects go through follows on the next page. Each step involves people management, financial management and marketing management skills.

Stop for a moment—think through your own business, identifying areas where you think you could improve. Following this self-evaluation, start the book at the beginning and, much like a novel, read it to the end. Then, study the topical outline in the table of contents or the index and concentrate on each area of particular interest to you.

The Kitchen/Bath Project Process

Client — Design — Design/Measure Fee — Showroom/Portfolio/Samples

Survey Appointment — Budget — Presentation/Budget — Designer Fee/Retainer

Material Selection w/Allowances
Cabinets/Tops Appliances, Fixture/Fittings, Decorative, Splash, Floor, Lights — Working Drawings
Before/Construction, Floor Plan, Elevations Design Detail, Perspective

Project Job Costing Estimate — Final Presentation — Contract Signing/Deposit Paid

Jobsite Verification — Order Acknowledgement — Schedule/Receive Material

Deliver to Jobsite/2nd Payment Made — Installation — Inspection — Change Orders

Punch List — Final Payment Made
Job Costs Analysis, Referral Marketing Program — After the Sale, Follow Through

For sales directors/managers or branch managers, think through "The Kitchen/Bath Project Process" detailed above. As you manage a sales team or a branch of your company, look for ways that you can increase the efficiency of the organization in specific areas, or improvements you might suggest to the business owner. You bring a fresh viewpoint and a new skill set to your management team—use your experiences to review the process that currently typifies your organization and set time aside with the company's principals or your manager to work on efficiencies of scale.

Common Business Traits of High Profit Firms

- Have solid growth on an annual basis
- Review and use monthly P&L statements as a management tool
- Owners spend time to learn to be better people managers
- Control their product mix and customers to avoid profit erosion
  1. Rely more on cabinets as a percentage of the total sale
  2. Select products that reflect your strategic business plan
  3. Charge design fee retainers
- Sell cabinets installed: view project as a package, not parts

- Have a higher median annual sales volume and a higher average job selling price
- Are paid quicker
- Complete job cost reviews in a timely manner on all projects
- Acheive superior personnel productivity
  1. Base commissions on gross profit and volume
  2. Use computers to aid design
  3. Offer company benefits with some employee contribution
- Acheive higher gross margins
- Do a better job managing overhead expenses

CHAPTER 1: Getting Started

Millions of people start their own businesses every year. Possibly you have already started yours or maybe you are just giving it serious thought. Whichever the case may be for you, there are many skeptics who will try and scare you with the statistics on how many new businesses fail every year, how hard you will have to work and how long it will take before you show a profit. If everyone listened to the skeptics … John Michael Kohler would not have started Kohler Company, Paul Wellborn certainly would not have expanded Wellborn Cabinet, Inc. and the seven Jacuzzi brothers would not have started the now multi-product Jacuzzi, Inc.

THE PROS AND CONS OF OWNING YOUR OWN BUSINESS

Owning Your Own Business – Pros

- You are your own boss. The sky's the limit.
- You can prove yourself.
- You will have a hand in all aspects of the business.
- You will be able to take pride in promoting and marketing your own business.
- You will be in control.
- You will have creative freedom.
- The more the company makes – the more you make.
- You cannot be fired, laid off or forced to retire.
- You will have the ultimate satisfaction of knowing you started and ran a successful business.

Owning Your Own Business – Cons

- There is no guaranteed paycheck.
- It's all on your shoulders.
- You cannot please everyone.
- You will work harder and longer than ever before.
- You will assume the risk of investment.
- There will be constant stress and pressure.
- You will have to adhere to all the laws and regulations.

DO YOU HAVE
WHAT IT TAKES?

It All Starts With an Idea

At some point it hits you, like so many other people, you could own and run your own business. You want to step out on your own and take control of your work and financial future. You are confident that you have what it takes to buck the odds and succeed. You also know that owning your own business comes with risks—all of which you are willing to take on.

Mrs. Field's Cookies
1/4 cup Passion
1/4 cup Perfection
1/4 cup Perseverance
1/4 cup People

A Business Success

Debbi Fields Rose, the founder and owner of Mrs. Field's Cookies, had her recipe for success: you could call it "The 4 Ps." Mrs. Fields defines each P this way:

- **Passion.** You have to absolutely and passionately love what you do. In your case you will have to love designing and selling kitchen and bath projects. Never go into business with your first priority being to make money. Money will be the by product of doing something you love and doing it well.

- **Perfection.** You must constantly strive for perfection because for your business to succeed and have staying power, you have to do it better than anyone else. Stay focused on constantly improving while stamping out mediocrity.

- **Perseverance.** Stick with it. What you need is guts. Guts to start and guts to believe in yourself. Guts to take on the many challenges, guts to face failure and guts to stick it out.

- **People.** No business can succeed without its greatest asset— people—no matter how good the products and services are. You are not designing and building kitchens and baths, you are helping make dreams turn into reality. To achieve this you will need a team that loves designing, selling and installing dream projects as much as you do.

Four Keys to a Successful Kitchen/Bath Business

The Business Foundation
- A qualified entrepreneur
- A researched business opportunity
- A detailed written plan
- A sufficient capital fund

Put all four of these together and you have a wonderful chance of success in owning and operating your own business.

Evaluating Yourself

While it is true that starting and running a business is difficult, it is successfully done all the time by many individuals and partners who have built both large and small kitchen and bath businesses. You probably know some of these people. If you do not, you can meet them by actively participating in your area NKBA Chapter events and other associations. Develop a networking opportunity for yourself: seek them out, introduce yourself and ask questions to learn what their keys to success are.

WOULD YOU HIRE YOU?

If you have just begun to think about starting your own business or you have been running one for a number of years, you might want to determine if you are the right person for the job.

The position in question is one of being your own boss and running the whole show—which includes bookkeeping, sales and marketing, customer service, supervising other employees, vendor relations and so much more. Most importantly, your job hinges on your ability to make key decisions (some on short notice) and to utilize your people skills because nearly every business involves interaction with others. You may not be skilled in all of these key areas. If you are not, you will have to find other people who can assist you by providing strength in areas where you are lacking.

LEADERSHIP TRAITS

Here is a checklist of traits and characteristics you may need to run a business successfully:

❏ The ability to make important decisions.

❏ The ability to stay motivated, even when the business has slow times and is not running as smoothly as it might.

❏ A knack for organization.

❏ Good time management skills.

❏ Good communication skills.

❏ Stick-to-itiveness, or the drive that keeps you working long hours to get the job done.

❏ Good physical health and stamina to survive the long hours and little sleep that may be part of the job.

❏ The ability to get along well with many different types of personalities.

❏ The ability to harness and manage anger and frustration.

❏ Confidence in your skills, knowledge and abilities to run a kitchen and bath business.

❏ The ability to find answers to questions you cannot answer easily.

❏ The ability to be firm or flexible so you can make adjustments or changes in your plans.

❏ The ability to do research and weigh options before jumping into a situation or making a hasty decision.

❏ The ability to balance a business and a personal life successfully.

EVALUATE YOURSELF

Be honest with yourself. Identify how many of these skills and talents you possess. How many will you commit to learning? How much of the above description just is not you? How many people will you need to hire to fill the void? If you need help with 40% or more, maybe you should reconsider starting your own business.

As you analyze yourself, keep in mind that although businesses do fail for a variety of reasons outside of the owner's control, more often the actions (or lack of action) on the owner's part leads to an unsuccessful venture. That is why entrepreneurs need to have a clear picture of both their skills and their short comings so they can build on their strengths and shore up their weak areas.

Complete the following Entrepreneurial Innovation Assessment to help you identify your entrepreneurial potential.

ENTREPRENEURIAL INNOVATION ASSESSMENT

Read each statement carefully, then mark the answer that most accurately describes your behavior, feeling and attitude as it actually is—not as you would like it to be, or think it should be. Try to mark your first reaction.

	Agree	Disagree
1. My parents encouraged me to take an interest in discovering things for myself.		
2. At least one of my close relatives is an entrepreneur.		
3. Throughout my education I had many part-time jobs.		
4. One or both of my parents had many unconventional or unorthodox ideas.		
5. If I were stranded in an unfamiliar city without friends or money I would cope well.		
6. I am curious about more things than most people are.		
7. I enjoy a venture in which I must constantly keep trying new approaches and possibilities.		
8. I always seek challenging problems to solve.		
9. I am not too painstaking in my work.		
10. I am able to work for extended periods of time, frequently to the point of exhaustion.		
11. When faced with a problem I usually investigate a wide variety of options.		
12. Before taking on an important project I learn all I can about it.		
13. When confronted with a difficult problem I try solutions others would not think of.		
14. Once I undertake a new venture I am determined to see it through.		
15. I concentrate harder on projects I'm working on than most people seem to.		
16. I cannot get excited about ideas that may never lead to anything.		
17. When brainstorming with a group of people I think up more ideas quicker than others.		
18. I have broader interests and am more widely informed than most people.		
19. When the chips are down, I display more personal strength than most people.		
20. I need social interaction and am very interested in interpersonal relationships.		
21. I find it easy to identify flaws in other's ideas.		
22. I regard myself as a 'specialist' not a 'generalist.'		
23. When evaluating information I believe the source is more important than the content.		
24. I am easily frustrated by uncertainty and unpredictability.		
25. I can easily give up immediate gain or comfort to reach long term goals.		
26. I have great tenacity of purpose.		
27. Things that are obvious to others are not so obvious to me.		

ENTREPRENEURIAL INNOVATION ASSESSMENT -continued-

	Always	Often	Sometimes	Rarely	Never
28. I get a kick out of breaking the rules.					
29. I become upset if I cannot immediately come to a decision.					
30. Ideas run through my head at night to the point that I cannot sleep.					
31. I get into trouble because I'm too curious or inquisitive.					
32. I am able to win other people over to my point of view.					
33. I tolerate frustration more than the average person does.					
34. I rely on intuition when trying to solve a problem.					
35. I can stick with difficult problems for extended periods of time.					
36. My problem solving abilities are stronger than my social abilities.					
37. A logical step-by-step method is best for solving problems.					
38. I can readily allay people's suspicions.					

39. Below is a list of adjectives and descriptive terms. Indicate with a check mark 12 words that best describe you.

Energetic	☐	Quick	☐	Organized	☐	Sociable	☐
Tactful	☐	Cautious	☐	Factual	☐	Self-Confident	☐
Dedicated	☐	Alert	☐	Polished	☐	Fashionable	☐
Stern	☐	Flexible	☐	Innovative	☐	Persevering	☐
Efficient	☐	Persuasive	☐	Inquisitive	☐	Good Natured	☐
Perceptive	☐	Modest	☐	Inhibited	☐	Habit Bound	☐
Egotistical	☐	Original	☐	Unemotional	☐	Absent Minded	☐
Curious	☐	Dynamic	☐	Clear Thinker	☐	Forward Looking	☐
Informal	☐	Practical	☐	Open Minded	☐	Understanding	☐
Involved	☐	Formal	☐	Courageous	☐	Self Demanding	☐
Predicable	☐	Poised	☐	Independent	☐	Well Liked	☐
Observant	☐	Helpful	☐	Thorough	☐	Enthusiastic	☐
		Realistic	☐	Resourceful	☐		

ENTREPRENEURIAL INNOVATION ASSESSMENT -continued-

Scoring Instructions

To score the test, circle and add up the values for your answers.

Statement	Agree	Disagree
1.	4	1
2.	3	1
3.	4	1
4.	3	1
5.	4	1
6.	4	1
7.	4	1
8.	3	1
9.	0	4
10.	4	1

Statement	Agree	Disagree
11.	4	1
12.	3	1
13.	4	1
14.	4	1
15.	4	1
16.	4	1
17.	1	4
18.	4	1
19.	4	1
20.	4	1

Statement	Agree	Disagree
21.	1	4
22.	3	1
23.	1	4
24.	1	4
25.	1	4
26.	4	1
27.	4	1
28.	4	1

Statement	Always	Often	Sometimes	Rarely	Never
29.	2	3	5	1	0
30.	0	2	3	5	1
31.	2	4	5	3	0
32.	3	4	5	1	0
33.	3	4	5	1	0
34.	3	4	5	1	0
35.	5	4	3	1	0
36.	4	5	3	1	0
37.	4	5	3	1	0
38.	1	2	5	3	0
39.	3	4	5	1	0

ENTREPRENEURIAL INNOVATION ASSESSMENT -continued-

40. The following characteristics score 2 points each: *energetic, observant, persevering, resourceful, independent, dedicated, original, perceptive, enthusiastic, innovative, curious, involved,* and *flexible.*

The following score 1 point each: *self-confident, forward looking, informal, courageous, thorough, open minded, alert, dynamic, self-demanding,* and *absent minded.*

Interpreting Your Score

125 – 186   If you scored in this range you are probably a highly innovative person. Ideas come readily to you. On the whole you take an innovative approach to solving problems. You also discern possibilities and opportunities in areas where others find little potential. You are original and individualistic, and you have no problem resisting pressures to conform. You have the courage to pit yourself against uncertain circumstances.

77 – 124   A score in this range indicates that you are moderately innovative. While you lack some of the autonomy, self-sufficiency and self-confidence of the highly innovative entrepreneur, you compensate with your predilection for method, precision and exactness. You also have faith in the successful outcome of your present and future entrepreneurial efforts.

27 – 76   If you scored in this range you may be more successful operating a franchise or working for someone else than you would be starting and owning your own business. However, remember: innovative abilities can be developed and cultivated either through on-the-job training or by attending workshops or seminars. If you are determined to own your own business—do not give up.

BEFORE YOU START

Now that you have done the self-evaluation exercises and you still want to pursue owning your own business—or if you are already an owner and "passed" the self-evaluation—you have several more things to consider.

What are your career and business goals?

Where are you today? Where do you want to be in 3-5 years? How do you plan to get there?

What are your goals? Yes, you want to make money—but how much and how fast? Do you see yourself running a small business (less than 10 employees), or one with multiple stores and more employees? Is it a business that you would hope your spouse, children or other family members might want to work in and take over at some point? Or do you want to work hard for 10-20 years then sell it and retire? How will you mix personal and business in order to achieve a good balance in your life?

Knowing where you want to end up is important to consider before you even start. Many experts will tell you to start planning your exit strategy the day you start your business.

Separate Home From Business

If your only activity is your business, it is likely your family and social life will suffer. We all know people who are divorced today because of problems resulting directly from the pressures of starting and operating a business. Do not let this happen to you.

Think about these words from Lord Chesterfield (1773-1894), "Few people do business well who do nothing else." What this quotation tells us is that you are likely to lose some of the very qualities that will make you a business success if you do not remain well-rounded in other aspects of your life. You already know you have to spend a lot of time with your business—but it is imperative that you also set aside time for family, friends—and yourself. Without this relief, you are likely to "burn out" long before you attain the success you want.

Here are a few specific suggestions for ensuring a successful "marriage" between your business and home life.

- Plan for the future, but live in the present. Do not let the good times pass you by.

- If you do any work at home—designate an area for work only—do not infringe on other areas of the home.

- Keep your hobby alive. Your hobby can be an excellent source of relaxation.

- Maintain some type of physical activity. Exercise is a wonderful way to reduce tension and clear your mind.

- When socializing, try not to talk about business-related topics unless asked by others.

- Keep your significant other informed about your business activities, but do not make it the only topic of discussion.

- Although you will be putting in long hours on business, regularly set aside time for activities with family and friends.

- And, remember—problems with family and friends can spell disaster for your business. Be sensitive to their needs, as well as your own. Stay involved in activities other than your business to the greatest extent possible.

How Well Do You Understand Business?

You do not need to have an MBA, be a CPA, or read the *Wall Street Journal* from cover to cover to be able to own and operate a successful business.

A Business Example from Hank Darlington's "Early" Career

When I was eight years old a neighbor playmate, Sally, and I opened up a lemonade stand. A couple of other kids had started one about eight blocks away so we did market research on the best location, then purchased lemons, sugar, cups and napkins (inventory). We needed a table, chairs, and signage (assets). We established a sell price that was greater than cost which generated a gross profit. We had a serious human resource issue which was who would be the boss. (I was older so I won the job.) In the end we had all the ingredients of a kitchen and bath business and could have generated a profit and loss statement and balance sheet. As I remember, the hot spell lasted about two days and our interest level was just about as long. Thanks to family and neighbors I'm sure we put a few coins in our piggy banks. That was my first entrepreneurial experience. I loved it then and love it still!

Beyond operating a lemonade stand when you were a kid, do you have any "hands-on" business experience? Do you really know all the things involved in running a business? There is a lot to it. Things like bookkeeping, taxes, payrolls, accounts receivable and payable, marketing, signing contracts, making deals and operating in accordance with all government laws and regulations.

According to an analysis by Dunn & Bradstreet, experience and aptitude count for a whole lot. Dunn & Bradstreet suggest that poor management is the leading cause of business failure. They estimate that a lack of managerial experience and aptitude accounts for almost 90% of business failures.

WHY MANY COMPANIES DO NOT MAKE IT

Since so many small businesses do fail in the first six years, it is important to look at the reasons why this happens:

Why Many Business Ventures Don't Make It

- Running out of money
- Lack of business planning
- Inefficient control of costs
- Quality of product and services
- Insufficient inventory control
- Under pricing of products and services sold
- Poor customer relations
- Failure to promote and maintain a favorable public image
- Bad relations with suppliers
- Terrible management
- Illness of key personnel
- Reluctance to seek professional help
- Failure to minimize taxation through tax planning

- Inadequate insurance
- Loss of key personnel
- Lack of staff training
- Insufficient knowledge of the industry
- Inability to compete
- Failure to anticipate market trends
- Inadequate cash flow
- Growth without adequate capitalization
- Ignoring data on the company's financial position
- Incomplete financial records
- Overextending credit
- Over borrowing
- Over due receivables
- Excessive demands from creditors

FAILURE FACTORS AND CHARACTERISTICS OF ENTREPRENEURS WHO HAVE FAILED

Since the failure rate of new businesses exceeds the success rate, it is important to look more closely at typical characteristics of businesses which did not make it.

- **Lack of Management Experience.** Many entrepreneurs do not understand the intricacies of running a business. Too many kitchen and bath dealership owners have entered into business with good design and sales experience, but little or no management experience. Lack of skills in financial, human resource and marketing management can lead to failure.

- **Poor Financial Planners.** A major cause of failure is not having the expertise to write a comprehensive business plan, develop annual budgets and generate and analyze monthly financial statements. This, plus poor planning in terms of capital requirements, can be the downfall.

- **Poor Location Choice.** For a kitchen and bath dealer, finding the right location should be one of the most important decisions. Spend the time and money to be sure the business is in the right area.

- **Ineffective Business Controllers.** Lack of written policies, procedures, systems and job descriptions, along with poor controls in accounting, job costing, accounts receivable and inventory control can kill a business before it even gets started.

- **Being a Big Spender.** Buying all new equipment and furnishings vs. leasing or buying used is not wise unless the finances allow. Do not over-spend on displays and building improvements. Driving fancy cars and taking too much salary can all contribute to a downfall.

- **A Lack of Commitment and Dedication.** In the early years of a new business, the lack of willingness to spend the needed hours or give up non-work related activities will have a negative impact on the enterprise. At times, family life will be disrupted as the founder works long hours creating a strong foundation for the business.

- **An Impulse to Over-expand.** Okay, the initial business gets off to a great start. The first impulse is to expand—locations, products, services, customer base, etc. Trying to do too much, too quickly can lead to a decline in services rendered, quality of product and employee performance. Plus, the issue of available capital plays an important role in any expansion. A word of advice: go slowly and be sure before undertaking any expansions.

SUCCESS FACTOR CHARACTERISTICS OF ENTREPRENEURS WHO HAVE SUCCEEDED

To succeed, you must define your skills. To help you determine your level of expertise in each category, here is a summary of the skills needed to succeed.

- **Business Planning:** The ability to establish and achieve short term (1-3 years) and long term (3-5 years) planning goals for the business.

- **Finance:** The ability to manage money, create and interpret financial statements, develop and update annual budgets, manage accounts payable and receivable and successfully seek out funding sources for the business.

- **Accounting:** The ability to accurately record and interpret the income and expenses of the business in a timely manner (preferably monthly). If the business includes installation as one of its services this would include job costing.

- **Marketing:** The ability to identify target markets (area and clients), plus putting together a package of products and services that will be attractive to these clients. Marketing also includes knowing your competition and responding positively to them.

- **Sales:** The ability to close sales once clients have been attracted to the business through marketing efforts and the presentation of a solution-slanted functional design plan. This would include learning and teaching sales skills to all salespeople.

- **Advertising, Promotion and Public Relations:** The ability to create plans, budgets and campaigns that successfully sell the offerings of your business—and attract potential clients to the business.

- **Design:** The ability to create space solutions that work.

- **Installation:** The ability to manage a design/build kitchen/bath project with in-house installations or subcontractors.

- **Product Knowledge:** The ability of knowing your products and services better than your competition, identifying and selling numerous features and benefits of your company, your products and your services.

- **Human Resource Management:** The ability to recruit, hire, train, motivate, manage and fire people.

AVOID THESE COMMON MISTAKES

Instead of making mistakes and learning the 'hard way' you can learn from the mistakes of others. Here are some of the pitfalls and common mistakes to be aware of:

- **Being married to your ideas.** Learn to be flexible, and be able to adjust and roll with the changes.

- **Not identifying your target audience.** Are you going to market kitchens and baths to the "high end," "middle" or the "lower end" buyer? It is unlikely that you'll be able to be all things to all people. Select your niche carefully and thoughtfully.

- **Acting impulsively (i.e., not doing the proper research).** You will need to learn everything possible about the kitchen and bath industry and the marketplace you plan to serve. Take time to learn as many details as possible. Have the facts—do not operate on impulse.

- **Not having a business plan.** You will need one that includes a marketing plan, financial projections, and human resource needs.

- **Ignoring the competition.** Study them, "mystery shop" (i.e., visit competitors incognito), research them. Know what their target market is, what main products and services they offer, what price point they offer, what image they project, etc. In other words, learn everything you can—then use it to your benefit.

- **Underestimating your timeframe to profitability.** Having a business plan, knowing your competition, knowing your customers and offering the right mix of products and services will definitely lead you to profitability in a shorter timeframe.

15

- **Trying to be a "one person show."** Yes, it is your business. No, you cannot do it all by yourself. The most successful business people surround themselves with competent people to assist them. Good management is getting the job done through other people.

- **Cutting the wrong corners.** Spending all of your money to build a great showroom but not having money left over to advertise and promote will not get the job done. Be prudent, but be smart.

- **Focusing too much on technology and too little on people.** While technology can do wonders it will not substitute for good customer, vendor, and employee relations. Do not spend all your time and money on the latest and greatest CAD system while you should be training, motivating and appreciating your employees.

- **Trying to do too much all at once.** Take the whole process one step at a time. Prioritize, set budgets and time lines. Then proceed in an orderly fashion.

GETTING HELP FROM ADVISORS AND MENTORS

Do not try to build a business in a vacuum. Take advantage of the feedback, suggestions, directions and opinions of others; they can be extremely valuable to help get a business started or to grow an existing business. Certainly seek advice from related trade professionals but also utilize your banker, attorney, accountant, insurance agent and friends to help in your venture.

A FEW SOURCES TO CONSIDER CONTACTING:

American Association of Entrepreneurs   Phone: (202) 659-2979
655 15th Street N.W.   www.albertine.com/entrepreneurial.htm
Suite 400 / F Street Lobby
Washington, DC 20005

United States Small Business Association   Phone: (202) 205-7701
403 3rd Street S.W.   www.sba.gov
Washington, DC 20416

The National Association of Self-Employed   Phone: (800) 232-6273
P.O. Box 612067, DFW Airport   www.nase.org
Dallas, TX 75261-2067

The American Institute for Small Business   Phone: (800) 328-2906
7515 Wayzata Blvd., Suite 129   www.aisb.biz
Minneapolis, MN 55426

THE RESOURCES FOR MARKETERS AND ENTREPRENEURS ARE INFINITE. HERE ARE A FEW TO GET YOU STARTED:

American Express   Phone: (888) 792-0279
Small Business Exchange   www.americanexpress.com/smallbusiness

BizAdvantage   Phone: (800) 223-1026
                                              www.bizadvantage.com

SCORE (Service Corp of Retired Executives)   Phone: (800) 634-0245
409 3rd Street, SW, 6th Floor   www.score.org
Washington, DC 20024

SmartBIZ   www.smartbiz.com

CHAPTER 2: Planning Your Business

WHAT TYPE OF KITCHEN AND BATH BUSINESS ARE YOU GOING TO OPERATE?

Whether you are starting new, have stepped into the family business, bought an existing business or been operating a business for some time, you need to evaluate (or maybe re-evaluate) the type of business you want to own.

There is no "right" answer to the question: "What's the best business model for a kitchen/bath firm?" However, there are several "typical" business models. Although other different models do exist, the following outline is an overview of companies found throughout North America.

BUSINESS MODEL NO. 1 — A DESIGNER'S STUDIO

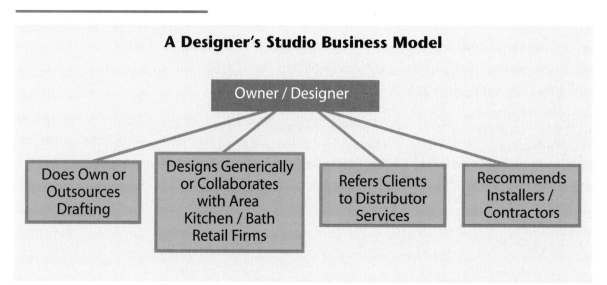

A Designer's Studio Business Model

Owner / Designer

- Does Own or Outsources Drafting
- Designs Generically or Collaborates with Area Kitchen / Bath Retail Firms
- Refers Clients to Distributor Services
- Recommends Installers / Contractors

An independent kitchen designer operating out of his/her home or a studio location provides design services for a fee. The designer may work closely with area kitchen specialists representing products* or may provide only generic plans. Installation is rarely provided. Oftentimes, contractors/installers are recommended. The individual is the branded image in the community.

*Individual business ethics guidelines and state/province laws determine whether the independent designer can derive income from products purchased by the consumer from referred sources.

BUSINESS MODEL NO. 2 –
A DESIGN PRACTICE FIRM

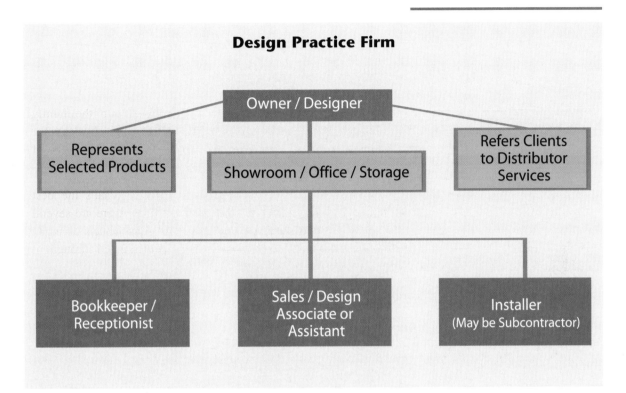

Design Practice Firm

Owner / Designer

Represents Selected Products

Showroom / Office / Storage

Refers Clients to Distributor Services

Bookkeeper / Receptionist

Sales / Design Associate or Assistant

Installer (May be Subcontractor)

A design practice firm represents cabinets and counter surfaces. The firm may also provide appliances, fittings and fixtures. Installation services are offered through in-house staff or subcontractors. The business may be in a destination location, part of a home-based business, or in a retail "strip mall" environment. The owner is typically the only designer, or the primary designer, for the firm. Both the firm and the owner are known in the community, with the owner as an individual—the better recognized—identity.

BUSINESS MODEL NO. 3 –
A DESIGN BUSINESS FIRM

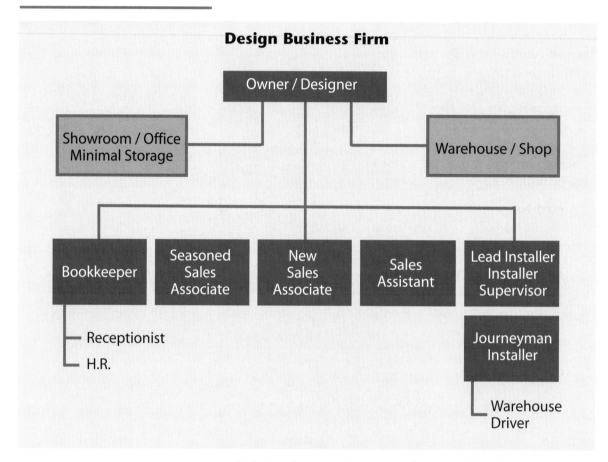

Design Business Firm

Owner / Designer

Showroom / Office Minimal Storage

Warehouse / Shop

Bookkeeper

Seasoned Sales Associate

New Sales Associate

Sales Assistant

Lead Installer Installer Supervisor

Receptionist

H.R.

Journeyman Installer

Warehouse Driver

A design firm is a larger organization with a showroom and an attached or remotely located warehouse/shop facility. The business may be a department of a larger business: the kitchen/bath section of a large lumberyard for example. Such department style organizations normally use a reference program directing clients to installation specialists, rather than maintaining an installation department. Another model is a comprehensive "design/build" firm where in-house crews or subcontractors provide a "turnkey" operation.

The owner/manager leads the company and significantly contributes to the sales volume. However, it is the firm that has the branded image, not the individual. Once again, this firm may be in a destination environment, a retail shopping community, or in a trade/retail design center.

This type of firm might have more than one branch location—more than one showroom. The organization may also have a tier of middle-management: a sales manager/director may head the team of sales associates and assistants. The organization may have a branch manager at each remote location who is part of a leadership management team. The sales director/manager and branch manager bring a wealth of knowledge to the organization: their input about ways to streamline the operation's work procedures, as well as their ability to assist the owner in managing the business, is extremely valuable.

YOUR BUSINESS SELECTION CRITERIA

Select your ideal business model based on your market research, strategic marketing plan, long-term goals and exit strategy.

A good business idea should be one that will bring you a good profit. Beyond that, a good idea for business should meet some or all of the following criteria:

- Fill a void and/or meet a customer need.

- Offer a faster, better, easier or higher quality product and service than is currently available.

- Be realistic—within the scope of something that you can do.

- Have a defined target audience.

- Don't over-saturate the marketplace.

- Be legal.

What to Do After You Have an Idea

To determine the merits and shortcomings of your business idea, research, crunch numbers and examine all the practical and not so practical aspects of making your idea a reality. Nurture this idea and help it grow into a full-fledged written plan. Then put together the elaborate puzzle that takes your idea from the drawing board and turns it into reality.

DECIDING ON THE RIGHT BUSINESS

There are a number of significant factors that will be part of your decision-making process as you set about finding the right type of kitchen and bath business for you. Here are a few of these factors:

- What will you enjoy doing every day that will earn the greatest profitability and return on your time and money?

- Will people pay for the products and services that you plan to sell?

- How much financial help will you need and where can you get it?

- What resources (people, vendors, mentors, etc.) can you gather to help run the business?

- How much time and effort can you put into the business without sacrificing other aspects of your life?

Whether starting new or taking a fresh look at your existing business—step back and try to design the perfect scenario for yourself.

No, you probably won't end up with the exact same thing, but at least you will have an idea what it is you want to achieve. If after five or ten years you find yourself running a business that is close to what you pictured—then you have done very well indeed. But it all starts with a picture and a plan.

CHOOSING A NAME FOR YOUR BUSINESS

The name of your business is the key to your brand image in your customer's mind. Chosen well, your name will reflect an image that is unique, memorable, appropriate, likeable, and capable of advancing a promise for your business.

Following are several questions to ask yourself before committing to a name for a new business or changing the name of an existing business.

- **What kind of name do you want?**

   1. **Owner's Name:** Darlington Kitchen and Bath Design Studio

   2. **Geographical Name:** Northern California Kitchen and Bath Center

   3. **Alphabetical Name:** D & D Kitchens, Baths and Custom Cabinetry

   4. **Descriptive Name:** Creative Cabinetry

- **What do you want the name to convey?** Words such as quality, creative, premier, factory direct?

- **Is the name you want available?**

  1. Screen the name for trademark ownership. Check the Patent and Trademark Depository Library (PTDL) at www.uspto.gov.

  2. Check if the name is available as a domain name (www.networksolutions.com).

  3. Protect the name if it is available. An attorney can do this for a reasonable fee.

- **Is it easy to spell?** Is it phonetically pleasing? Is it a name that works well in normal business conversation?

- **Is it original?** Check several telephone books and check the Internet. Aim for an original name that stands apart from the "pack."

- **Is it memorable?** Look for a name that reflects a distinct aspect of your company.

- **Can you live and grow with the name?** You are going to have to live with this name for a long time, so the most important questions are, "Do you like it? Will it adapt to your future?"

- **Are you ready to commit to a name?** Once you have settled on a name and determined that people can spell it, say it, remember it and relate well to it – you are ready to take the following steps:

  1. Register the name and trademark in your state/province.

  2. Register the domain name.

  3. Create a professional logo to serve as the "force" of your name.

  4. Look for new ways to advance your name and logo—on vehicle signage, clothing, store signage, letterhead, note cards, advertisements, etc.

Do all you can to make your name part of your brand.

STAGES OF COMPANY GROWTH

Just as people go through many stages in their lives, companies evolve and change over their years of operation. As you prepare to write a business plan be sure that you know what stage of growth your business is in—from brand new to well-established. Following are the natural evolutionary stages that almost all companies go through. Make sure your plan places you in the right stage.

Stages of Company Growth

- Idea
- Planning
- Funding
- Start-up
- Ramp-up
- Evolution
- Sustaining

Idea Stage

When you first start thinking about going into business for yourself and what kind of business it will be.

Planning Stage

This is taking the idea and documenting how the start up will actually happen. The goal here is to develop a plan that convinces you and others that your idea is a good one and worthy of both the time and money invested.

Funding Stage

Where you acquire the money needed to start or change your business. Many kitchen and bath businesses are self-funded (i.e., the owner put up all the money). If you need additional funding, you will become the salesperson and evangelist to banks, partners, family and any reasonable source. A good job of developing a comprehensive written plan will help immensely in the fund raising stage.

Start-up Stage

This is where you put your plan and funding into action. You select vendors, a location, build the showroom, hire help and kick-off the marketing plan.

Ramp-up Stage

The word is out. Clients are coming in because of referrals and the business really starts to take off. This is good—but a word of caution is in order: managing growth can be just as difficult as managing a business down-turn. You may need more people or more equipment to become technologically in tune. This stage could last from six months to two years.

Evolution Stage

When you reach this stage, you will find yourself asking "What will we do next year?" instead of "Will we be around next year?" Your future survival is no longer a major concern. This is where you step back and look at your product and service offering. Just because things have gone well up to this point does not mean you can become complacent or sit back and rest on your laurels. You must be creative and innovative all over again. Take the next steps that will keep you ahead of your competition and in front of your target audience.

As an example: maybe you have been marketing and selling kitchen and bath design and a selection of higher end products, but you have not offered installation. You are finding more and more clients looking for "turnkey" projects and a few of your competitors are offering this. As a part of your evolution stage you may want to add installation to your services and you may want to expand products to include countertops, appliances and lighting. After reviewing your projects you find 90% have been kitchens—you might consider marketing to grow bathroom design and sales.

You cannot stay at the same level in business. You are either moving ahead or you are falling behind.

Sustaining Stage

This is when you are all grown up. When you reach this stage you will be an accepted, recognized "player" in the marketplace, and, hopefully a leader. People will look at you as one of the companies to beat when starting a new business. And they will look at you as one of the companies to emulate when doing their business. Even when you reach this stage, the planning, budgeting, and market research does not stop. It is an ongoing, never-ending process.

SHORT AND LONG TERM PLANNING

Nothing happens in the long term without short-term plans and actions that move you toward your desired outcome. These short-term actions cannot help you achieve any particular goal if no goals have been set or no plan has been developed.

You must know where you are going before you can figure out a route to get there.

- Taking the time to determine your own goals, your company's long-term mission and objectives will guide your daily actions. Without this framework, you and your employees may be busy but the business will not move forward because everyone is pulling in separate directions.

- Making sure everyone knows and understands the goals and objectives of the company will make life a lot easier—for you as well as your employees.

> For example: You are a CKD. You love designing kitchens enough to win awards. You are okay with the selling process because you know that is what really pays the bills. But now you are involved in the whole business management as well and you have found you are designing less and hassling with installers more, i.e., you are not having fun anymore. This might have been prevented and, in fact, still can be changed by hiring an installation manager, someone you can turn that side of the business over to. Now you can get back to designing and selling—and having fun too.

AGAIN, WHY DO YOU START WITH A DETAILED PLAN?

- Setting goals helps you identify actions you must take to get from A (where you are) to B (where your goals are).
- A plan analysis shows you if your idea is viable or not. It saves you time, money and heartaches.
- You and your business associates use the plan as a road map.
- The plan begins as a start-up then becomes the "evolution" plan followed by the "sustaining" plan.
- To make it achievable, be honest, accurate and reasonable.

Before tackling the step-by-step process of creating a plan outlined by Hank Darlington, we invited industry marketing expert Leonard V. Casey to share his views on the importance of concentrating on the marketing strategy first. Len, an industry veteran with experience leading the DuPont Corian team, running a major cabinet company and contributing to the strategic planning of a variety of businesses in the kitchen and bath industry, suggests the following business focus.

HOW TO CREATE A STRATEGIC BUSINESS PLAN FOR A KITCHEN/BATH DEALER

By Leonard V. Casey, MBA

We all have our own important reasons for going into business—none of these reasons include paying bills, dealing with banks, understanding suppliers or writing a business plan. However, over the next few pages you will find a new and valuable view of a planning process leading to greater enjoyment for your real passion and reasons to have your own business.

A strategic business plan may sound like a lot work and perhaps a little boring. But—if done well—it becomes the business owner's best friend: a place where the owner can think through his or her ideas without day-to-day pressures clouding the view. The strategic business plan also helps gather support from other stakeholders such as employees, suppliers and advisors—even customers—by providing a clear view of where the organization is headed.

It allows the business owner to evaluate events not as a reaction to short-term opportunities (sometimes turning out to be long-term nightmares), but to measure opportunities versus your strategic yardstick, better selecting the "good" and jettisoning things not fitting your plan. This will save time and money, and greatly reduce stress.

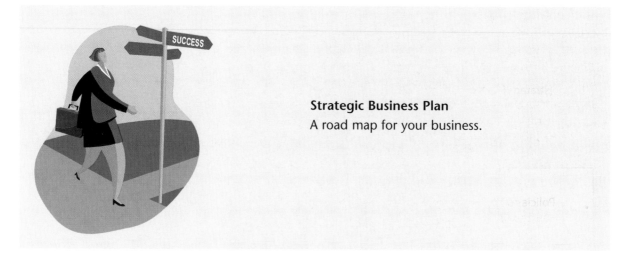

Strategic Business Plan
A road map for your business.

A Road Map

A strategic business plan is much like a road map for your business. It allows you to look ahead in such a way as to anticipate needs and the outcome of your actions. Take full advantage of your strategic business plan and you will have the opportunity of thinking through what you are contemplating, thereby reducing risks and greatly improving chances of success.

In today's business world, there is a great deal of opportunity—far more than perhaps ever before—across a broad spectrum of market segments. A well-engineered, strategic business plan will help the business owner and other employees focus on the most important opportunities for the business, consistent with your values and strengths. It will also give you the conviction to avoid other interesting opportunities that are not a strategic fit.

USE THE MAP

Business plans are often large documents filled with financial data that find a permanent resting place on a shelf, never to be read again once written. But a useful strategic business plan is quite different. It will be read, used and understood by all stakeholders of the business. It will become a valuable asset. Producing a useful business plan is not easy and involves a great deal of thought, discipline and understanding of your market, but it is worth it.

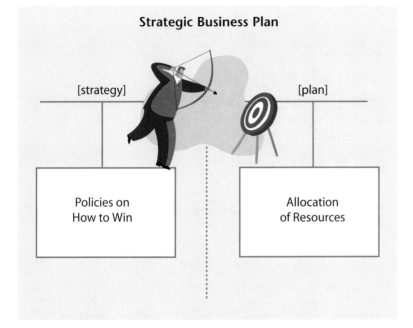

The Difference Between Strategy and the Plan

The name "strategic business plan" implies something more than just the business plan itself. It is made up of two distinct but inseparable parts: first, the strategy and then the plan.

- The strategy of a company is the collection of the important policies designed to allow the business to "win" (i.e., to meet or exceed its business plan goals and objectives) in the desired marketplace.

- The plan is the allocation of the company's scarce resources of money, time and people to implement the policies the business is using to "win."

The two are inseparable because a business plan not based on a clear strategic direction has no chance of being successful.

Profit is the Reason For a Business to Exist But Offers No Direction

Many businesses focus a lot of their attention on the notion of the company's profit objective. They will sometimes break down the profit into quarterly, monthly or even weekly objectives trying to aim the organization towards the whole idea of earning profit. This, however, may result in a misuse of the concept of profit because it can lead the business in too many directions, wasting resources and, therefore, ultimately producing poor results.

An alert: Sometimes talking about the concept of a misuse of profits leads to confusion because companies should earn profit - this is the reward for being successful. However, focusing much of the organization's time on profit itself provides no direction on how to make that profit and does not automatically lead an organization to meaningful solutions.

Look at this concept from another angle. Think of:

Profit is to business as fun is to a vacation.

*They are both the desired result of specific actions
(working, vacationing).*

Profit in business has a similar role as fun has to a vacation—it is the goal (the reason you do it). However, both profit and fun offer no direction as to how you are to accomplish the goal. Therefore, they are not useful in shaping your actions. Indeed, in some cases, the quest for profit can even harm the organization because we may think we know where we are headed when we do not.

Conceptual Vacation

For example, two friends decide they are going to spend vacation together this winter starting on February 1st to "have fun." They agree to meet but when they arrive one is wearing full winter snow gear while the other is clad in a bathing suit and carrying a surfboard. Something was missing in their plan—it was the lack of strategic intent for what it was they wanted to do (how was fun to occur).

Now, look at this situation with only one improvement—a single element of strategy. The two discuss in advance their desire to have a vacation together and decide they are going to meet in Key West on February 1 (of course, to have fun). If this is the only discussion concerning their vacation, they will accelerate their good experience exponentially. The two could have probably added other items of value such as booking flights together, saving money on rental cars, and a whole list of things. However, if nothing else did occur, these two will have a good chance of having fun because they have a strategic intent.

It is the same with business profit: profit is the very reason we are in business. However, profit is non-directional. Making profit sounds like the right thing to do, and members of the organization may go off in their individual directions—trying to earn profit. But such unfocused efforts may do just the opposite because of the various actions taken. For example, reducing inventory to improve profit may be a good idea. However, if it results in a stock-out, unacceptable delivery delays and—worst of all—a lost customer, the slight savings in inventory could mean disaster for the company.

Profit Is The Result of a Successful Strategy

Organizations need to understand how they will make profit before they can start out.

Once you know where you are going you can measure if you are getting there, and, along the way, you can make improvements to make the profit projections even better. The entire profit opportunity of the company becomes real, measurable and achievable when you have a clear sense of strategic intent. For example:

- "This year we will increase the total number of kitchens we will complete from 20 to 25 with an increase in the average profit margin from 39% to 42%."

- "We will improve our customer referral from 60% to 85% during the next two years."

Both of the above statements are strategic and directional. Once the organization uses measurable and achievable action elements, the entire profit opportunity of the company becomes real.

Strategy is the things you will do to make profit. Profit is the result.

Break up the process of our strategic business plan into its individual parts.

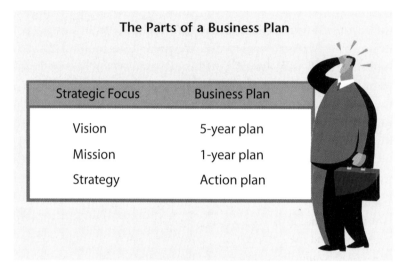

The Parts of a Business Plan

Strategic Focus	Business Plan
Vision	5-year plan
Mission	1-year plan
Strategy	Action plan

The strategic focus of a company is made up of three important areas: vision, mission and fundamental strategy. Collectively, these are the most powerful tools a business has. Let's have a look at each individually and how they are interconnected as building blocks with their own hierarchy.

The Vision and Mission of Your Company

The vision is the core purpose of why the company exists. It can be said it is the "soul" of the company. While it says nothing about the day-to-day activities of the organization, it guides everything we do. A company vision functions much like the *Constitution of the United States* which does not tell us what we are to do—it guides everything we do.

Without a clear vision, a business will wander from opportunity to opportunity, never reaching its true potential. With a clear and shared vision, every employee will be enabled to focus their energy on the proper variables leading to the success of the business. The vision is only the beginning of the strategic process, but it is the first step. Without it, you can go no further.

Vision/Mission
Much like the Constitution
of the United States

THE VISION COMES FROM THE TOP

The vision comes from the top—the founder, the chairperson, the president, and the key people responsible for the business—and must be shared by all. Visions were not always thought of in the formal way we are speaking of today, but visions were always present in all successful businesses. While a vision may not have been articulated on paper, great businesses have been headed by a leader who was a "visionary." Such a leader had a personal vision that permeated the total atmosphere of the day-to-day life of the organization.

One example: John Hollingsworth, a successful merchant in the mid-1800s, decided to go into the growing business of ship building in Newport News, Virginia. In the first days of his company, standing on the steps of his new office in front of his small staff, he said,

> *"We will make good ships here, at a profit if we can, at a loss if we must, but always good ships."*

The importance of John Hollingsworth's words became clearer every day. He set the standard of the way the company existed and why it should exist: "To make good ships." This was his vision. Can you imagine in a bad year a smart purchasing agent who thought he could help profits by purchasing a lower grade of lumber, thereby improving profitability? Hollingsworth's words would go a long way in guiding his purchasing agent and others to look for better solutions and not waste important time on debates about things outside his vision. John Hollingsworth's Newport News ship building company went on to become the most successful ship building company in the world. His vision surely helped. (Source: Customer Driven Company)

Oftentimes, people use the words "vision" and "mission" interchangeably, or reverse the order of hierarchy. There is good logic on both sides but, in the end, it is mostly semantics. If the vision of a company is the first building block and the most important abstract view of where the business is going, the mission is the beginning of how we are going to set about the task ahead. Therefore, the mission is the value and belief standards of the organization. The mission statement will help to communicate the organization's belief as an outgrowth of the vision itself.

Below is an example of a vision and mission statement by a leading faucet and sink manufacturer:

Vision

KWC is known by kitchen and bath consumers, interior designers, architects and kitchen specialists as the provider of innovative performance-driven water appliances with uncompromising quality, design and service.

Mission

To reach out to the design professionals in the kitchen and bath industry through a series of design and support programs. KWC will be understood, advocated and the product of choice for the design community.

Strategy

WHAT IT IS

The strategy of a business is the written statement of the policies, services, procedures, pricing, etc. that the company will use to be successful reaching its goals in the selected market. In its simplest form, a business can only make decisions covering four major areas. They are:

STRATEGY

- What products do we offer? Products include physical items, as well as services.

- At what price will we sell these products?

- Where will the transaction take place?

- How do we communicate our message in a manner to stimulate a sale?

(Courtesy of Eugene McCarthy, Author Principal of Marketing)

FOUR KEY PARTS

While this may seem over simplified, all decisions made in business stem from one of these four areas.

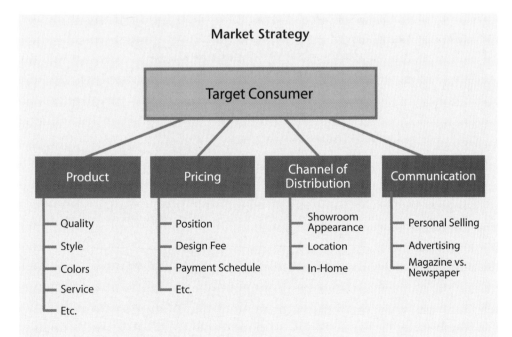

On a day-to-day basis, we do not speak of the four decisions of product, pricing, channel of distribution or communication policies. We tend to find ourselves asking questions such as:

- What is the quality and style of the products we are handling?

- Do we provide full installation services? Or, offer turnkey construction services?

- What about price?

- Do we charge a design fee? When, if ever, do we give away the plans?

- What is a reasonable payment schedule?

- What about location? How should the showroom look? Where should the showroom be located? Where is the consumer most comfortable?

On a practical basis, these and many other questions are answered day in and day out. And the questions are interrelated: you cannot offer the best in design without some type of advance payment system. Installation cannot be offered if the price does not allow for a profitable installation department. The question, then, is how do we balance the four important variables of price, product, location and communication in such a way to insure we are on the correct path forward?

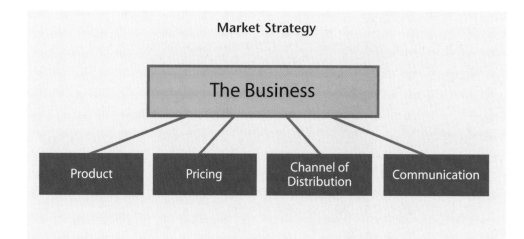

The Answer is Found When We Identify the Target Consumer

WHO IS A TARGET CONSUMER?

The key element in a business strategy is the proper identification of your target consumer. Without doing so, the balance of your efforts will not work. The more clearly you can identify your target consumer, the easier the answers will become, thereby improving the understanding and execution of your strategy.

Who Is a Target Consumer?
This group should be small enough in size for you to have a clear understanding of their true needs and values, yet large enough to be financially interesting.

A target consumer should be a homogeneous group who shares a common sense of quality, values and needs.

Decisions around these four important variables are interrelated. The answers come from a common denominator: the target consumer you strive to attract. Therefore, the way to ask and answer the questions is to first identify your target consumer and then ask:

- What products does this consumer group need and want?

- What are they willing to pay?

- How does this target consumer learn about products?

- What do they need to know to say "yes"?

- What service offering does this consumer group want in order to complete the transaction?

When successfully balancing your four major decisions in harmony with your target consumer group, you will have completed your "business strategy."

A COMMENT ON THE CURRENT KITCHEN/BATH BUSINESS ENVIRONMENT

As you identify your target consumer—realize that in today's kitchen and bath market it is difficult to serve all types of clients interested in a new kitchen, bath or other fitted furniture. The old target of trying to offer "good, better, best" selections of products and services is simply too hard to manage in our complex industry today. This outdated business model leads to a few yearly "monuments" or projects that are unprofitable, as well as to time wasted on over-designed projects for entry level clients.

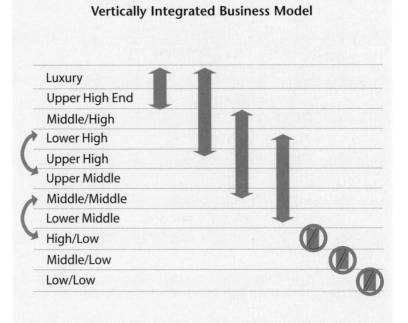

Vertically Integrated Business Model

Luxury
Upper High End
Middle/High
Lower High
Upper High
Upper Middle
Middle/Middle
Lower Middle
High/Low
Middle/Low
Low/Low

Industry leaders suggest a vertically integrated business model is more successful when it focuses on a limited series of related segments of the market, such as the upper end of the market, the upper middle of the market or the middle-middle of the market.

When you are successful in segmenting your target consumer, you will find the answers to the questions of product, price, etc. faster and easier to get to. You will clearly know what policies you must follow for a profitable venture. Further, consumers who are similar in nature, values and needs are your best source of repeat and referral business in the same market segment.

Outdated Good/Better/Best Business Model

Luxury	Leads to designing unprofitable monuments
Upper High End	
Middle/High	Under designed for client, over designed with mid-range products
Lower High	
Upper High	
Upper Middle	
Middle/Middle	Over designed for budget, too much time spent with client
Lower Middle	
High/Low	Wasted time with poorly qualified clients
Middle/Low	
Low/Low	Leads to confusing product mix

ENGAGE YOUR STAKEHOLDERS IN THE PROCESS

When looking to produce your business strategy, it becomes helpful to use your key stakeholders to help you think through the process. Stakeholders should take part in the development and review of the strategy. The end result is a written document describing your target consumer and a policy statement for key business variables of product, price, location and communications. Once this has been completed, the business plan becomes a much easier task and alive with insight.

After Developing the Strategic Plan Based on Your Identified Target, Develop the Business Plan

When armed with a clear strategic focus, the work needed to produce your business plan is easier, less time consuming, more meaningful, and receives faster agreement among all stakeholders in the organization. The purpose of your business plan is to drive your business forward to reach the strategic goals you and your organization have set.

THE GOAL IS BOTH FINANCIAL AND DIRECTIONAL

By now, you can see the goal of the strategic business plan is not merely financial—it is directional. A financially successful company is the result of producing a valued offering to a target consumer group. Without providing consistent value over time, the business will fail. The business plan becomes the allocation of your important and limited resources of people, money and time to perform the necessary work to create the value described in your business strategy, resulting in winning the loyalty of your target consumer. The focus of the plan then becomes describing the tasks or work to be accomplished in a measurable and achievable manner.

The Secret to a Successful Business Plan
- The plan must be measurable and achievable
- Realize it is not easy to write the plan
- Make the plan without fear
- Keep the plan short

Some important considerations to remember when writing your business plan:

- **The plan must always be measurable and achievable**. Therefore, care needs to be taken to insure the plan is written in an objective way and is not subjective in its nature.

  For example, someone could include in their plan, "We will actively promote the value of our organization to the community's opinion leaders throughout the year." When reading this statement, it sounds important and like a good idea. However, statements like this are subjective, impossible to measure and the implementation often wastes valuable resources of time and money. People within the organization will be trying to do what they think you mean by this statement.

An alternative statement that is measurable and achievable might be: "In order to become known by the community's design leaders (Wilson Design Group, Johnson Interiors, All American Architects) we will host three receptions during May and June for the owners and their staff." By making this change, your organization is more empowered to do the intended work. Everyone on your staff now knows who the community leaders are and when the work of courting them will be done. Everyone can add to the list or challenge the validity of the selection. Everyone knows when the effort will take place, and the outcome itself is measurable.

Once you make work objectives, as in the above example, time will not erode the true meaning.

- Developing the plan is not easy—it will take discipline and careful assessment from all the stakeholders as to the strategic intent driving your target market.

   1. You will need to involve everyone in the process. This will give the plan the best 360 degree view, improving its ideas, performance and its outcome.

   2. You must develop the support staff's agreement and buy-in for the tasks, as well as their understanding of the relevance and importance of their work to the whole.

   3. All actionable plan items need to have dates of completion and a clear identification of who is responsible.

   4. There must be a willingness by all to upgrade the plan.

   5. The plan must be understood by all stakeholders.

- **The plan must be without fear.** If the plan is used in a negative way to judge people, then the plan will not be embraced by the organization. For example, the people taking on the project of working with the design community leaders (Wilson Design Group, Johnson Interior, All American Architects) are responsible for the events agreed upon, but should not be judged on whether the design community leader uses their services. The people responsible for the plan will tend to only include things they know are easy, therefore, you will not get the best from your employees and suppliers. (Make it fun!)

- **Short is better than long.** The shorter your plan is, the easier it will be to read and to communicate and so the better the opportunity for success. Short plans also have a way of exposing a lack of substance. A short plan can offer a complete understanding of the organization, i.e., the goals, strategy and direction of the business.

Your business plan must:

- Translate strategy into action.

- Allow your resources to be efficiently and properly proportioned.

- Provide better communications to associates, customers and suppliers.

- Provide a timely measurement of success.

- Provide the rationale for financial goals—not just the numbers.

- Establish priorities.

- Be the means of selecting alternative opportunities.

- Be the basis of new plans.

BUSINESS PLAN RESPONSIBILITIES

Who is responsible for the business planning process?

- Business owners are the starting place for planning responsibility, accountability and leadership. Business owners are responsible for the essence of the plan, not just its financial goals. Unless the owners and the top management of the firm become intimate with the plan, the organization will never assemble the resources to achieve the financial rewards.

- Management—at all levels of the firm—must be part of the development of the path forward, as well as agree to its potential achievability.

- Designers will perform better when they are engaged in the development of the central theme of the organization (its business strategy), and will select customers, develop referrals and perform closer to the goals if they understand and participate in the development of the plan.

- All support groups, such as accountants, subcontractors, suppliers, etc., need to be part of the planning process. Each support member can see the opportunity from its own unique vantage point. Further, second-guessing from support groups can be detrimental to the potential success.

Formatting the Business Plan

While the format might not be the most important aspect of a strategic business plan, a consistent format is part of the necessary discipline helpful in delivering the important information to keep the organization on-track to achieve success. The following format is highly recommended.

The format consists of:

- 5-year View

- 1-year View

- 1-year Action Plan

- Review Process

- Judging the Business Plan

FIVE-YEAR BUSINESS STATEMENT

This is a broad view of where your business is to be five years from now, including a list of the critical events necessary to achieve the five-year business position.

- Keep the broad view to one or two paragraphs, stating both the strategic and financial consequences of your efforts, plus the key events.

- Keep the five-year view in place for the entire time, until it is accomplished (unless it is clearly known to be unsuccessful). This keeps all stakeholders responsible for their efforts and improves the plan's performance.

Follow the five-year view with a ...

ONE-YEAR VIEW

The one-year view is also a broad statement of what must happen during the first year of business to be on-course for the successful completion of the full five-year plan.

43

- Write it in terms of its consequences of your actions (always measurable and achievable), followed by the key events to meet the one-year positioning.

- Write it in one or two paragraphs, followed by a list of the three or four most critical events or programs needed to happen in order to successfully complete the one-year plan.

  State the most critical events as one-liners and spell them out in greater detail for those directly involved in their implementation.

- These should be done as an attachment outside the body of the plan itself. This will allow for the necessary details needed by users without fatiguing the plan itself.

For example, as part of a five-year plan:

"It is mandatory we gain a strong repeat and referral basis which will constitute the majority of our future business growth by year five."

However, you will need to get started; therefore, a one-year plan states what the important elements are:

"We will implement our 'Customers-R-Forever' program during the second quarter."

For many of the readers of this plan this may be enough information—just knowing the "Customers-R-Forever" plan will be implemented during the second quarter.

However, for the plan's "drivers," you would have a separate document with a full explanation of what is meant by the "Customers-R-Forever" program, including details of what the plan is, how it will be implemented, how you measure its success, the cost/rewards, and the financial effect of the program.

Through the use of the document, the "drivers" can refer to the program's details without the need to go through the entire business plan, while other stakeholders and support members can see the entire plan in its context without being distracted by the details of important programs.

The five-year and one-year views of the business plan are useful to allow stakeholders and support groups a view of the organization's definition of success. They also allow the supporters to see from their own vantage point how they can help. The document is short, clear and concise.

ONE-YEAR ACTION PLAN

This is a list of the most important items to be accomplished throughout the year, who will be responsible, and when these items will be accomplished. The format for this action plan is simple: it should list items, a date and the name of the person responsible. Sometimes the action items may need to be spelled out in order for others to assist.

Involve the full organization in the business development and its review. Make the central themes of the review: team work, support, upgrading and fun. Plans and the plan review can often lead to uncertainty by some, and fear of being judged wrong. This can—and should be—eliminated. Hold quarterly or monthly reviews. A review should be a celebration of the firm's progress. Stakeholders should look forward to the review, positive reinforcement of work done, and the opportunity to learn from each other.

ACTION PLAN SPREADSHEET

Action Items	Person Responsible	Start Date	Completion Date	Amount

ACTION PLAN SPREADSHEET

Action Items	Person Responsible	Start Date	Completion Date	Amount

JUDGING THE BUSINESS PLAN

Judge the plan in advance. This may sound hard to do, however, it is not only do-able, it is necessary. Waiting for the end of a five-year business plan to judge the plan as unsuccessful is obviously too late. The best way to judge the plan in advance is to dissect it into its important work and to be sure the work needed to meet the goals of the plan happens in a timely way.

The following is a way to judge a plan in advance of the outcome.

AGREEMENT IS A KEY TO SUCCESS

Here is what to look for and gain agreement to.

- **Submit the plan on time.** A plan—no matter how ingenious it may seem—will never reach its full potential if it is late. Therefore, spell out all plans and key elements in a timely manner.

- **Sign off on the plan before implementing.** All plan stakeholders, particularly senior management, and writers of the plan need to sign-off on the plan in advance of its implementation. The recognition by sign-off and the commitment of the plan's resources of time, people and money makes the plan more firm. No one should be willing to sign-off on a plan if they do not believe in it. A "sign-off" is a literal signing of the document at a kick-off meeting.

- **Complete all action items on time.** After the sign-off, the action items are a promise to all stakeholders you will do what you say. This should be an important part of the monthly review.

- **Review plans either quarterly or monthly.** The plan review meeting needs to be a celebration of the plan and should be fun. The plan review meetings are the time and place to honor good performance and to offer help where needed.

Judging a plan in advance of its end point will go a long way in helping employees and other stakeholders to stay focused on real issues without second-guessing. The discipline of staying on time for all important plan parts and the "sign-off" commitment of resources will help the total organization keep focused on what they agreed to do. There is no better way to assure your plan will have a higher opportunity of success.

Judging a plan in this manner will go a long way in gaining a greater understanding by the whole organization in advance of the starting date. The plan will clearly be used as a vehicle for success, not as an indictment for failure. A strategic business plan is much more about events leading to a successful organization, rather than the financial rewards. If the events happen, the financial rewards will occur.

After considering Len Casey's business planning process, industry leaders suggest the following systematic approach to the business plan development process.

The key to operating a successful business is to combine your interest and knowledge of a business with the needs of other people in a particular market. After you have determined what type of kitchen and bath business you want to be, the next step is making sure there is a market.

RESEARCHING THE MARKET

Researching the Market
- Analyze how viable your business idea is in your market
- Determine the size of your market
- Evaluate your competition
- Study the upside potential of the industry
- Identify current and future lifestyle trends for your targeted consumer

Getting Help

You can ask and pay for outside help in understanding your market but most likely you will do the majority of market research yourself. Here are a few places you can go to find information:

- Trade publications
- Your local Chamber of Commerce
- The Internet
- Individual company websites
- The Small Business Association
- Other kitchen and bath business owners
- Your National Kitchen & Bath Association Chapter

Knowing What To Look For

Through all of this research you should be looking for substantial information that supports your ideas and your business plan. In essence, you are conducting a study to see if your plan is feasible based on the current market, economic and competitive climate—and for future prospects.

Examining Your Market Potential

Get an idea of the size of your potential market. Because you will be catering to a specific market by selling a specialized product and service, you will want to know what's happening in new home construction and remodeling.

- **Industry Information.** It is important to gauge the overall industry and where it is headed.

- **Competition.** How many competitors are there? Are there already too many players? What companies are capturing the lion's share of the market? What impact have and will the large multi-branch retailers make? Can you find a niche that the others have overlooked? What can you do to differentiate yourself from the competition?

- **Industry Trends.** In addition to gathering industry information and competitors roles, look at trends (past, present and future), both in business and in lifestyle. Facts tell us that do-it-yourself (DIY) is on a decline and do-it-for-me (DIFM) is on the rise. Statistics demonstrate remodeling accounts for approximately 80% of all kitchen and bath products being sold today. We also know that the kitchen and bathroom have become the two most important rooms in the home. Add these trends together and it bodes well for kitchen and bath businesses.

PREPARING YOUR BUSINESS PLAN

Hank Darlington adds the following details to the overview provided by Len Casey:

You have evaluated yourself, your idea, your marketplace and still believe that starting your own business is a good idea. The next step and one you cannot skip is writing a detailed business plan. Buildings have blueprints, teachers have lesson plans, ball clubs have game plans and projects have network diagrams. Like so many other endeavors, businesses need a plan of action.

A good business plan will not only keep you on track, but, like a good outline for a screenplay or novel, it will allow you to put your thoughts and ideas on paper and manipulate them until they are just right. You will then continually expand, change and "tweak" them as the business takes shape. When it is complete, the business plan will, like a good mystery novel, answer all the pertinent questions and tie up all the loose ends—which, in your case, will be the details that are part and parcel to running a successful business.

THE PARTS OF A BUSINESS PLAN

- The overall vision of the business
- Goals and objectives
- Overview of the industry
- Company and executive summary
- Market information and analysis
- Comprehensive description of the products and services
- Marketing plan with strategies
- Overview of the competition
- Financial plan and information, including projected income and expense figures
- Overview of key personnel

The degree of detail and the manner in which the plan is written will vary from business to business and writer to writer. Plans will include varying information depending on what is necessary to tell the overall story of how the business will be formed or, if an existing business, how it will proceed over the next 3 to 5 years.

The business plan does not have to be written in the order listed above. You may start with the areas that you feel the most comfortable or familiar with. The executive summary which comes near the beginning is often written near the end.

Getting Ready

Writing a business plan the first time may seem like a daunting task. However, if you set aside some quality quiet time and take it one step at a time you will find it is not as hard as it might seem. You'll start with an outline, then move on to a rough draft and, as it comes together, you will make revisions and changes. You should share the plan with other people to get their input and feedback. Many find they are overwhelmed at the beginning of the writing process, but as the plan progresses, begin to enjoy learning about themselves and look forward to carrying out the plan.

- **Where to Find Guidelines.** Since thousands, if not millions, of business plans have preceded yours, do not feel like you have to reinvent the wheel. There are numerous books and CDs on the subject and by going online you will find a lot of information to help your effort. You will find sample business plans that will help you understand and plan yours. One of the best places to look for sample business plans is on the Internet at www.bplan.com. This website offers numerous plans for a wide variety of businesses.

- **Make it Clear.** Even though kitchen and bath businesses are generally small "mom and pop" operations, do not be afraid to develop a longer and more detailed plan. And, remember, the best plan for you does not need have the most jargon, most pages, or most use of buzz words like network, leverage or equity. The best business plan is one that clearly paints the picture of your business and demonstrates how and why it will be successful, grow and—most importantly—be profitable.

- **Make it Professional.** Whether you are doing your plan for just yourself or for more formal reasons (to present to a bank or investors to help secure financing) do a professional looking business plan—complete with a cover page and binding. Be sure to proofread and edit the document. Graphs, charts and even illustrations or photos can enhance the plan. Do not do this to just fill up space. Do not cut corners and do not load it with fluff—include pertinent information.

- **Use It.** Far too many businesses fail each year because they either did not have a business plan or had a plan, but left out some key elements that might have helped. You would never start a long driving trip to unfamiliar destinations without a map so why would you start a business without a detailed business plan?

HOW TO FORMAT THE BUSINESS PLAN

- Title page
- Table of contents
- Executive summary
    1. Business concept
    2. Financial features
    3. Financial requirements
    4. Current business position
    5. Major achievements
- Business description and mission
- Market and industry analysis

- Competitive analysis
- Marketing strategy
- Operations and management
- The leadership team
- The financial plan
- Summary and conclusion
- Appendix and supplementary materials

A Step-By-Step Guide

In the following sections you will find all the information you need to write a plan.

Step 1 – Title Page: This is the reader's first impression of your plan. It should look professional. Show the name of the company, the name(s) of the principal(s), address, telephone, fax and cell phone numbers, email and website addresses and, finally, the date. If you have a logo or company colors, use them.

Step 2 – Table of Contents: A table of contents (TOC) provides an easy way to find key information. The TOC presents an organized overview of what is included within the business plan. It lets readers go back and find each subject without having to look through the entire plan. Keep it simple and straightforward and try not to exceed one page.

Step 3 – Executive Summary: The executive summary is the single most important section of the business plan. Many business owners write this last, because they want to be sure that they have covered and included all the most important points of the plan.

It consists of one paragraph (at most) to describe each section of your plan. The whole executive summary should be just one and a half to two pages long. If a banker or investor is looking at your plan, this summary helps them make the decision to continue reading on or stop there. Therefore, your summary needs to catch and hold the reader's attention.

Your executive summary should touch on the following key elements:

- **Business Concept:** Describe the business, its products and services, the market it serves, and the business' competitive advantage.

- **Financial Features:** Include financial highlights such as sales, margins and profits.

- **Financial Requirements:** State how much capital you need for start-up or expansion, how it will be used and what collateral is available.

- **Current Business Position:** Furnish relevant information about the company, its legal form of operation, when it was founded, the principal owners, and key personnel.

- **Major Achievements:** Point out anything noteworthy such as awards, major projects, new products or services, unique marketing trials, etc.

Include your strongest selling points. Your location, uniqueness. Trend-setting, award-winning, etc. Throughout the whole summary—be concise. The fewer words, the better.

Step 4 – Business Description and Mission: This section of the plan explains your products and services and how they meet the needs of your market. Describe exactly what it is you will be selling and why people will buy it. How will your products and services be different from similar products and services already being offered in the marketplace? If yours is a really revolutionary concept, explain why the market needs this new breakthrough.

Spell out your company's mission. Tell people why the company exists. This simple statement covers, in just a few sentences, the reason for your company's existence. It provides an overall umbrella under which all other goals and actions fall. It says what your company does and who it does it for.

A typical mission statement for a kitchen and bath business might be the following:

"To provide award winning, functional designs, quality products, service and installation for kitchens and bathrooms in both new construction and remodeling projects, with the very best one-on-one personalized service from conception to completion."

Notice that this statement is brief and to the point, determining the overall direction of the company. It also sets limits. The statement says "kitchens and bathrooms" which eliminates room additions, patios, garages, etc.

One of the best, most concise, and to the point mission statements is one used by the Ritz Carlton Hotel chain. These folks build and operate only five-star properties. Their mission statement, which every employee knows and practices, is "Ladies and gentlemen serving ladies and gentlemen."

Your mission statement not only explains why you are in business and what you do—it explains to employees, customers, vendors and everyone else exactly who you are and what you do.

When writing the business description section do not get side tracked into talking about all the great things that you believe about the company. You may be writing this for a bank or an investor and they do not need to hear you sounding like a proud parent bragging about a child. Stick to the facts and focus on what the outsider needs to know to entice them to invest in or loan money to your business.

Start by describing your products and services. Explain what your products and services will do for your clients, what benefits you offer and why clients will want to buy from you. If you offer unique products and services describe them (i.e., home offices, entertainment centers, and fireplaces so you might market these as quality custom "Furniture" for the home).

You may want to include a history subsection here that describes how the company was started and how it has evolved over the years.

Talk a little bit about the industry, where it has been and where it is going. Needless to say you will have to do the necessary research in this area so as not to include incorrect or misleading information.

Tell the reader what the legal entity of the business is: sole proprietor, partnership, S-Corporation or C-Corporation. Continue with information on who your main clients are, how big the market is and how the products and services are distributed and marketed.

Step 5 – Market and Industry Analysis: In this section you present your business in conjunction with the overall industry in which it falls—kitchen and bath remodel and new construction. Here you take a step back and look at the big picture, the industry as it currently stands and the projected future developments. You will need to do a fair amount of research, with a bit of looking into your crystal ball, before putting this part of the plan together. It will be important to make note of the size and growth of the overall industry.

You can use charts, graphs or text to explain the various trends culled from your research. In addition to the broader overall industry news, you need to clearly illustrate the market in your area, including growth of remodel and new construction, Baby Boomers starting to gray and spend money on their homes, etc. Then tie in your business with the marketing demands and trends.

The end result of this industry analysis should demonstrate why your business will be able to take a nice "piece of the pie." This is also important for you, the entrepreneur, to see clearly. If you cannot picture a potential market share you will have trouble selling others on what will make your company successful.

Step 6 – Competitive Analysis: This is the section where you discuss the competition. You should find this to be a fun exercise. You will need to do some investigative research so that you can adequately describe these businesses. The best way to do this is to go visit them. Do it from the point of view of a customer as well as a competitor. You will want to discuss how their businesses operate, their location, products, services, share of the market, whether they market to the higher end or mid- to lower-priced market, and if they install and charge design fees. Do they only market kitchens and baths or have they expanded in other areas of the home, and what selection of products do they show and sell?

The next step is to describe and make comparisons to your business and explain how you will improve on the products and services offered by the competition, stating what makes your business unique. Study what the market wants and show how you can provide solutions in a better way.

You are not trying to denigrate other businesses—you are simply trying to separate what you do from what is being done by others. In your plan let people know that you are prepared to carve out your own segment of the market, and how you propose to do it.

Step 7 – Marketing Strategy: If nobody buys your products or services you will be out of business quickly. Nothing ends a business faster than no customers. In this section of your business plan you need to explain how you intend to attract customers. You can have the best products and services in the world but if you do not spread the word and attract customers, you will not be successful.

In this section you need to explain who your target market is. For example: higher priced older homes that are ripe for remodel and mid to higher priced new construction. Since your business will be geared to reach a certain market segment, your marketing effort will have to be geared to that market. You will not be able to be all things to all people, so do not try and market your business to too large an audience.

Gather as much information as possible to support the demographics of your area. Then channel your marketing effort to that group which will be interested in your products and services.

Finally you will need to explain how you intend to capture a portion of that market. Detail the methods and media you will utilize to market your business. What forms of advertising and promotions will you use? Then assign a budget to your marketing program. A general guideline in the kitchen and bath industry is 3% to 5% of your sales. (This would include any manufacturer co-op monies you can negotiate.) It is very important to justify your marketing plan and to show others and remind yourself that you are not throwing money away on a poor marketing strategy. Since you'll be trying to create a specific image for the business, you should describe what that image is, and how your marketing plan backs it up. You might also describe, in some detail, any unique or special promotional advertising activities you will use to attract clients.

A good marketing plan takes a fair amount of time and careful consideration to produce. It should be the culmination of researching industry trends and your target market, and a careful evaluation of the proper media and promotional choices for getting your message to your target audience. Whatever you do, be totally realistic in your projected marketing plans.

Step 8 – Operations and Management: This section of your plan is designed to describe how the business functions on a continuing basis. It explains who does what and how and where they do it. It tells who is responsible for each aspect of the business. It describes how you work with clients, from meeting and greeting to the finished project (design, selection of products, quotation, writing the order, getting a deposit, installing the products, etc.). Explain the distribution channel for the various products and services such as cabinets from several manufacturers, countertops from a local fabricator, appliances, lighting and flooring from local distributors, and some installation (in-house and subcontracted), etc.

Each company's organizational structure will vary somewhat—so it should be divided into several broad areas:

- Marketing, Design, Sales and Customer Relations

- Installation and Production

- Administration, Finances and Human Resources

Expand this section with details and add capital expenditure areas. Possibly include showroom construction and updating costs, new delivery truck, new CAD system for designing and so forth.

When a person finishes reading this section, he or she should have a clear picture on exactly how your business operates.

Step 9 – The Management Team: The kitchen and bath industry is comprised mainly of "mom and pop" firms, so the management team section may be short. The owner oversees everything and usually sells, orders and mentors. There may be a need for a bookkeeper/office manager. If the business offers installation there may be an installation supervisor. List all the key players with short bios and what they bring to the company. This will be an important but relatively short section.

If you have a Board of Directors or use outside mentors, mention them and what they do because they are important to your success.

Step 10 – The Financial Plan: Everything else up to this point was presented as the foundation for the financial analysis. If it is a new business you need to spell out the actual investment required and when and how the business will make enough money to pay it back. If an existing business, you will use historic financial data to help build your financial projections for the next 3 to 5 years. These pro formas, as they are called, will project sales, margins, expenses and the bottom line.

There is a fair amount of looking into the crystal ball for this part of the plan. Doing this exercise and doing it well will help you manage your business more accurately and professionally. It helps you understand cash flow in advance, when to hire or let people go, when money will be available to make capital expenditures, when you will be able to update the showroom and much more.

This section includes an income statement, balance sheet and cash flow analysis. If you are starting from scratch or planning to expand and need to borrow money to do it, this is the section that gains either a positive or negative response. Be as realistic as possible because almost everything you do in the business will be guided by what the bottom line tells you.

Do not be afraid to get help with this section. Ask your accountant and/or banker to help you. In a later chapter you will find more detailed information on how to develop an annual budget and how to generate and read profit and loss statements, balance sheets and cash flow analysis. Review these before tackling this section of your business plan.

Step 11 – Summary and Conclusion: Some people do not include this section in their business plans, but it is beneficial to summarize the many details in this special and final section. The summary reiterates what was presented in the Executive Summary but adds additional insight because the reader is now informed on the idea, the market, the competition and the financial requirements of the business. In this section, you can tie-up the plan in a neat package and ensure that readers understand your view of the overall opportunity instead of letting them try to figure it out on their own.

Step 12 – Appendix and/or Supplementary Materials: The appendix and supplementary materials are often referred to throughout the plan and then appear as detailed references at the end. You might include charts, graphs, resumes and whatever literature is necessary to convince the reader or investors that you have done your homework. It is important to include this information at the end of the plan in order to avoid bogging it down with too much detail.

Ethics and Your Plan

Be totally honest in everything you present. If you are trying to interest a bank or investor in loaning you money it will never happen if they do not trust you or believe the information presented in your plan.

Reviewing Your Plan

Review your plan carefully when it is complete. Make sure you included all the key points, that it reads clearly and that all spelling and grammar is checked and edited. Be sure the plan is printed on quality paper, it is bound and has a professional appearance.

The completed plan will probably run between 20 and 40 pages. Double space it and allow wide enough margins so the type does not look cramped. Make sure the pages are numbered and double check that they match up to the Table of Contents.

Remember, the business plan needs to be a realistic portrait of your business and not an abstract design. If the pieces do not fit together or the numbers do not add up, not only will the plan not work but neither will the business.

CHAPTER 3: Business Start-Up Issues

If you are just starting a business you have a lot of important decisions to make. If you have been in business for several years there are a number of topics that you might revisit. This chapter covers topics such as legal structures for businesses, licenses and permits, paying taxes and registering your business name.

CHOOSING THE BUSINESS LEGAL STRUCTURE

Choosing the legal structure of a business is usually done right in the beginning, but it is not uncommon for an owner to reevaluate the original legal structure he/she selected. Maybe you started as a sole proprietorship and now it makes better business sense to change to a corporation or vice versa.

Choosing the Business Legal Structure
- Sole Proprietorship
- Partnership (limited or general)
- Corporations (S or C)
- Limited Liability Company

TYPE OF BUSINESS: A Quick Reference Chart

Sole Proprietorship

The sole proprietorship is the most common form of business organization. You own and operate the business and have sole responsibility and control. Essentially, you, the owner, are the business. The profits of the business are considered as personal income and, therefore, are taxed at your personal tax rate.

Advantages

- Ease of formation; fewer legal restrictions, usually less expensive than a partnership or corporation.
- Flexibility: quick response to business needs
- Profits: you have sole ownership of profits
- Exclusive control and decision making; you are in charge
- Tax deductions: losses are tax deductible

Disadvantages

- Unlimited liability: you are responsible for the full amount of business debts, and this liability extends to your personal assets
- Unstable business life: business could be crippled or terminated by your illness or death
- Limited investment; investment in the business is limited to the resources that you can raise

Partnership
A. General Partnership
B. Limited Partnership

A limited partnership is a partnership formed by two or more persons with at least one general partner and at least one limited partner. It has some of the attributes of a general partnership and a corporation. A partnership is the association of two or more people as co-owners of a business. It is a legal mechanism that allows for profits and losses to be divided among a group of investors.

When forming a partnership, you should have a partnership agreement developed that specifies the legal obligations of each partner. A partnership agreement will:

- Stipulate the initial amount of funding each partner will contribute to the business;
- Determine how management decisions will be made and authority will be divided;
- Establish methods for settling disputes among partners;
- Set up a procedure for selling out. Specify how each partner's interest will be valued; establish restrictions on selling partner's interest to a third party;
- Specify what would happen to your business if one of the partners dies or becomes physically or mentally incapacitated;
- Specify the rights of the partner's spouse.

In general partnerships, partners participate in the management of the business and are personally responsible for all debts.

Advantages

- Ease of formation
- More skills and capital available to boost performance and growth
- Flexibility and decision making with relative freedom from government control and special taxation
- Losses are tax deductible

Disadvantages

- Unlimited liability
- Personal liability of a solvent partner for the actions of unscrupulous partners
- Unstable life of business, partnership is dissolved if a partner dies or withdraws, unless specifically prescribed for in the written agreement
- Buying out a partner may be difficult unless specifically prescribed in the written agreement
- Potential for disagreements between partners could lead to costly dissolution

Limited partners in limited partnerships are liable only to the extent of their investment and do not share in the management of the business.

Advantages

- A person can invest capital in a partnership business and reap a share of the profits without becoming liable for all debts of the partnership or risking more than the amount of capital contributed.

Disadvantages

- Must have at least one partner who is liable for all debts of the partnership, and other (limited) partners whose liability is limited to their investment in the partnership
- No voice in the management of the partnership
- There are other legal and tax considerations involved, and legal advice is necessary in choosing this form of organization
- Formation and operation requires more formality than the formation and operation of a general partnership. Must file with the state.

TYPE OF BUSINESS –continued–

Corporation

The most complex form of business organization is the corporation, which is made up of three groups of people – shareholders, directors and officers. The corporation can borrow money, own assets and perform business functions without directly involving you or the other corporate owners.

Advantages

- Limitation of the stockholder's liability to a fixed amount, usually the amount invested
- Business looks more credible than a sole proprietorship to potential suppliers, employees and bankers
- Ownership is readily transferable
- Separate legal existence
- Relative ease of securing capital in large amounts and from many investors

Disadvantages

- Activity is limited by the corporation's charter and various laws
- Extensive government regulation and burdensome federal, state and local reports
- Considerable expense in forming corporation
- Greater administrative expenses on an annual basis

The legal structure you choose depends on a number of things involving your type of business, individual situation, goals for the business and a number of other personal and financial factors. Before deciding what is best for you, discuss your situation with your accountant and attorney. Make sure you are prepared to describe your business plans in some detail. It will be money and time well spent. Making the right choice can help you avoid a mistake that can be costly in terms of possible future liability.

There are three basic options to consider and each has its own unique advantages and disadvantages.

Sole Proprietorship

This is the most popular legal structure for a small business. According to the Small Business Administration, almost 75% of the 23 million small businesses in the United States are sole proprietorships. As the name implies, ownership is totally with one person. It is the easiest structure to establish because no legal formalities are necessary. The only business requirement may be a license from your local jurisdiction.

ADVANTAGES OF A SOLE PROPRIETORSHIP

- Easy and quick and usually the least expensive to establish.

- You have total ownership and control of the business.

- All profits of the business belong to you, the owner.

- No additional Federal taxation on business profits—meaning no double taxation.

- No periodic business reporting to the IRS or other government agency is required.

- Income tax filing is simply part of your annual personal tax return. (You would use a Schedule C or Canada Revenue Agency Form T4002.)

DISADVANTAGES OF A SOLE PROPRIETORSHIP

- The owner is personally liable for all business debts and the liability is not limited to just the business. You are personally liable for any and all business debt you incur.

- It is generally more difficult to borrow money or obtain outside investment than with other types of legal structures.

- If the owner is incapacitated for any reason, the business is likely to fail.

- All management responsibility is with the owner, which can be a heavy burden.

- You must pay self-employment tax on the business's net income.

Note: If you are a designer doing business from home (i.e. a "home business") then you are most likely a sole proprietor. However, just because you conduct business from your home does not exempt you from possible legal or other liabilities.

Partnership

This type of business is just what the name implies: business ownership is divided between two or more partners. The general partnership is the most common and is formed to conduct a business with two or more partners fully involved in the operation of the business. All the partners share both the profits and the liabilities. A Limited Partnership, as the name implies, provides for limited liability of partners. This liability can be no greater than the partner's investment in the partnership. In a Limited Partnership there must be at least one general partner who remains liable for all the debts of the partnership.

ADVANTAGES OF A PARTNERSHIP

- Synergy as a result of pooling partners, different areas of expertise.

- The partnership does not pay Federal income taxes.

- An informational tax return (IRS form #1065 or Canada Revenue Agency Form T4002) must be filed which shows the pass through of income/loss to each partner.

- Liability may be spread among partners.

- Investment can come from the partners in the form of a loan which creates interest income for the partners and a business deduction for the partnership.

DISADVANTAGES OF A PARTNERSHIP

- Formation and subsequent changes in structure are complex.

- Problems with partners stem from misunderstandings, different goals, etc., and can adversely affect or destroy the partnership.

- Limited partners are liable for debt if they are active managers in the business. General partners have unlimited liability, and you may also be liable for commitments of the partners. Limited partners are not liable for the debts of the limited partnership unless they are active managers in the business.

Corporation

There are two types of Corporations: the C-Corporation (regular Corporation) and the S-Corporation (or "S-Corp"). Both of these forms of corporations are complex legal entities. Their detailed structure may vary from state/province to state/province. Incorporating a business in a given state/province allows you to conduct business only in that state/province. It is essential for you to obtain legal advice if you are thinking about forming a corporation. Because each state/province has its own set of corporation laws, contact the appropriate office in your state/province. Usually the Office of the Secretary of State will provide additional material and procedures.

Most people immediately think of incorporating in order to minimize their personal liability. The liability of stockholders (owners) in a corporation is limited under certain and complex conditions. Today, with the Tax Reform Act of 1986 and other legislation there are really few good tax reasons to incorporate (with the exception of dividing corporate profits as noted below). The reason for incorporation is, in fact, the limited liability. However, there is no such thing as a total insulation from liability resulting from doing business as a corporation.

Record keeping and tax matters for a corporation are complex and time consuming tasks usually requiring the services of an accountant. Keep this in mind when considering operational costs for your business.

Avoid "do-it-yourself" incorporation guides. The process is complex and not a task you should take on by yourself. Legal fees for setting up a corporation can run from $350 to $1,500, assuming it is relatively straightforward.

REGULAR CORPORATION

The corporation is a taxable entity and as such pays taxes. This results in the "double taxation" you may have heard about. The corporation pays corporate taxes on its profits and then you, the owner (shareholder), pay personal taxes on the wages and dividends the corporation pays you. This is one of the biggest disadvantages of a corporation.

On the other hand, incorporating your business usually makes it easier to establish credit with suppliers and to borrow from banks. If you expect to use outside investors for business capital, a corporation is necessary.

ADVANTAGES OF A REGULAR CORPORATION

- Shareholders (the owners) enjoy personal limited liability.

- It is generally easier to obtain business capital.

- Profits may be divided among owners and the corporation in order to reduce taxes by taking advantage of lower taxes.

- The corporation does not dissolve on the death of a stockholder (owner) or, if the ownership changes, it has perpetual existence.

- Favorable tax treatment for employee fringe benefits including medical, disability, and life insurance plans.

- Seventy percent of any dividends received by corporation from stock investments are deductible as long as they weren't purchased with borrowed money.

- Shares in corporation are easily transferable (unless limited by Shareholders' Agreement).

DISADVANTAGES OF A REGULAR CORPORATION

- More expensive and complex to set up than other legal structures.

- Completing tax returns usually requires the help of an accountant.

- Double taxation on wages and profits paid to owners.

- Recurring annual corporate fees.

- Tax rates are higher than individual rates for profits greater than approximately $75,000.

- Twenty-eight percent accumulated earnings tax or profits in excess of $250,000.

- Businesses losses are not deductible by the corporation.

S-CORPORATION

The S–Corporation offers the limited liability advantages of a corporation but does not pay Federal taxes. All of the earnings of an S-Corporation are passed through to the shareholders (owners). Losses can also be passed through if the shareholder has basis. It is a popular form of incorporation in the start-up years of a business, but there are some subtle disadvantages that need to be considered as you grow. To qualify as an S-Corporation, a corporation must file IRS Form 2553 in a timely fashion; some states require a separate election. Again, because of the complexities involved, talk with your attorney and/or accountant.

ADVANTAGES OF AN S-CORPORATION

- Owners enjoy personal limited liability as in a regular corporation.
- No Federal income tax liability and in most cases no state income tax.
- Profits are passed to owners with no double taxation.
- Losses are passed through to the owners if shareholder has basis.
- Wholly owned subsidiaries are permitted.

DISADVANTAGES OF AN S-CORPORATION

- More expensive and complex to set up than other legal structures.
- Maximum of 75 shareholders (usually not an issue in our industry).
- Only one class of common stock is permitted and no preferred stock.

Limited Liability Company (LLC)

This type of entity blends the tax advantages of a partnership and the limited liability advantages of a corporation. Owners of an LLC are called "members." The LLC has some limitations also. Get information from your state/province and consult with your attorney and accountant to see if an LLC is the way to incorporate your business.

ADVANTAGES OF AN LLC

- Limited personal liability for the owners, like a Corporation and unlike a Partnership.

- No Federal taxes, like a Partnership.

- No limit on the number of stockholders, unlike an S-Corporation.

- More than one class of stock is permitted, unlike an S-Corporation.

- Business losses may be deducted on your personal tax return, like an S-Corporation.

- The IRS and most states allow for a single member LLC for those sole proprietors who want limited liability but do not want to incorporate.

DISADVANTAGES OF AN LLC

- Earnings are generally subject to self-employment tax.

- State law may limit the life of an LLC.

- Lack of uniformity in LLC statutes. Businesses that operate in more than one state may not receive consistent treatment.

- Some states do not tax partnerships, but they do tax LLCs.

- Conversion of an existing business to LLC status could result in tax recognition on appreciated assets.

Making Your Choice of Legal Structure

It is impossible to give advice on this important decision in this volume because every situation is unique. Assess the advantages and disadvantages described here based on your particular situation. In any case, it is important to discuss your plans with advisors, including both an attorney and an accountant before making your final decision.

When discussing your plans with advisors keep in mind the following points:

- The LLC is worth looking into.

- Saving on taxes is one of the most important considerations for selecting a business structure. Keep in mind there are generally few tax advantages with a corporation if your total taxable business income is more than $75,000.

- Do not select the corporation structure based on possible tax advantages of profit-sharing plans because the 401(k), SEP and Simple IRA plans available to sole proprietorships are equally beneficial.

- If you consider a partnership, be certain to have a complete partnership agreement drawn up by your attorney.

- Consider an S-Corporation if you expect business losses for the first year or two. These losses can be passed through to the owners as tax relief but they provide no current benefit in a regular corporation if a shareholder has basis.

OTHER REQUIREMENTS AND CONSIDERATIONS

There are a number of items to address when starting and operating a business, regardless of the legal structure and type. Review the following list so that you stay compliant in all areas and do not overlook important acts or issues.

Business Licenses and Permits

Depending on your type of business and your location, various licenses and permits may be required. Check with your state, city and county/municipality governments for information on these items. Be diligent because fines could be levied for any omissions.

Business Name

Once you have selected the business name, if you are a sole proprietorship or partnership, be sure to register for a "fictitious name" with your state/province. "Fictitious" because the name most likely will not be your own full legal name. Filing with the state/province costs from $10 to $100. Be sure no one else has selected the same name or one very close to it. If you develop a logo for the business, you can apply for a copyright for this. If you think you will ever do business in more than one state/province, register the name in each state/province.

Tax Payments

You will be required to make periodic estimated Federal and, sometimes, State/Province tax payments regardless of your business legal structure so you must obtain a tax ID number from the tax authority. The requirements vary so discuss with your accountant. Late tax payments will accrue costly penalties.

Collection of Sales Tax

Most kitchen and bath businesses sell products to end-user customers (the public) which means it is likely you will collect sales tax for the state/province and or local government. Check with your state/province and local tax departments on the requirements because every state/province is different. You will probably have to apply for a sales tax identification number that will identify you to the local and state/province government as a seller of goods. The process is easy and usually no cost is involved. There may also be monthly reporting requirements.

Operating in More Than One State/Province

Assume that your business grows and you want to operate with stores or offices in more than one state/province. The good news is—this is possible. The bad news is that you may need to perform some filings and registrations to qualify in each state/province where you do business. In addition, you will have to file tax returns in each of these states/provinces as well. Once again, get professional help in this area.

LOCATION, LOCATION, LOCATION

Business Location Choices
- Home-based location
- Studio/boutique location
- Destination location
- Shared location
- Retail shopping location
- Trade/retail "mart" location

If starting a new business, be sure to select the best location. If you are already in business, step back and look at your present site.

Not all locations are created equal. And not all businesses need a great location. But, for a kitchen and bath business that wants to attract homeowners, interior designers, contractors and architects, the location is important. Visibility, access and exposure are all essential to consider.

The first thing to ask is, "Have you targeted the right community?" Consider:

- Is the population base large enough to support your business?

- Does the demographic profile closely match that of the market you wish to serve?

- Does the community have a stable economic base that will promote a healthy environment in which your business can operate?

- What are the community attitudes or outlook?

The answers to these questions require that you know the demographic profile of your potential clients. Look for:

- **Purchasing Power:** What is the percentage of disposable income within the community? This would include the income levels of the homeowners.

- **Residences:** Are the homes owned or rented? What is the current and projected value of homes in this marketplace?

- **Means of Transportation:** Do your prospective clients own vehicles or use public transportation?

- **Age Range:** What is the age range of your target audience? Generally, you will be looking for homeowners in the 35+ age bracket. Are they aging Baby Boomers, young professionals or retirees?

- **Family Status:** Are the residents mostly married or are there more who are single?

- **Leisure Activities:** What type of hobbies and recreational activities do people in the community participate in?

Other considerations for your location:

- **Traffic and Accessibility:** Is your location easy to get to? Will a lot of drive-by traffic help the business? (Usually, yes.)

- **Competition:** How many competitors are in this marketplace? Where are they located?

- **Related Building Product Businesses:** Being close to tile/granite, lighting, appliance, flooring, window and door businesses is usually a big plus. Clients like one-stop shopping whenever possible.

- **Visibility:** Is the location easily seen from the street or highway?

- **Signage:** Good signage is invaluable. Check local restrictions and regulations.

- **Facilities:** Do the area and building project the image you want and need? How is the parking, lighting and landscaping?

- **The Landlord:** Is the landlord responsive and easy to work with or just the opposite?

- **Rent:** Cost is important. Can you afford it? Conversely, if it is a great location, can you not afford it? Plan to provide references to the landlord.

- **Miscellaneous:** Storage of merchandise, shipping and receiving areas, regulations regarding garbage, pick-up and deliveries, snow removal, etc. Utilities, office and support space, windows for displays, ceiling height, public restrooms, good security and neighbors, and additional fees if in a mall type location are all things to consider.

The ideal location would be in an area that meets many of these needs and one that offers growth opportunity, terrific demographics for your products and services, little direct competition and is in an area where you feel safe and can attract the high level of experienced personnel you will need to help make the business a success.

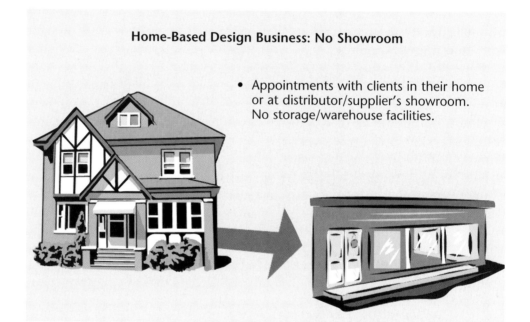

Home-Based Design Business: No Showroom

- Appointments with clients in their home or at distributor/supplier's showroom. No storage/warehouse facilities.

Design/Build Destination Showroom

- Appointments in showroom
- Separate storage and/or shop facility on site or a distance away

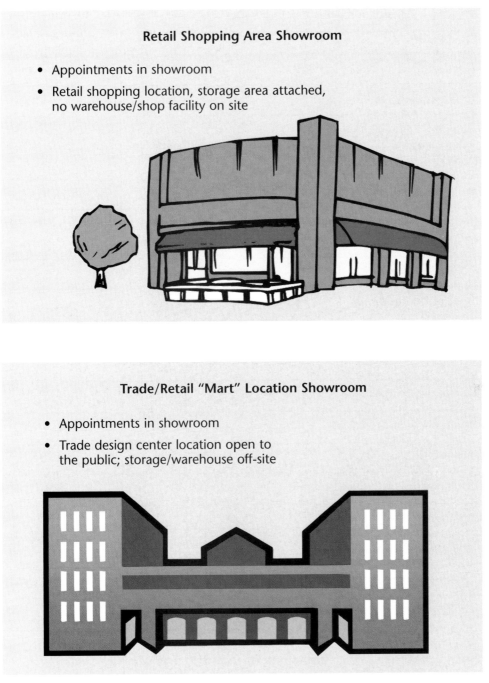

Retail Shopping Area Showroom

- Appointments in showroom
- Retail shopping location, storage area attached, no warehouse/shop facility on site

Trade/Retail "Mart" Location Showroom

- Appointments in showroom
- Trade design center location open to the public; storage/warehouse off-site

Following is a "Location Checklist" that you might use to help you in this important decision. Add any other items that would be important to you.

LOCATION CHECKLIST

Answer each question on a scale of 1-3, with 1 being "Good," 2 being "Fair" and 3 being "Poor."

Questions	Good	Fair	Poor
1. Is the facility large enough for your business?			
2. Does it meet your layout requirements?			
3. Does the building need any repairs?			
4. Are leasehold improvements completed?			
5. How accessible is the facility to your target audience?			
6. How convenient is it for employees in terms of commuting, parking, comfort and safety?			
7. How consistent is the facility with the image you want to project?			
8. How safe is the neighborhood?			
9. How likely will neighboring businesses help attract clients?			
10. How close are competitors located to the facility?			
11. Can suppliers conveniently make deliveries?			
12. Does the facility allow room to expand?			
13. Rate the visibility and signage.			
14. Are there windows to show off your displays?			
15. Is there plenty of convenient parking?			
16. Is the outside and inside lighting sufficient?			
17. Will the public restrooms meet your needs?			
18. How is the car and foot traffic?			
19. Are the lease and rent terms favorable?			
20. Is the location zoned for your type of business?			
21. Can you live with all regulations, restrictions?			
22. Are other building product businesses near the facility?			

Your numerical ratings combined with your good judgment when weighing the relative importance of each item will assist you in comparing potential sites.

Tax Ramifications of Claiming an Office in Your Home

Some designers choose to operate from a home office. This might be the ideal business location for an independent designer.

Too often, people automatically assume working out of their home provides specific tax advantages. When certain conditions are met, the Internal Revenue Service/Canada Revenue Agency allows you to deduct the costs associated with using a portion of your home for business.

THE CONDITIONS

In most cases, you must use your home office exclusively for business activities. In other words, you cannot use the area for both business and personal purposes. The area could be a room or another identifiable space.

The area generally must be either your principal place of business or a place where you meet with clients or customers. However, a separate structure (such as a garage) that you use in connection with your business also may qualify.

IF YOU'RE AN EMPLOYEE

If you are an employee who works out of your home, you may qualify for a home office deduction if all the above requirements are met and you are using the office for your employer's convenience.

WHAT'S DEDUCTIBLE?

Deductible expenses include a portion (based on the percentage of space in the home used for business) of real estate taxes, mortgage interest or rent, utilities, depreciation, insurance and maintenance costs.

WHAT IF I SELL MY HOME?

Consult a tax professional regarding the ramifications of selling your home if you claim a portion of it as a home office.

FINANCING THE BUSINESS

Once again, whether you are considering a brand new business or you have been in business for some time, the "money hunt" is never ending. Cash is king during good times and bad, during expansion and cutbacks. Because it is so important, spend time thinking about how to keep your business well financed.

Having the money available to finance your dream or to continue to grow it can only happen if you have a solid foundation in-place. If you are thinking about securing funds from a lender or an investor, you should know exactly how much money you need to get started or to grow and stay open. Knowing this will put you well ahead of most other small business entrepreneurs. The big question is—where will you find the money to start or grow your business?

A number of sources provide funding.

- Banks, venture capitalists.

- Personal loans and individual investors.

- Your own savings. (However, if you are using some of your own savings, do not take away from living expenses or savings earmarked for college tuitions or retirement.)

If you have the money to invest—use it cautiously and stick to your business plan.

> **A Word of Experience from Hank Darlington**
>
> Even if you are going to self fund the business, either through savings, selling assets, credit cards or some other plan, this foundation is no less important. It is the basis for creating a solid kitchen and bath business.

Packaging Your Loan Proposal
- Who are you?
- What are you going to do with the money?
- When and how do you plan to pay it back?
- Does the amount requested make suitable allowances for unexpected business developments?
  1. Your management ability
  2. The ratio of business debt to net worth
  3. Your debt paying record
  4. The company's past earnings
  5. The value and condition of your collateral

Packaging Your Loan Proposal

By Melvin Pfeif

Mark Twain once said that a banker is a fellow who lends his umbrella when the sun is shining and wants it back the minute it rains.

While there may be some truth to that thought, it is important to remember that bankers WANT to make loans. Making loans is how the banks earn a profit. But keep in mind that the banker wants to make loans to businesses that are solvent, profitable and growing. Your job is to convince the banker that you fit (or soon will fit) that description.

Many different outlines are available for preparing a loan proposal. The Small Business Administration, SCORE, your bank and others have developed guidelines for clearly and effectively communicating your financial needs and anticipated sources of prepayment. Which outline is the "right" format is a matter of preference.

Regardless of your choice, always begin your proposal with a cover letter. Clearly and quickly explain who you are, what your background is, the nature of your business, and amount and purpose of your loan request, your requested terms of repayment, how the funds will benefit your business and how you will repay the loan. Keep it simple and direct. You have the rest of the package to fully explain the details of your proposal.

Then, follow your chosen outline to provide more depth and discuss the specifics at length. Don't assume the reader is familiar with your industry and your individual business. Take the time to include the details, industry information and anything else that will make the reader comfortable with how your business works and what the industry trends are.

Keep in mind that the loan officer must feel satisfied with the answers to the following questions:

Who are you?	Your character comes first, then your ability to manage your business.
What are you going to do with the money?	The answer to this will determine the type of loan, short or long-term. Money to be used for the purchase of seasonal inventory will require faster repayment than money used to buy fixed assets.
When and how do you plan to pay it back?	Your banker's judgment of your business ability and the type of loan will be a deciding factor in the answer to this question.
Does the amount requested make suitable allowance for developments?	The banker decides this question on the basis of your financial statement which sets forth for the unexpected condition on your business and on the collateral pledged.
What is the outlook for business in general and for your business particularly?	When assembling this information, pay close attention to the preparation of income and cash flow projections to support your ability to repay the loan. These projections are critically important for a new venture or a business that has not yet established a track record of profitability to clearly substantiate repayment. When you have compiled your loan proposal package and carefully prepared your projections, think about some of the factors the lender will consider.

Your management ability.	If you are starting a business or purchasing an existing business, you will generally be expected to demonstrate previous management experience in your field. Without this prior background, the potential risk of business failure usually precludes conventional bank financing or an SBA loan.
The ratio of business debt to net worth.	The lender will look closely at your tangible dollar investment in the firm. Don't expect a bank or the SBA to finance a venture you are unwilling to risk your funds in. For startups or buyouts, you should plan to invest at least one dollar of your own funds for each two dollars of loan. The more debt a firm takes on, the more risk to the business owner and the lender.
Your debt-paying record to suppliers, banks, home mortgage holders and other creditors.	Check your credit rating. Your banker will. Contact business and personal credit reporting services and ask for a copy of your file. You may have to pay a fee for this information, but it may be money well spent. Errors and inaccuracies in these reports can occur. It is easier to correct the mistakes before you apply for a loan rather than try to provide explanations to your lender after the problem arises.
The company's past earnings.	If these earnings don't support your ability to repay the loan, you have your work cut out to convince the lender. Remember to emphasize what the loan will do for the firm. Point out the benefits of the loan and what will happen to the company as a result. And remember to support your projected figures with clear, logical explanations.
The value and condition of your collateral.	Every loan must have at least two identifiable sources of repayment. The first source is ordinarily cash flow generated from profitable operations of the business. The second source is usually collateral pledged to secure the loan. Keep in mind that lenders will typically view business assets such as inventory, accounts receivable and equipment as much less than you might think. If YOU can't sell the inventory, imagine how difficult it will be for the lender to find a buyer at a reasonable price!

When all is said and done, take another look at the proposal to make sure you have included everything necessary. If your proposal is fairly complex, it may take a substantial amount of material to complete the presentation. But remember that excessive quantity may sometimes be a "red flag" in itself. The lender will want to read everything that is pertinent to the proposal, but may become impatient if it appears that superfluous material is presented just to make an impressively thick package.

Investors, regardless of who they are will be looking for:

- A good idea.

- A solid, comprehensive business plan.

- Someone with the experience, drive, determination and skills to make that plan happen.

And you will be looking for:

- Someone who understands your idea or shares the same vision.

- Someone who will let you maintain control of your business.

- An individual or institution with the funding to help you make your plan happen.

A Warning

Obtaining financing is often tied to control issues.

- If you obtain a loan, arrange to pay back the money with interest, but with no other strings attached.

- Realize that if you take on an investor, be it a friend, relative or stranger, you may have to give up some degree of control over your business and some percentage of the profits.

Therefore, whenever taking on investors, determine specifically what they want for their investment. Are they seeking profits, control or some of each? Try to reach an agreement that makes you feel comfortable—and put it in writing!

Funding Sources

BANKS

The bank will not want any ownership or control of the business—they will leave the day-to-day business decisions to you. The bank will want to secure its loan with collateral on your part. In simple terms, they will want to know that they will get their money back one way or another. The bank will want to see a complete and detailed business plan. The bank will want to know specifically what the money will be used for (i.e., expanding your displays, new furniture, equipment, inventories, etc.). They will want to know exactly how much money you want. No rough estimates.

Your background, character and capability to run a business and to repay a loan are other key factors. Your past financial statements, credit history and references are also important information to back up your loan application.

Several programs featuring loans for small businesses are also available through the Small Business Association (SBA). Check with your local banks or look at their various loan programs on their website (www.sba.gov).

You can also join a credit union and apply for a smaller, shorter-term loan through them.

VENTURE CAPITAL FIRMS

Most venture capitalists are more interested in helping mature businesses with growth and expansion, although some will work with start-up businesses.

Once again, you will have to show them a sound business plan and prove your worthiness. They will expect to earn a reasonable rate of interest on their investment and may want to exert some control. Remember, this is not a loan—these firms are making an investment.

INDIVIDUAL INVESTORS

This is where finding backing for your business gets interesting, to say the least. Individual investors can range from family to friends to neighbors. Once again, regardless who the individual investor might be, present your proposal and plan in a professional manner. Pitch your idea to them exactly the same way you would to anyone else.

Should you elect to take this route, put the entire agreement in writing. If it is a loan with interest, document this. If it is an investment in future profitability or part ownership, spell out the details and cover the control issue.

STOCKHOLDERS

In order to secure financing, and if your business is a corporation, you may need to sell a piece of the business to investors. They would become shareholders and would most likely expect to receive some share of the profits on a regular basis, usually yearly. If the business is sold, the number of percentage of shares the investors hold determines how much of the selling price they receive. Once again, be sure to cover the control issue. Put all of this in writing to eliminate any misunderstandings.

Financing Your Business
The Six C's of Credit
- Capital
- Collateral
- Character
- Capability
- Coverage
- Circumstances

THE SIX C's OF CREDIT

Bankers use what they refer to as the six C's of credit. The higher you rate in these categories, the greater the likelihood of getting your loan approved. And, the better the rate will be!

- **Capital** – The amount of money already invested in your business or available for future investment.

- **Collateral** – The assets you own that could be used to secure your loan.

- **Character** – Your personal experience, reputation and credit history.

- **Capability** – Your ability to repay the loan based on past, current and future income flows.

- **Coverage** – The insurance or safety precautions needed to protect the lender's investment.

- **Circumstances** – Both the current financial situations of your business and the economy as a whole.

If deficiencies exist in any area of your business, do not try to hide them. Be open and honest. Show what you are doing to correct the problem and emphasize other favorable factors. Bankers want to lend money and handle your banking needs, but it is up to you to demonstrate that you are a good risk. If the first bank you visit turns you down, learn by your mistakes, correct them, and go visit another bank.

When You Have The Money

Now that you have obtained a loan from a bank or investor, the money is yours to do with what ever you choose, right? Wrong. You requested this money for a specific purpose and that is exactly where that money needs to be spent. The bank and/or investors will want to stay informed about what is happening. Do what you say you are going to do at all levels. You may need to revisit this source again in the future and you will want a favorable response. Look at these sources of funding as "partners" in the business even though legally they are not.

A LOOK AT TAXES

While you most likely will not welcome the tax man with open arms, you do need to know how to prepare for tax payments once you become a business owner. There will be federal, state/province, county and city taxes to be paid. Other than the Internal Revenue Service/Canada Revenue Agency, the rates and regulations will vary by area. You, your bookkeeper (if it's someone other than yourself) and your accountant will all need to be informed and involved. Here are just a few tips to help you remain legal and to help you minimize your tax obligations.

Keep Good Records

One of the most basic principles of paying taxes is sound preparation, which entails good record keeping. Studies show that more people run into problems with their various tax returns because of their record keeping system than for any other reason.

Your record keeping system provides a clear picture of all income and expenses. Keep information on all sales transactions, receipts and cancelled checks for all purchases and expenses made for the business. Make sure all paperwork is dated and filed according to categories such as rent, utilities, auto expenses, advertising, accounts payable by vendor and so on. Your system should be easy to follow, to update and to access.

What You Need to Pay and When

The legal entity of your business dictates when, at what rate, and how much you have to pay. Whether you operate on a calendar or fiscal year also has some bearing.

Your bookkeeper, accountant, or both will help with taxes, but the end responsibility is yours. The Internal Revenue Service/Canada Revenue Agency, states/provinces and other agencies are unforgiving when it comes to not paying taxes. Do not delegate and forget. Be sure to pay your taxes in a timely and correct manner.

There are lots of opportunities and temptations where taxes are concerned. Do not jeopardize your business or personal life by taking short cuts—play it straight.

Obtain Good Professional Help

The tax laws and regulations are long and varied so it is in your best interest to obtain the best professional help you can find. A good tax professional can advise you how to legally minimize both your business and personal taxes. Avail yourself of this expertise. Here are a few tips to use when looking for the right tax professional. Choose someone:

- Who you trust implicitly.

- Who will take the time to review your situation and provide you with advice and guidance on an on-going basis.

- Who has all the necessary credentials in the field.

- Who is familiar with your type of business on a broad level.

- Who likes working with small business owners.

- Who knows the federal, state/province and local regulations and requirements.

- Who is willing to be your financial mentor on an on-going basis.

A good tax professional can quite literally mean the difference between success and failure in business. So take your time and choose someone you believe can help you make the right tax decisions and devise the best tax plan for your business.

SELECTING
VENDOR PARTNERS

One of the most important marketing decisions you make is selecting the products you want to sell. Because yours is a kitchen and bath business, cabinets will be one of those products. Your market research should have told you what other products you might add to your product package. Many kitchen and bath businesses are showing and selling countertops (natural and synthetic), some show and sell appliances, tile, plumbing, lighting, flooring, doors and windows. What is or will be your product offering?

Once you have made this important decision you must decide who your vendor partners will be. Make your decision almost as if you are entering into a marriage, because the attributes that make for a strong personal marriage are similar in a business marriage. Good communication, openness, honesty, commitment, loyalty and respect all apply to both.

Part of the decision process will be selecting your niche—luxury, high end, middle range or entry level (most competitive).

Some try to combine two or three of these niches; however, it is very difficult to be all things to all people. It is easier, less costly and more productive to be a specialist in just one area, with the possibility of overlapping into another area just a bit.

Once you have selected your niche, start looking for vendors that supply this price and quality range of products. There is such a wide range of wood species, styles, colors and finishes, as well as a variety of custom offerings from manufacturers, that you may have to select three or four cabinet partners. Some businesses elect to work with just one or two cabinet suppliers and others have seven to ten. One or two lines may not give you all the offerings you need, seven to ten may dilute the amount of business you can give to each; remember, you want to be an important partner to them.

There is a long list of items to use to rate the various vendors. Not each line item will be of equal importance to you and this will vary by business so you should assign your own weighting for each item. To rate importance you might use the numbers 1 – 5, with 5 having the most value to your business and 1 the least. When comparing like vendors, use the guide to rate each. Do not fall into the trap of "I like the rep." The rep who calls on you is important, but it is only one of the items rated on the following list. There are many other factors to consider. When feasible go visit the vendor, take the tour, meet their people and check their financial statements. They will insist on seeing yours so it is only fair, and good business too, to review theirs.

Countertops, appliances, plumbing and the many other products you might decide to show and sell will most likely be supplied by more local vendors or distributors. Choose the very best partner wisely as you will want the 'marriage' to grow and last.

VENDOR SELECTION CHECKLIST

Rate each area on a scale of 1 to 5, with 1 being the lowest value to your business and 5 being the highest value to your business. Or come up with your own rating. Feel free to add any other items that would be important to you at the bottom of the list to prioritize the results. Assign weight to each item to the degree of importance to your business.

Review Product Line by the Following:	Weight	X	Rating	=	Total
Breadth and depth					
Quality					
Price Point					
Overall Service					
Style of Product					
Brand Recognition					
Purchase Cost (Multiplier)					
Sales and Profit Potential					
Exclusivity					
Market Share					
Company History and Growth					
Company Financial Status					
Product Warranty Program					
Local Representative					
Terms of Purchase					
Cash Terms					
Days Due					
Delivery					
Lead Times					
Freight					
Co-op Programs					
Training					
Volume Rebate Program					
Special Event Dollars					
Literature and Brochures					
Order Placement Procedures					
Vendor Advertising and Promotions					
Do they sell to multi-brand retailers?					
Do they sell through buying groups?					
Display Programs					
Return Goods Policy					
Customer Testimonials					
Quality of Reps					
Total Score					

BUYING GROUPS – SHARING EXPERTISE

While buying groups have been around in most industries for decades, the kitchen and bath industry is still a relative newcomer to the buying group concept. There are two major buying groups that have been participating in our industry since the mid-1990s.

Buying Groups Offer You:
- Sharing expertise/networking
- Receiving industry specific financial information
- Participating in shared expense marketing programs
- Receiving rebate financial rewards

Advantages of Participating in a Buying Group

- Monetary benefits—rebates, cash and other discounts generally not available to individuals.

- A direct and greater voice to the top management of vendor/supplier partners.

- Access to kitchen/bath industry focused marketing programs.

- The opportunity to network with fellow professionals at the one or twice-per-year buying group meetings.

- The opportunity to attend kitchen/bath industry-focused educational conferences.

- Assistance with business management issues by individuals completely focused on the kitchen/bath industry.

- The opportunity to participate in a consumer magazine program.

Although the financial benefits are normally the top reason dealerships join buying groups, members often cite other advantages that become more important as they participate.

- **The opportunity to share financial information with businesses following a similar model.** Some consider receiving focused advice on how to improve financial performance from one meeting to the next a major benefit. To gain this benefit, participants must be willing to share accurate—and, oftentimes, confidential—financial information.

- **Networking opportunities with others in the same business.** Learning how to expand your business, or being introduced to business practices or marketing programs in a more focused environment rather than association meetings or other activities that have a more diverse business membership. As one individual said, "It becomes an ongoing school for finding best practices in the industry and sharing them."

- **The opportunity for national exposure through consumer publications oftentimes published by the buying group.** These "advertorial buy a page or two-page" formats have proven successful for participating dealers. The consumer values the information and examples of great kitchen design and considers these books on a par with shelter publication's special interest issues.

Why Dealers Have Not Joined Buying Groups

- Do not understand the membership fee structure or the rebate program.

- Do not want to pay annual dues, and do not like the idea of submitting a letter of credit.

- Feel they currently can buy just as competitively on their own. Are not interested in carrying the product lines represented by the buying group.

- The buying group does not represent enough of their vendor partners.

A buying group may not be in the best interest of dealerships whose business models are quite different from the majority of the buying group's membership. For example, a boutique business with an annual sales volume of less than $1 million and who focuses on the high-end might not benefit from a buying group catering to larger retail organizations.

SELECTING VENDORS IS A GROUP RESPONSIBILITY

As reported in *Kitchen & Bath Design News* magazine, dealers are typically hesitant about joining buying groups because of concerns about the supplier partner elements of the group.

> *"To be successful, a buying group must do a volume of business with specific vendors. This means all members must participate and purchase all or some of their product mix from the participating manufacturers. In all groups, the members actually choose the manufacturers to represent. Additionally, while members are encouraged to buy from this select group (and receive greater rebates when they do), members certainly can still choose to buy other products from non-member vendors: assuming they make their minimum purchase requirements for the buying group."*

MEMBERSHIP REQUIREMENTS VARY
BUT ARE TYPICALLY BASED ON ...

- A one-time membership fee and some type of annual fee. (The annual fee may be used for other buying group services, or may be waived based on the minimum purchasing level met by the dealer.)

- A minimum yearly annual sales volume from the participating manufacturers.

- The firm may be required to have a showroom and not belong to a competing buying group.

- There may be a minimum annual sales volume requirement.

- Participating members must attend at least one of the buying group's two conferences held each year.

JOINING THE BUSINESS COMMUNITY

By virtue of being located in a community, you are now part of it. You will have to follow local ordinances and pay local taxes. There will be various business and civic organizations to join for both learning and networking opportunities, such as the local Chamber of Commerce. They offer seminars and learning opportunities for small business owners and, by being a member, you can network with other small business entrepreneurs.

By joining a community and becoming involved, you will develop relationships that can help you and your image, leading to good public relations. Support from leaders in the community can help your business draw attention to itself. Sponsoring an event to help a charitable organization will enhance your public image.

By contributing to your community, you will draw positive attention from the media. They, in turn, will reflect to the public a positive image of you and your business.

You will be busy running your business so you may not be able to initially afford the time to become one of the leaders of the various organizations, but being an active member and supporter can only create positive results.

TAKING ADVANTAGE OF OUTSIDE HELP

It is difficult to build a business in a vacuum. The feedback, suggestions, opinions and guidance from others can be valuable in helping you run your business. The sources and resources are innumerable. Some help you may have to pay for (attorney, accountant, consultants, etc.) and other help may be free for the asking (banker, Chamber of Commerce, the Small Business Association, etc.).

Consider Your Banker a Key Business Associate

Your bank is more than a place where you keep a checking account. They provide many important services that will be required for your business operations. Choose carefully.

- Is the bank in a convenient location?

- Does the banker understand your business?

- Is the bank small enough so you can deal with senior management?

- Will your banker be willing to act as a mentor and be willing to coach you?

- Does the bank have an SBA loan department?

- In the United States, is the bank a member of FDIC and the Federal Reserve Bank? In Canada, is the bank a member of the Canadian Investor Protection Fund (CIPF)?

- Does the bank provide the services
  you will need now and in the future?

- Is the bank's capitalization/asset ratio greater than 6%?
  (This is a good measure of the bank's health.)

- What are the fees for various transactions?
  Are they competitive?

- What are the fees and interest rates associated
  with their credit cards? Are they competitive?

- What balances are required on
  interest bearing checking accounts?

The National Kitchen & Bath Association

One great resource is the National Kitchen & Bath Association. Local and national activities provide invaluable networking opportunities. As you meet and become acquainted with other owners at NKBA events, you will be able to pick up the phone or fire off an email to discuss almost any issue that may surface. Do not try to reinvent the wheel, just improve on it. There is no better way than by sharing experience with folks who "have been there and done that."

An Advisory Board

Establish an advisory board for your business. Include your accountant, attorney, banker and add a friend or relative who may have small business management experience. If you work with an advertising or public relations firm, ask them to be a member. Bring the group together quarterly or as necessary. Have an agenda and start brainstorming. It may cost you a few dinners and a gift during the holidays, but the results will be more valuable than you could imagine. Help is out there—go find it.

CHAPTER 4: Accounting and Record Keeping

Behind the excitement and anticipation of a great business success comes a more mundane, yet vital task. Business accounting is your way to keep score on how well the business is doing. If the main purpose of operating a business is to make a profit then proper business accounting is required so you know how well you are doing, and if you really are generating profits.

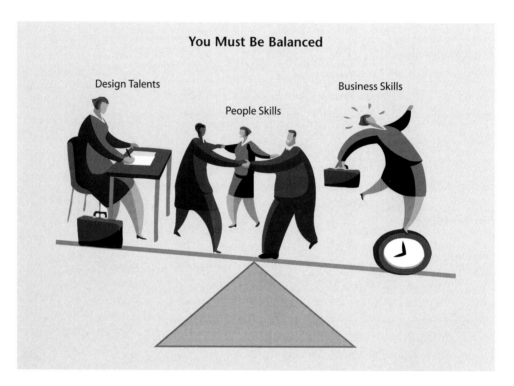

You Must Be Balanced

Design Talents

People Skills

Business Skills

Remember, there are two parts to your business: the things you love (designing, selling, creating dream kitchen and bath projects), and the things you must do (accounting, managing people, making problems go away, etc.). Accounting falls into the latter group. Bookkeeping is not glamorous and it is not the reason you went into business, but it is the backbone of a successful business. Without accurate books and business records and without the skills to generate and analyze these records, you will be unable to get a clear picture of just how well, or how poorly, your business is doing.

Most kitchen and bath business owners fall short in this all important area. But the difference between just eking out a living and a successful business is often an owner's involvement and understanding of this area of the business.

What can you do to become a good financial manager? Be a balanced business owner.

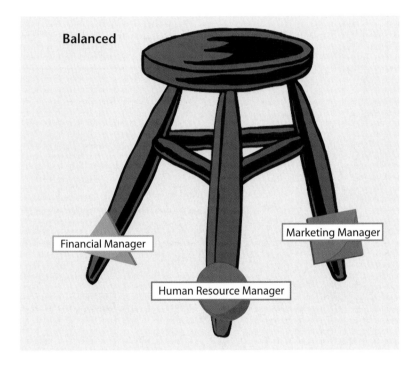

Every business consists of three parts:

• Marketing Management

• Human Resource Management

• Financial Management

All three areas need to be equally strong for a business to be truly successful. Most kitchen and bath owners are fairly strong in the marketing segments (design, sales, advertising, promotion), but are weak and too often reluctant to improve upon the human resource (people management) and financial areas (budgets, financial statements, cash flow) of the business.

Marketing Manager

From his experience, Hank advises:

"This may seem a bit strong but I believe that owners who do not go to "school" and become stronger in the human resource and financial management sides of their businesses will most likely not be in business five or ten years from now. The stronger and better managed competitors, may they be large or small, will out perform them and squeeze them out of the marketplace."

WHY YOU NEED TO KEEP GOOD RECORDS

It is elementary that good bookkeeping and record keeping are essential to operating a small business. When you own a business, you need to know why these daily chores are important so you will be motivated to keep up with them. And, if you are like most owners in our industry, you will need all the motivation you can get. Here are a few reasons why good record keeping is important.

Keeping Good Records Helps You:
- Monitor and track performance of your business
- Pay the right amount in taxes
- Pay yourself and others
- Manage the business
- Sell the business
- Borrow money

Monitor and Track Performance of Your Business

Close monitoring tells you whether you are making or losing money. Monitoring allows you to gauge what products and services are selling and which are not. It tells you which are profitable and those that are not. Monitoring will give you a firm understanding of expenses and allow you to manage them accordingly.

All business decisions should be based on where you stand financially. Before you change out a display, take on new products, expand your services, hire more people, buy a new truck or do anything that requires a financial outlay, you need to know how your decision impacts your business financially. Good bookkeeping and record keeping provides you with this much-needed information that is easily retrieved when you need it.

To Pay Your Taxes

It is much easier to calculate tax return figures and pay taxes when you are working from a set of accurate financial records. If you are a corporation, you will have to pay quarterly taxes in a timely manner. In addition, the many rules and regulations governing sales taxes and payroll taxes will be much easier to comply with if you know where to look for the correct numbers.

Paying Yourself and Others

The rule should be to pay yourself first. But how much? You cannot pay yourself or distribute profits to other partners or investors if you do not know what the profits are.

Managing the Business

Good accounting and the ability to interpret the numbers will tell you when it is appropriate to expand or necessary to cut back. It allows you to truly manage the business to maximize profitability and the return on your investment.

Selling the Business

You will need up-to-date and accurate accounting if you ever decide to sell the business. You will need it yourself to help arrive at a fair selling price and the prospective buyers will need to know how the business is doing before they can make an educated decision on whether to move ahead with the purchase.

If You Need to Borrow Money

To pursue investors you will need to show accurate financial statements. Good, solid bookkeeping is the only way to produce the information everyone will need.

ESTABLISHING BOOKKEEPING PROCEDURES

The newness and size of your business will dictate whether you have to keep the books or whether you can afford to hire a bookkeeper to handle the responsibilities. The size and volume of the operation will determine whether you can have someone on staff full time or if someone working part-time can perform the duties.

Basic bookkeeping starts on a day-to-day and sale-by-sale level. The wide variety of excellent software packages available make much of the work quite simple. Whether you are using a software program or doing the bookkeeping manually, you will need to keep a journal of sales and cash receipts. This allows you to see your sales totals, know what products and services were sold on credit and keep track of when you received payment for each sale.

Your cash disbursements journal (or expense journal) will provide you with information on how much you are spending and to whom you are paying the money.

Do not defer all financial and accounting questions and decisions to the bookkeeping department or an outside accountant. This can lead to trouble. Bookkeepers provide you with accurate books; an accountant will help you prepare financial statements and make recommendations. But it is up to you to make final and informed decisions. Therefore, get in the habit of meeting with your accountant and/or bookkeeper on a regular basis to get updates on what your financial situation is.

You may want to seriously consider taking a basic accounting class or two at your local community college. No, you do not have to become an accountant. Yes, you do have to gain a basic understanding of accounting and financial management.

CHOOSING AN ACCOUNTING SYSTEM

There are two basic types of accounting methods: the cash method and the accrual method.

The Cash Method

In the cash method, you record income only when you receive it from your customers. Likewise, when you write a check or pay cash out, you record that as well. This system is simple because you are keeping track of cash in or out of hand. However, most businesses, including kitchen and bath businesses, are not cash-only businesses. It is common today to extend credit to customers, or, in the case of kitchen and bath businesses, to take deposits for products and services to be rendered at a future date. A cash accounting system does not account for these types of transactions. Therefore, you do not have the whole picture of what you have actually earned or spent.

The Accrual Method

Much more common today, especially with kitchen and bath businesses, is the accrual method of accounting. Here, each transaction is recorded when it occurs, regardless of whether you have received the cash or spent the cash at that moment. This will generally provide you with a more accurate picture of your profits and losses, especially where deposits are received, product purchased, work performed and invoices paid at varying intervals. To get the best picture of where you stand in your kitchen and bath business, you will benefit by using the accrual method. If you maintain inventory you do not have a choice: the Internal Revenue System says you must use the accrual system.

Selecting A Single or Double Entry System

Another choice you may have is whether to use a single entry or a double entry accounting system. Most software programs come with the double entry system already built in. In these programs, you make one entry and the programs make the second: both a debit and a credit entry are made for each transaction. Another reason the double entry system is preferred is it provides a checks and balance system (credits must equal debits), allowing you to find errors more easily.

Establishing Your Fiscal Year

An accounting "period" is a set amount of time where the financial reports of the business can be compared with those from another set amount of time. The accounting period can be months, quarters or years. One year in a company's financial life is called a **fiscal year**. A fiscal year can follow a yearly calendar (January 1 – December 31) or any other 12-month period you select (e.g. March 1 – February 28). S-Corporations typically have to be on a calendar year.

There Are No Shortcuts

Be leery of accountants, bookkeepers, or any online offers that solicit dramatic shortcuts to handling the tasks of record keeping. While technology can speed up your accounting methods, anything that appears to be too fast or takes too many shortcuts is probably missing some vital steps that may come back to haunt you later on.

WHAT TO KEEP TRACK OF

What To Keep Track Of
- Accounts receivable
- Accounts payable
- General ledger
- Balance sheet
- Operating income statement
- Job costing

Choosing the right system is one thing, but after you make that decision, you need to know what to keep tabs on. Otherwise your accounting system will not do you any good. Here are the important things you will want to track:

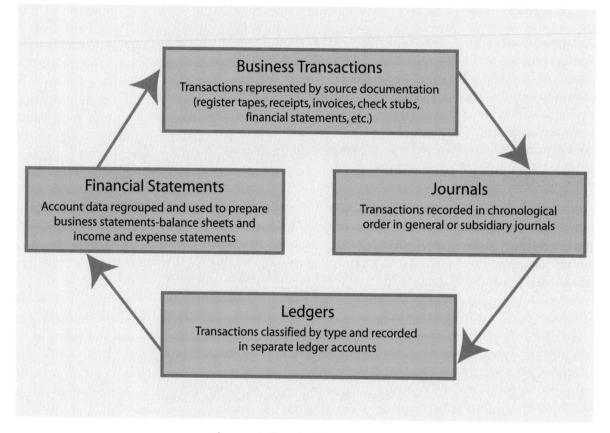

Business Transactions
Transactions represented by source documentation (register tapes, receipts, invoices, check stubs, financial statements, etc.)

Journals
Transactions recorded in chronological order in general or subsidiary journals

Ledgers
Transactions classified by type and recorded in separate ledger accounts

Financial Statements
Account data regrouped and used to prepare business statements-balance sheets and income and expense statements

Accounts Receivable

You will need to keep track of all accounts receivable, i.e., the money owed to you by customers. For each customer you will keep an individual list of account receivables. This will allow you to know how much you are owed by each customer and in total. It will also tell you whether this money is due or overdue.

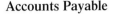

Accounts Payable

The money that you owe and need to pay to others is your accounts payable. You may owe money to suppliers and vendors or others from whom you have purchased merchandise, equipment, or services. By keeping a separate ledger account for each supplier or vendor, you will be able to see exactly to whom you owe money and how much you owe at any given time. This will allow you to plan your payments and to take advantage of any cash discounts offered.

General Ledger

Here is where you start to organize your financial statement. The general ledger summarizes data from other journals, including cash disbursements or your expense journal and your sales and cash receipts journal. Here you will find the balance between debits and credits when you finish posting your entries.

Balance Sheet

The balance sheet is one of the key financial statements to prepare based on your bookkeeping and accounting procedures. This will present you with an overview of your business at the present time. All your assets and liabilities are included on a balance sheet. The balance sheet will result after posting to the general ledger, adjusting entries, and completing the trial balance.

As the name would imply, the balance sheet will need to balance, meaning your assets will equal your liabilities plus your capital. The balance sheet tells you who owns the majority of your business, you and your investors or the banks, vendors and other creditors. See Chapter 5 for more details.

Operating Income Statement

This is the statement that will generate the most attention from you in running your business, as well as any banks or investors you might be working with. This financial statement, also known as the operating or income statement, shows your net income or loss and gives you an overall perspective on where the business stands in terms of making money and reaching your goals.

The profit and loss statement is simply a final, rounded off (to the next full dollar) summation of what you have earned and what you have spent. The main items shown on the profit and loss statement are: sales, cost of goods sold, gross profit, expenses, and net income or loss. This report gives you the all important "bottom line." (This is the final line of the report showing a profit or a loss.)

You will find more detail and examples on this important financial statement in Chapter 5.

Job Costing

Job costing is one record keeping activity often overlooked by business owners who also design, sell and supervise installations (see Chapter 11). It is important that your estimating forms flow into your accounting records so that as invoices are received they can be "matched up" with the estimated costs for that aspect of the project. It is not unusual for a high-volume seller to actually generate fewer profits than another member on the team who does not generate as much cash, but does a better job estimating and managing the project, resulting in a more profitable business opportunity.

Modern technology requires the right software for the right task, whether it is for design, project management, inventory, graphics, communications or financial management. An accounting software package should be easy to learn and should include features pertinent for your particular business. Make the decision on which financial software package would be best for you with your accountant, as well as other well-established kitchen and bath business owners. Keep in mind that the software will have to be compatible with your computer system.

There are a number of programs and online services available, ranging from those under $100 to programs costing several thousand dollars. Following are a few of the more popular programs that should cover most of your small business accounting needs while not costing you a fortune. As a result of the popularity of software packages for small businesses, most accounting professionals are now offering assistance with these programs as part of their services.

Accounting Software

One of the most popular accounting software packages, QuickBooks includes many key accounting features. You can navigate between reports and documents easily, email and fax invoices, enjoy online banking privileges, manage files, modify reports and essentially handle all your bookkeeping needs with one program. Its website www.quickbooks.com lets you view each feature and click for support and service help.

From the general ledger to your accounts payables and receivables right through to more advanced accounting features, Peachtree is another good choice. Peachtree First Accounting includes more than fifty predefined reports and statements designed to provide you with a comprehensive look at the financial picture of your business. Support and services are also offered. Visit www.peachtree.com.

MYOB helps you "mind your own business" with a variety of powerful features including multi-user capabilities, professional time billing, a fully integrated payroll system to take the headaches out of payroll calculations and much more. The program is easy to navigate and MYOB provides support. Visit www.myob.com.

Two other programs you might want to look at are:

Oracle Small Business Suite
www.oraclesmallbusiness.com

ACCPAC Simply Accounting
www.accpac.com

In your haste to get your bookkeeping into your computer system, do not forget to carefully review your computer system's requirements for any software package, as well as upgrades you may have to purchase. The last thing you want is to invest money in software that your computer system is too outdated to run.

RECORD KEEPING AND ADMINISTRATIVE NEEDS

Besides all the financial records of sales, expenditures, profits and losses, you will need to maintain other records. These would include the names and addresses of your suppliers, accurate client records, and up-to-date employee data. If you keep any inventory and other such records in your computer, it is in your best interest to also keep hard copies of key information as a backup.

Your personnel files should include:

- All necessary tax information for each employee, including his/her social security number.

- Personal contact information, including emergency numbers in case of injury or illness.

- Employment history including resume, initial job application, etc.

- Employment record with your company, including pay rate, dates of pay changes, sick days and vacation days accrued.

For clients and customers you will need to maintain files including:

* All up-to-date contact information.

* Copy of credit application with signed personal guarantee, if appropriate.

* All correspondence.

* All records of transactions.

Other files that should be on hand:

* Permits, licenses and registrations.

* Property lease agreements.

* Equipment leasing contracts or receipts for purchases.

* Important correspondence with landlord, regulatory agencies and government officials.

* Supplier contact information and term of purchase, including any specially negotiated deals.

* Contact listings for all local and industry governing bodies, including NKBA, the local Chamber of Commerce, zoning committee, etc.

* Legal papers including claims you've made and claims against your company.

* Lease/property/equipment insurance (i.e., the insurance needed to operate, etc.).

Even though much business is transacted through email it is important to take the time to run hard copies of all key documents and to store them safely in your files. Businesses that rely solely on their computers are taking enormous risks. Have back-up data available at all times.

One of the biggest—yet least discussed—causes of business failure is poor record keeping. And this does not mean strictly financial records. Businesses shut down because they let licenses and registrations lapse. Companies find themselves in financial trouble because they neglected legal matters. It is vital to have a solid record keeping and filing system in place from the beginning.

How Long Should You Retain Your Records?

Corporate Records	Retain
Bylaws, charter, minute books	Indefinitely
Capital stock and bond records	Indefinitely
Checks (Taxes, property and settlement contracts)	Indefinitely
Contracts and agreements (current)	Indefinitely
Copyrights and trademark registrations	Indefinitely
Deeds, mortgages and bills of sale	Indefinitely
Labor contracts	Indefinitely
Minute books of directors/ stockholders (including bylaws and charter)	Indefinitely
Mortgages, notes and leases (expired)	8 Years
Patents	Indefinitely
Property appraisals	Indefinitely
Proxies	Indefinitely
Retirement and pension records	Indefinitely
Stock and bond certificates (cancelled)	7 Years
Tax returns and working papers, revenue agent reports	Indefinitely

Correspondence	
General	3 Years
Legal and tax	Indefinitely
Routine (customers, vendors)	1 Year

Personnel	
Contracts (expired)	7 Years
Disability and sick benefit reports	6 Years
Employment applications	3 Years
Personnel files (terminated)	6 Years
Withholding tax statements	6 years

Accounting	Retain
Auditors records	Indefinitely
Bank reconciliations	1 Year
Bank statements and deposit slips	3 Years
Cash books	Indefinitely
Chart of accounts	Indefinitely
Cancelled checks	8 Years
Depreciation schedules	Indefinitely
Dividend checks (cancelled)	6 Years
Expense reports	7 Years
Financial statements (end of year)	Indefinitely
Fixed assets detail	Indefinitely
General ledgers and journals	Indefinitely
Inventory of products, materials and supplies	7 Years
Payroll	
Time cards	3 Years
Individual earnings' records	8 Years
Records and summaries	7 Years
Petty cash vouchers	3 Years
Physical inventory tags	3 Years
Subsidiary ledgers (A/R and A/P)	7 Years
Trial balances (monthly)	7 Years
Vouchers for payments to vendors, employees, etc.	7 Years

Insurance	
Accident reports	7 Years
Claims (after settlement)	Indefinitely
Policies (all types – expired)	4 Years
Safety reports	8 Years

Purchasing/Sales	
Purchase orders	7 Years
Requisitions	7 Years
Sales contracts	7 Years
Sales invoices	7 Years

Because a number of owners have a hard time dealing with the financial aspect of their businesses, they need professional advice and help in this all-important area. They may be award-winning designers, outstanding salespeople and great marketers, but ask them to analyze a profit and loss statement and their eyes glaze over. Even the best and most powerful accounting software is useless if you cannot input or understand the data. So, most of the time, hiring an accountant or bookkeeper is smart business.

While accountants or bookkeepers cannot guarantee your success they can be an important adjunct to your business. Their basic services include keeping track of how much your business owes, how much it is owed, creating financial statements (such as balance sheets, income statements, cash flow statements, etc.) and reconciling bank statements. Beyond that, they might handle:

- **Taxes:** A good accountant/bookkeeper can save your business and, perhaps you, thousands of dollars through proper tax planning.

- **Payroll:** Although often this is out-sourced.

- **Financial Statement Preparation (Compilation, Review or Audit):** This may be required if you have bank loans or outside investors.

- **IRS Audits:** This other type of audit is another instance where accountants and bookkeepers can be invaluable.

- **Business and Financial Planning:** A CPA can help with business succession and estate planning or help to prepare and value the business for sale.

So, where do you find a good accountant or bookkeeper? Referrals are the best source. Network within your local industry. Consult other small business owners, as well as your friends, banker and attorney.

After you get a few names, set up appointments and interview them to find out:

- **Their experience.** You want someone who deals with small businesses, especially in your field.

- **If timely service is delivered.** Numbers are constantly coming in from your business so make sure they will get reports to you at least monthly. (No later than the 10th of the month.)

- **Who will service your account?** Will it be the person you are meeting with or an associate you do not know?

- **What service you can expect beyond reporting?** Will they handle your taxes, payroll, etc.?

- **If you will be able to get business consulting as well.** A good accountant or bookkeeper should become a valuable member of your team.

- **How much will it cost?** You should know fairly accurately how much time they will put in each month and what you should expect to pay.

- **How well will you relate to this person?** Is their personality one you can work with? Do you have other interests in common and can you become friends as well as business associates?

In addition, this person should become a dependable business advisor, and someone you can trust implicitly.

Accountants are professionals and their fees are not inexpensive. Knowing this, there are a few ways to keep your accounting costs down.

- **Keep great records.** Keep receipts organized. Maintain a legible and current ledger. If possible, automate your records.

- Handle the small things in house.

- Use a bookkeeper for the daily and monthly accounting and use the accountant for taxes, audits and year-end reporting.

BUDGETING FOR PROFIT AND CASH FLOW

A business cannot open its doors each day without having some idea of what to expect. And it cannot close its doors at the end of the day not knowing what happened. The Boy Scouts have a great motto, "Be prepared." A business should follow the same motto. It should plan and be prepared for its future and it should control its actual performance to reach financial goals.

Business owners/managers have two broad options:

- They can wait for results to be reported to them on a "look back" basis; or,

- They can look ahead and plan what profit and cash flow should be and then compare actual results against the plan.

The latter option is the essence of budgeting.

What is a Budget?

Please be careful with how you use the term "budgeting." Budgeting does not refer to putting a financial straight jacket on a business. Rather, business budgeting refers to setting specific goals and developing the detailed plans necessary to achieve those goals.

Business budgeting is built on realistic forecasts for the coming period and it demands that owners/managers have a thorough understanding of the profit blueprint of the business and the financial effect of profit-making activities. A business budget is an integrated plan of action, not simply a few trend lines on a financial chart.

What is the Difference Between Budgeting and P&L Statements?

Financial statements (see Chapter 5) are prepared after the fact, i.e., after sales, expenses and profits are recorded. Budgeted financial statements, on the other hand, are prepared before the fact and are based on future transactions expected to take place based on the profit strategy and financial goals of the business.

Note: Budgeted financial statements are not reported outside the business; they are strictly for internal management use. The only exception to this would be if you needed a bank loan. The bank would most likely want to see some projected numbers, also known as "pro formas."

Doing an annual budget has become much easier with the advent of some great accounting software. Here again, using the computer beats the old "do-it-by-hand" method.

How to Develop a Business Budget

If yours is a new business your budget will be all "crystal balling." You will not have the historical numbers of a more mature business. A business that has been operating for several years offers the budget preparer (owner/manager) the advantage of real numbers documented for management and tax purposes. Therefore, you can build your budget on historical data using statistical growth formulas.

The first time you sit down to do an annual budget it will seem like a daunting task—to some degree it is. It takes quiet and time. If you operate on a calendar fiscal year January 1 through December 31, you should start the process two months before the end of your fiscal year, meaning you would start work on your budget November 1.

Start by having the financial statements from the past two or three years in front of you. Then do some futuristic market survey information collecting. Ask your sales staff what they believe next year will bring. Ask your suppliers the same question. Check what other small business owners in your marketplace see for the future. Call other kitchen and bath business owners and get their input. Contact your local Chamber of Commerce and see what they believe the business climate will be in your area for the next 12-month period. In other words, ask anyone and everyone for their opinions.

First, The Revenue Stream: A Sales Plan

A sales plan is simply a compilation of the amount of product and/or services that the company anticipates selling over a defined period of time.

Experienced sales managers in the kitchen and bath industry offer these general rules for the generation of a sales plan:

- Agree that a defined period of time is one year.

- Because of the cyclical nature of kitchen and bath sales, it is easier to forecast sales on a calendar basis.

- Base sales forecasting on incoming orders (orders signed and sold for the period), rather than the accounting definition of invoiced sales.

- Forecast yearly sales by month and by quarter. Geographic areas vary; a typical quarterly breakdown for kitchen and bath sales is:

  1st Quarter is 20%

  2nd Quarter is 25%

  3rd Quarter is 30%

  4th Quarter is 25%

- Chart sales monthly, by salesperson.

- Industry experience suggests salespeople should be capable of generating between $500,000 to $750,000 in sales per year. This consists of cabinets, countertops, delivered and installed. After identifying the average time from lead ➪ contract ➪ deposit and ➪ final payment, you will be able to estimate the number of months it will take a new salesperson to be at peak performance during your sales forecasting annual period. (In a number of well-run businesses the salespeople achieve sales of $750,000 to $1 million per year.)

If you are not dramatically increasing or decreasing your sales force, once you have a "feel" for what the next year may bring, apply it to your historic data. If your sales have been growing at 10% a year and the forecasts are for more of the same, use a 10% increase in sales as your numbers for the next year.

Study Your Expenses

The third step in developing a budget is to zero-in on the expenses your firm incurs during normal operation of business and in executing every project you sell.

Follow this by looking at every line item on your income statement and reviewing expenses. Will they go up or down? Will rent increase? Will health and medical expenses continue to climb? Will you have to hire another salesperson or installer because sales are projected to grow? After you have made your best, most informed guess on each of these items, add it all up and see what the bottom line says. Will it meet or exceed your expectations?

For start-up businesses or those in an evolutionary stage, look at every line item and review expenses. For businesses on a "fast track" growth pattern, decisions about the marketing plan may dramatically affect the expenses. For example, if you are predicting a large increase in sales you may need to hire more people to handle that increase: this will dramatically increase your cost of doing business.

Your operating expense reporting is dramatically influenced by how you pay yourself and what you pay your sales/design staff. Please study the information in Chapter 8 to better understand the importance of paying yourself a salary commensurate with the work you are performing as a member of your company's leadership and sales team, as well as to learn from an in-depth discussion about the pros and cons of various salary/commission compensation packages for your sales/design staff.

Here are two different presentations of the same numbers generated by Acme Kitchen:

Acme Kitchens, Inc.
Income Statement – 6 Months – Period 01/01/05 - 06/30/05

Net Sales	$ 555,819	100.00%	$555,819
Cost of Sales			
Product Repairs/Warranty	432	.08	432
Repair Contract Labor	112	.02	112
Repair Product	1,264	.23	1,264
Installation Costs	2,662	.48	2,662
Supplier Purchases	360,230	64.01	360,230
Purchases - Warranty and Repair	54	.01	54
Purchase Discounts	[660]	[.12]	[660]
Freight Out	3,510	.63	3,510
Total Cost of Sales	367,604	66.13	367,604
Gross Profit	188,215	33.86	188,215
Operating Expenses	180,164		*110,550
Net Income Before Other Items	8,051		77,665
Interest Income	98		98
Interest Expense	5,550		5,550
Rental Income	2,850		2,850
Net Income (Loss)	5,449		75,063

*Does not include owner wages and fringe benefits.

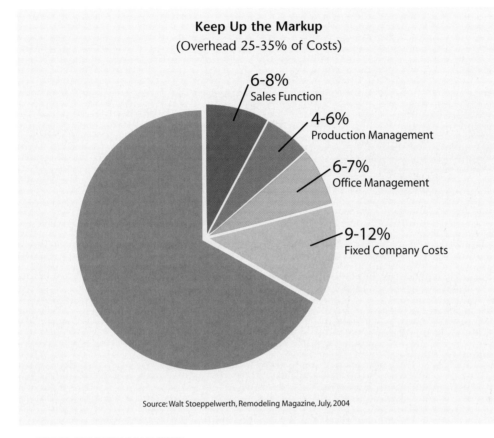

Keep Up the Markup
(Overhead 25-35% of Costs)

6-8%
Sales Function

4-6%
Production Management

6-7%
Office Management

9-12%
Fixed Company Costs

Source: Walt Stoeppelwerth, Remodeling Magazine, July, 2004

KEEP UP THE MARKUP

Just what are average overhead factors in our industry? Overhead is at least 25% to 35% of the total project costs for most firms that offer installation.

- The sales function accounts for 6% to 8%.

- Production management for 4% to 6%.

- Office management for 6% to 7%.

- Fixed company costs for 9% to 12%.

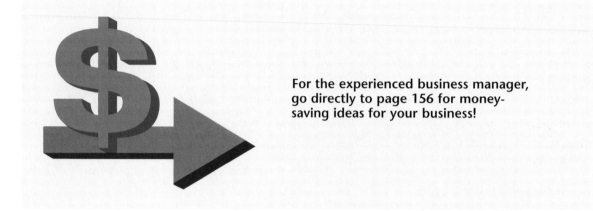

For the experienced business manager, go directly to page 156 for money-saving ideas for your business!

Once you have completed your sales forecast, margin analysis and expenses review, run the numbers. If your before-tax profits are below expectations you can:

- Raise Sales Forecasts

- Raise Margin Goals

- Lower Expenses

The balance of this chapter explains how to initiate one of these three profit producing business initiatives.

The Budget Is Your Roadmap

The budget should be on a spread sheet that shows all 12 months and a total. The budget should look exactly like your income statement, balance sheet and cash flow statement. (Yes, you will prepare a projected balance sheet and cash flow analysis from the information you gather.)

As the actual numbers of the new year are reported you will match these to your budgeted numbers. Some will be high and some will be low. If at the end of the first quarter you are way off with some budgeted numbers, then adjust them—they are not cast in concrete.

The big advantage of doing an annual budget is that it eliminates surprises. It helps you to plan when you will have to hire more people. It tells you when you will be able to afford to update part of your showroom or buy a new truck. And, more importantly, it sets sales, expense and profit goals that help you maximize your investment in money and hard work.

Budgeting has advantages and ramifications that go beyond the financial dimension and have more to do with business management in general. Here are a few additional benefits of budgeting:

- Budgeting forces owners/managers to better forecast.

- Budgeting motivates managers and employees by providing useful yardsticks for measuring performance.

- Budgeting can assist in communication between the owner, supervisors and employees.

- Budgeting is an essential piece of the all-important business plan (see Chapter 3).

Following is a sample budget spreadsheet to guide you in your annual budget preparation. If your current chart of accounts is detailed enough and works well for you, use your own format.

SAMPLE BUDGET SPREADSHEET

Income	Description	Jan	Feb	Mar	Apr	May...	Total
Sales	Sales						
	Cabinets						
	Countertops						
	Plumbing						
	Lighting						
	Appliances						
	Installation						
	Freight Income						
Cost of Goods Sold	Cost of Goods Sold						
	Cabinets						
	Countertops						
	Plumbing						
	Lighting						
	Appliances						
	Installation						
	Freight and Delivery						
Gross Profit	Gross Profit						
	Cabinets						
	Countertops						
	Plumbing						
	Lighting						
	Appliances						
	Installation						

Expenses

Operating Expenses	Operating Expenses						
	Personnel						
	Officers						
	Payroll – Exempt						
	Payroll – Non-exempt						
	Commissions						
	Bonuses/Incentives						
	Overtime						
	Payroll Taxes						
	Insurance – Health/Medical						
	Insurance – Workers' Comp						

SAMPLE BUDGET SPREADSHEET -continued-

Expenses (continued)	Description	Jan	Feb	Mar	Apr	May...	Total
Facilities and Equipment	Facilities and Equipment						
	Depreciation						
	Car/Truck Rental						
	Fuel						
	Office Equipment Rental						
	Building Rent						
	Vehicle Maintenance						
	Building Maintenance						
	Insurance – Fire & General						
	Insurance – Vehicle						
	Utilities						
	Property Taxes						
Other Operating Expense	Other Operating Expense						
	Advertising – Publications						
	Advertising – Newspaper						
	Advertising – Radio & TV						
	Advertising – Direct Mail						
	Advertising – Yellow Pages						
	Advertising – Other						
	Promotions						
	Conventions and Meetings						
	Travel and Entertainment						
	Dues and Subscriptions						
	Legal Fees						
	Accounting Fees						
	Supplies						
	Postage						
	Phone (Less Yellow Pages)						
	IRA – Pension Contributions						
	Provision for Bad Debt						
	Bank – Service Charges						
	Donations						
	Licenses – Auto and Business						
	Computer Expenses						

SAMPLE BUDGET SPREADSHEET -continued-

Expenses (continued)	Description	Jan	Feb	Mar	Apr	May...	Total
	Employee Training						
	Showroom Expenses						
	Cleaning Services						
	Alarm Expenses						

		Jan	Feb	Mar	Apr	May...	Total
Total Expenses							

		Jan	Feb	Mar	Apr	May...	Total
Total Net Operating Income							

Other Income/Expenses

Other Income	Discounts and Purchases						
	Interest Income						
	Refunds and Adjustments						
Total Other Income							
Other Expenses	Interest on Line of Credit						
	Interest Expense						
	State Income Tax						
Total Other Income							

Net Other Income							
Net Income/Loss Before Taxes							

Net Income							

CHAPTER 5: Financial Controls

Communication is a wonderful thing when it works. Communication takes on a new importance when it's about money. Money is a necessity of life, and most people treat threats to their money as threats to their person. Accounting procedures and statements provide a standardized way for people to communicate about financial and business situations.

The purpose of the highly structured world of accounting is to provide the business owner/manager and others with the information they need to manage a business or evaluate their investments. Accounting is how businesses keep score and just like keeping score in sports, there are numerous rules and procedures to accurately reflect the results of actions on the field.

UNDERSTANDING FINANCIAL STATEMENTS

Even if you have, or plan to have, an accountant or bookkeeper manage your financial records, YOU still need to understand basic financial terms so YOU can make reasonable financial decisions. In addition, if all of this understanding helps you make more money, you are going to learn to like it.

Understanding financial statements is not difficult. Using financial statements effectively along with a valid sales/profit/expense forecast gives you a preview of good times and bad times before they hit so you can take proactive measures.

The Basic Financial Statements

This chapter introduces you to financial statements and explains their basic purpose. There are three basic financial statements:

- The Income Statement, also known as Profit and Loss or Operating Statement

- The Balance Sheet

- The Statement of Cash Flow

The income statement shows you the sales revenue, expense and net income (or loss) of your company during a specific accounting period, which is usually a fiscal month, quarter or year. The balance sheet shows you how much you own and how much you owe at a particular point in time. This is usually calculated at the end of a fiscal quarter and on the last day of the fiscal year. The statement of cash flow shows exactly how much cash you actually received and how much cash you spent on a periodic basis. You really need to watch your cash flow statement carefully because it tells you how much money you have or will have in the bank, so you can pay your bills. Most likely, your accountant has or will advise you to operate your business on the accrual method of accounting, mainly because you receive deposits from clients and not all your products and services are delivered at the same time.

So far, so good? If not, go back and re-read this section. It is a bit like learning algebra or a foreign language—if you do not get one part, none of what follows will make sense. Following is more on the main parts.

CHART OF ACCOUNTS

One of the procedures accountants use to make record keeping easier and more understandable is summarizing transactions so that similar transactions are grouped together. They do this by using a chart of accounts. This lists all the possible categories of transactions and then organizes them in such a way as to produce financial statements.

- Group accounts that summarize the assets and liabilities of the company to form the balance sheet.

- Group accounts that summarize the sales and expenses of the company to form the income statement.

- If you are using the accrual method of accounting, you also will require a financial statement that details cash flow activity, which is likely to be different from the activity shown on the income statement. Cash-basis companies might not need as elaborate an analysis to generate a good understanding of their cash flows, but they should still be aware that lags between billing and collection could adversely affect their cash position.

Those statements, taken together, describe the total financial condition and results of operations for the company. The statement of cash flow uses information from both income and balance sheet statements.

It is critically important to set up these accounts so that they are useful for tax purposes and so you can get the financial management information (reports) you need to make effective monetary decisions. Remember, you do not get to report any taxes on income if you do not manage your business successfully enough to have a positive net income at the end of the year.

Follow Industry Leaders

Do not feel like you have to reinvent the wheel when creating your chart of accounts. Talk to other successful kitchen and bath business owners and see if they would share theirs with you – not their financial numbers—just the chart of accounts by name and number. This would be an easy way to get started. The software package you decide on may even include it.

Following is a Sample Chart of Accounts that the typical kitchen and bath business might use. You are not limited to the number (quantity) of accounts that you want to use. Our recommendation would be to use as many as possible. The more you can break down the expense portion of the income statement the easier it is to monitor and control expenditures. Breaking out sales by product also allows you to track progress and profitability.

SAMPLE CHART OF ACCOUNTS

BALANCE SHEET

	Account No.	Description
Current Assets	100	Cash
	110	Savings Account
	120	Accounts Receivable
	130	Inventory
	140	Prepaid Expenses
	150	Other Current Assets
Total Current Assets		

	Account No.	Description
Long-term Assets	200	Land
	210	Buildings
	220	Equipment and Machinery
	230	Vehicles
	240	Furniture
	250	Other Equipment/Computers
	260	Other Long-term Assets
Total Long-term Assets		

Liabilities and Owner's Equity

	Account No.	Description
Current Liabilities	400	Notes Payable (Less Than 1 Year)
	410	Accounts Payable
	420	Client Deposits
	430	Taxes Payable
	440	Accrued Expenses
	450	Other Current Liabilities
Total Current Liabilities		

	Account No.	Description
Long-Term Liabilities	500	Notes Payable (More Than 1 Year)
	510	Mortgage Payable
	520	Installment Debt Payable
	530	Other Long-term Liabilities
Total Long-term Liabilities		

	Account No.	Description
Owner's Equity	600	Paid in Capital
	610	Retained Earnings
Total Owner's Equity		

Total Liabilities and Owner's Equity

SAMPLE CHART OF ACCOUNTS

PROFIT AND LOSS STATEMENT

Income	Account No.	Description
Sales	700	Sales
	700.10	Cabinets
	700.20	Countertops
	700.30	Plumbing
	700.40	Lighting
	700.50	Appliances
	700.60	Installation
	700.70	Freight Income
Cost of Goods Sold	800	Cost of Goods Sold
	800.10	Cabinets
	800.20	Countertops
	800.30	Plumbing
	800.40	Lighting
	800.50	Appliances
	800.60	Installation
	800.70	Freight and Delivery
Gross Profit	900	Gross Profit
	900.10	Cabinets
	900.20	Countertops
	900.30	Plumbing
	900.40	Lighting
	900.50	Appliances
	900.60	Installation

Expenses

Operating Expenses	1000	Operating Expenses
	1010	Personnel
	1010.10	Officers
	1010.20	Payroll – Exempt
	1010.30	Payroll – Non-exempt
	1010.40	Commissions
	1010.50	Bonuses/Incentives
	1010.60	Overtime
	1010.70	Payroll Taxes
	1010.80	Insurance – Health/Medical
	1010.90	Insurance – Workers' Compensation

SAMPLE CHART OF ACCOUNTS

PROFIT AND LOSS STATEMENT (continued)

Expenses (Continued)	Account No.	Description
Facilities and Equipment	1100	Facilities and Equipment
	1100.10	Depreciation
	1100.20	Car/Truck Rental
	1100.30	Fuel
	1100.40	Office Equipment Rental
	1100.50	Building Rent
	1100.60	Vehicle Maintenance
	1100.70	Building Maintenance
	1100.80	Insurance – Fire and General
	1100.90	Insurance – Vehicle
	1100.100	Utilities
	1100.110	Property Taxes
Other Operating Expense	1200	Other Operating Expense
	1200.10	Advertising – Publications
	1200.20	Advertising – Newspaper
	1200.30	Advertising – Radio and Television
	1200.40	Advertising – Direct Mail
	1200.50	Advertising – Yellow Pages
	1200.60	Advertising – Other
	1200.70	Promotions
	1200.80	Conventions and Meetings
	1200.90	Travel and Entertainment
	1200.100	Dues and Subscriptions
	1200.110	Legal Fees
	1200.120	Accounting Fees
	1200.130	Supplies
	1200.140	Postage
	1200.150	Telephone (Less Yellow Pages)
	1200.160	IRA – Pension Contributions
	1200.170	Provision for Bad Debt
	1200.180	Bank – Service Charges
	1200.190	Donations
	1200.200	Licenses – Auto and Business
	1200.210	Computer Expenses

SAMPLE CHART OF ACCOUNTS

PROFIT AND LOSS STATEMENT (continued)

Expenses (Continued)	Account No.	Description
	1200.220	Employee Training
	1200.230	Showroom Expenses
	1200.240	Cleaning Services
	1200.250	Alarm Expenses

Total Expenses

Total Net Operating Income

Other Income/Expenses

Other Income	1300	Discounts and Purchases
	1400	Interest Income
	1500	Refunds and Adjustments
Total Other Income		

Other Expenses	1600	Interest on Line of Credit
	1700	Interest Expense
	1800	State Income Tax
Total Other Expenses		

Net Other Income
Net Income/Loss Before Taxes

Net Income

The Income Statement

Your income statement (P&L statement or operating statement) tells whether your business is profitable. The income statement totals the amount of revenue and then subtracts the expenses associated with making that revenue. The result is the pre-tax profit. After taxes are paid, you will have your net income.

Income statements show you how much you sold and how much it cost you to create these sales during a particular period. Unfortunately, many kitchen and bath businesses only have their income statements prepared at year-end or once a year for tax purposes. This is the only time the owner knows for sure how the business is doing. We believe every kitchen and bath business should generate monthly income statements. This way, if something is "out of kilter" and the business has not been performing well, you can respond, act, change and correct whatever it is that is not good. Those who wait until year-end to learn the business has been operating at a loss will have a much tougher time turning it around. It is much easier to plug a hole in a rowboat when you first see the leak than it is when the boat is sinking.

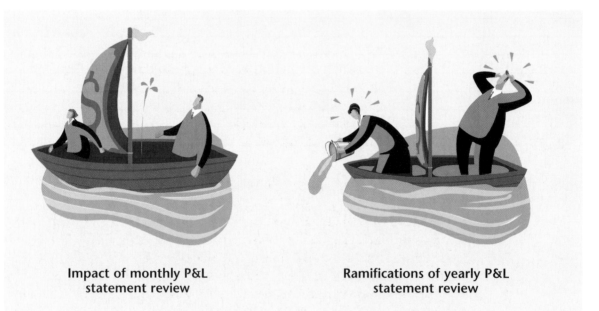

Impact of monthly P&L statement review

Ramifications of yearly P&L statement review

Once you and your accountant/bookkeeper have created your chart of accounts and you input the numbers into the software daily, it is easy and no more costly to run the income statement report monthly than it is once a year.

The key is that you, the owner/manager, have to discipline yourself to spend the half hour it takes to analyze the monthly income statement in a timely manner. You should get the statement by the 10th of the following month and you should have reviewed it within 2 or 3 days. This is your report card. It is the management tool that says either you are doing a great job and are earning a nice return on your investment, or you're doing a poor job and need to make some serious adjustments.

Once you learn how to read and analyze your financial statements you will look forward to getting them and you will benefit from spotting those areas that still need a little attention and work. If you are going to invest all the money to start the business and you are going to commit the bulk of your waking hours to it, shouldn't you try to run the best business possible?

If you cannot find a half hour or so each month to review how you are doing, the next book you read should be on time management. If you had invested $250,000 in the stock market, you would likely check the Dow Jones on a daily basis. Does not your business deserve the same?

The Sales Revenues

Sales revenues are the first numbers of an operating statement. They show what your sales are for a given period (monthly, quarterly, yearly). If you sell multiple products and services, break them out by category (i.e., cabinets, countertops, appliances, installation, etc.) so you will be able to track each category and make sound business decisions.

The Expenses

Expenses fall into two categories: cost of sales expenses and operating or fixed expenses.

COST OF SALES EXPENSES

Cost of sales expenses, also referred to as "cost of goods sold" or "COGS," are those directly related to your products and installation (if you install.) These generally include the cost of the products, namely, what you paid your suppliers. If you install, COGS are the cost of your labor and any outside subcontractors. You monitor these costs with timely job-costing reviews. Unmonitored, you may be suffering from gross profit margin erosion and not know what the cause is.

Categorized COGS will be exactly like sales to allow you to determine profitability by product category. Subtract COGS from the total sales to get your gross profit or gross margin. These are profit dollars you made on the sale. More about this all-important piece toward the end of this chapter.

OPERATING AND FIXED EXPENSES

The next part of the income statement is your operating and fixed expenses. These are the expenses associated with running your business. They include payroll (including your salary), rent, utilities, insurance and so on. Operating expenses also include a few items that are not necessarily fixed, but they still are shown in this section, like commissions or advertising expenses, which will vary from month to month. As mentioned earlier, the more chart of accounts (i.e., listing of expense items) that you show here, the easier it is for you to track and compare where the dollars are going.

The next and most important section of the income statement is the "bottom line" or net income. This obviously is the number that tells you whether making that monetary investment and working sixty to eighty hours a week has been worth it.

To summarize:

Net Sales	1,550,000	100.0%
- Cost of Goods Sold	990,000	64.0%
= Gross Profit	560,000	36.0%
- Expenses	490,000	32.0%
= Operating Profits	70,000	4.0%
- Taxes	21,000	1.4%
= Net Income (Profit)	**49,000**	**3.7%**

If the business is showing a net profit—the government will want its share. Do not fight it. In fact, be happy you have to pay taxes—it means you made money. Your accountant will work with you through good tax planning to help you minimize your taxes, both for the business and personally.

Following is a detailed sample of an income statement. It reflects the chart of accounts discussed previously and shows all of the parts that make up what might be a typical P&L statement for a kitchen and bath business. Compare this to what you currently generate. If it makes sense to make some changes, meet with your accountant and make them.

SAMPLE INCOME STATEMENT
PROFIT AND LOSS STATEMENT

Income

Income	Account No.	Description	Amount
Sales	700	Sales	
	700.10	Cabinets	
	700.20	Countertops	
	700.30	Plumbing	
	700.40	Lighting	
	700.50	Appliances	
	700.60	Installation	
	700.70	Fright Income	
Cost of Goods Sold	800	Cost of Goods Sold	
	800.10	Cabinets	
	800.20	Countertops	
	800.30	Plumbing	
	800.40	Lighting	
	800.50	Appliances	
	800.60	Installation	
	800.70	Freight and Delivery	
Gross Profit	900	Gross Profit	
	900.10	Cabinets	
	900.20	Countertops	
	900.30	Plumbing	
	900.40	Lighting	
	900.50	Appliances	
	900.60	Installation	

Expenses

Expenses			
Operating Expenses	1000	Operating Expenses	
	1010	Personnel	
	1010.10	Officers	
	1010.20	Payroll – Exempt	
	1010.30	Payroll – Non-exempt	
	1010.40	Commissions	
	1010.50	Bonuses/Incentives	
	1010.60	Overtime	
	1010.70	Payroll Taxes	
	1010.80	Insurance – Health/Medical	
	1010.90	Insurance – Workers' Comp	

PROFIT AND LOSS STATEMENT (continued)

	Account No.	Description	Amount
Facilities and Equipment	1100	Facilities and Equipment	
	1100.10	Depreciation	
	1100.20	Car/Truck Rental	
	1100.30	Fuel	
	1100.40	Office Equipment Rental	
	1100.50	Building Rent	
	1100.60	Vehicle Maintenance	
	1100.70	Building Maintenance	
	1100.80	Insurance – Fire and General	
	1100.90	Insurance – Vehicle	
	1100.100	Utilities	
	1100.110	Property Taxes	
Other Operating Expense	1200	Other Operating Expense	
	1200.10	Advertising – Publications	
	1200.20	Advertising – Newspaper	
	1200.30	Advertising – Radio and Television	
	1200.40	Advertising – Direct Mail	
	1200.50	Advertising – Yellow Pages	
	1200.60	Advertising – Other	
	1200.70	Promotions	
	1200.80	Conventions and Meetings	
	1200.90	Travel and Entertainment	
	1200.100	Dues and Subscriptions	
	1200.110	Legal Fees	
	1200.120	Accounting Fees	
	1200.130	Supplies	
	1200.140	Postage	
	1200.150	Telephone (Less Yellow Pages)	
	1200.160	IRA – Pension Contributions	
	1200.170	Provision for Bad Debt	
	1200.180	Bank – Service Charges	
	1200.190	Donations	
	1200.200	Licenses – Auto and Business	
	1200.210	Computer Expenses	

SAMPLE INCOME STATEMENT

PROFIT AND LOSS STATEMENT (continued)

Expenses (Continued)	Account No.	Description	Amount
	1200.220	Employee Training	
	1200.230	Showroom Expenses	
	1200.240	Cleaning Services	
	1200.250	Alarm Expenses	

Total Expenses			

Total Net Operating Income			

Other Income/Expenses

Other Income	1300	Discounts and Purchases	
	1400	Interest Income	
	1500	Refunds and Adjustments	
Total Other Income			

Other Expenses	1600	Interest on Line of Credit	
	1700	Interest Expense	
	1800	State Income Tax	
Total Other Expenses			

Net Other Income			
Net Income/Loss Before Taxes			

Net Income			

SAMPLE BALANCE SHEET

BALANCE SHEET

	Account No.	Description	Amount
Current Assets	100	Cash	
	110	Savings Account	
	120	Accounts Receivable	
	130	Inventory	
	140	Prepaid Expenses	
	150	Other Current Assets	
Total Current Assets			

Long-term Assets	200	Land	
	210	Buildings	
	220	Equipment and Machinery	
	230	Vehicles	
	240	Furniture	
	250	Other Equipment/Computers	
	260	Other Long-term Assets	
Total Long-term Assets			

Liabilities and Owner's Equity

Current Liabilities	400	Notes Payable (Less Than 1 Year)	
	410	Accounts Payable	
	420	Client Deposits	
	430	Taxes Payable	
	440	Accrued Expenses	
	450	Other Current Liabilities	
Total Current Liabilities			

Long-term Liabilities	500	Notes Payable (More Than 1 Year)	
	510	Mortgage Payable	
	520	Installment Debt Payable	
	530	Other Long-term Liabilities	
Total Long-term Liabilities			

Owner's Equity	600	Paid in Capital	
	610	Retained Earnings	
Total Owner's Equity			

Total Liabilities and Owner's Equity			

THE BALANCE SHEET

An income statement reflects the flow of money in and out of your business during a specific period, similar to how a videotape records events over a period of time. Alternatively, the balance sheet shows the amount of assets and liabilities at a particular point in time, similar to a camera taking a snap shot at a particular moment. The balance sheet is based on a fundamental equation of accounting: assets = liabilities + owner equity. (See page 134 opposite for a sample balance sheet.)

Assets

Assets are those items of value that the company owns, such as cash in the checking account, accounts receivable (money clients owe you), inventory, furniture, equipment, and property. Base the value of an asset on its initial purchase price minus any applicable depreciation (the account-tracked decrease in value that occurs as an asset ages).

LIQUID AND MIXED ASSETS

The definition of assets is broken out even further: some assets are referred to as liquid assets and others as fixed assets. Liquid assets include cash and anything you own that you can quickly convert into cash in less than 12 months (inventory, vehicles, furniture, etc.). Fixed assets are those that are more difficult to convert quickly (buildings, machinery, etc.).

Assets have three values:

- Initial purchase cost;

- Book value (purchase cost minus depreciation); and,

- Market value (what someone would pay for the asset today, disregarding any depreciated value.)

Liabilities

On the other side of the ledger of the balance sheet are the liabilities. These are the amounts of money that you owe. Typical liabilities might include accounts payable (reflecting the monies you owe to suppliers), loans (banks, credit unions, etc.), credit cards, taxes and any other people or institutions to whom you owe money.

Liabilities are broken out as:

- Short-term (or current liabilities) which are monies that will be paid back within a 12-month period; and,

- Long-term liabilities, which are monies that are not due within the next 12 months, i.e., those that will be paid back in 13 months or longer.

The next piece of the balance sheet is owner equity. This is the piece that makes a balance sheet balance. When you subtract liabilities from assets, it equals owner equity. It is taking what you owe away from what you own. Owner equity is derived by adding the initial investment of your company stock and the accumulated retained earnings of the business together. Retained earnings are the accumulation of each year's profit or loss from year one to the current year.

Retained Earnings
The retained earnings for this 5 year period would be $280,000

Year	$ Earnings/Loss
1	<10,000>
2	20,000
3	50,000
4	90,000
5	130,000
	$280,000

As your company grows, the numbers on your assets, liabilities and equity lines will usually grow larger also. This happens because you will be purchasing new equipment, computers, software and inventory (if you carry any). Accounts receivable will also be growing. Companies just starting out will typically have a small number on their assets, liabilities and equity lines. Your focus as an owner should be on generating positive net income. This creates positive and growing retained earnings, thereby, increasing the owner equity.

Here is a simplified example of a balance sheet:

Simplified Example of a Balance Sheet

Assets	
Cash	$25,000
Accounts Receivable	$100,000
Inventory	$25,000
Fixed Assets	$175,000
Total Assets	**$325,000**
Liabilities	
Short-Term	$65,000
Long-Term	$100,000
Total Liabilities	**$165,000**
Owner Equity	
Capital Stock	$10,000
Retained Earnings	$150,000
Total Owner Equity	**$160,000**

Assets ($325,000) = Liabilities ($165,000) +Owner Equity ($160,000)

Paying Taxes Is a Good Thing to Do!

Attention! All too often, small business owners will manage their businesses and finances so that they show a very small or negative income and, as a result, pay little or no taxes.

Since small, privately owned companies do not have to face the scrutiny of the publicly, larger investor-owned businesses, there is minimal pressure to show a positive net income. You too can take this approach with your business; however, be prepared to answer some pretty tough questions if you ever need to present your negative income financial statements to outside investors, such as bankers, venture capitalists—or, worse, the IRS.

Moreover, if you decide you want to sell your business it will not command a good selling price . Many buyers include a multiplier of 3 to 7 times earnings as part of the formula to value a business they are considering. EBIDA (Earnings Before Interest, Depreciation and Amortization—a formula banks and business brokers use to value a business) reflects that 5 x Nothing = Nothing. Once again, get your professional accountant's advice in this area.

CASH FLOW ANALYSIS

A cash flow analysis can be a very important financial statement because it tells you whether you have or will have enough cash to pay your bills. Never forget, cash is as important to your business as air is to you. The key challenge is keeping more cash coming in than is going out.

A cash flow analysis or statement of cash flow looks a lot like an income statement. The major difference is that your income statement focuses on earnings from operations, whereas the cash flow analysis also reflects investments, borrowings, repayments of loan principals and other balance sheet changes. Cash flow from operations might also be significantly different from reported earnings, especially if you are using the accrual method of accounting. Remember also that your income statement might be based on accrual accounting methods, whereas your cash flow statement is based on actual cash in and out flows.

The reason you need both an income statement and a cash flow statement is that you might have a good month of sales followed by a bad month of sales. So bad, in fact, that you may have to get a loan to cover your expenses.

By watching your cash flow analysis, you can see in advance when you will start to run out of cash during that month. However, because an income statement is based on an accrual basis of accounting records when obligations are made, and not when the cash is either spent or received, the good months and bad months often even themselves out. You would not know by looking at your income statement that August (the bad month) almost put you out of business due to lack of available cash. However, your monthly cash flow analysis would alert you to potential problems before they would become real problems. Therefore, it is imperative that you use all three financial statements to get an accurate picture of your company's financial condition.

Cash flow is your lifeblood—without it, your business will suffocate and die. One more reason, then, to create a budget is to insure you will have adequate cash flow. Without consistent, sufficient cash flow to buy inventory, pay bills, handle payroll, pay yourself, do marketing—you will go out of business. Preserving and defending your cash flow, therefore, is critical.

Aside from creating a budget, there are three more ways to control your cash flow.

- **Live by this rule:** Without your business oxygen (cash), your business will suffocate and die.

- **Create cash flow projections.** You need to know what will come in and when. Realistic cash flow projections are essential. The question is, "What do you expect your cash balance to be in six months?"

- **Keep the pipeline open.** A client or customer you acquire today may sign your contract and give you a deposit, but it may be several months before you finish the work and collect the final payment. You have to keep acquiring clients and doing work today to keep the cash flow "spigot" open.

A cash flow crunch is usually the result of poor planning. All businesses have "cycles" so plan for them. Most kitchen and bath dealers experience cyclical sales: slower Winter sales and stronger Spring, Summer and Fall sales. Sales and promotions should occur during the slower period to help balance out cash flow.

Cash flow can be difficult in both good and bad times. Knowing in advance—through good forecasting—will help you stay on top of this critical piece of your financial plan.

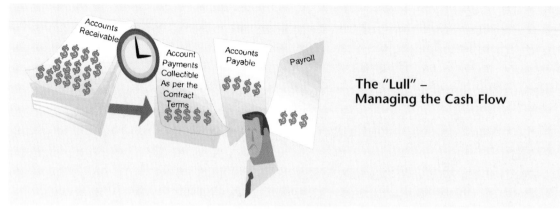

The "Lull" –
Managing the Cash Flow

The Cash Flow Forecast

(Source: "Managing Your Kitchen and Bath Firm's Finances for Profit," Don Quigley)

Once you have completed your sales and operating statement forecast you can move onto the all-important cash flow forecast.

The statement of cash flow is important to you, as the owner or manager of a kitchen and bathroom firm. It is the one statement you can use most effectively to guide your business through the maze of hidden costs. Without such a plan, you may have to pay interest and penalties, if you do not pay your bills and taxes on time. Or, if you estimate a job, based on a discounted price for materials, and then fail to take advantage of that discount because you do not have the funds available. Too often, people confuse cash flow with profits, but they are not the same thing. You may operate your business unprofitably for a long time before you realize you are in trouble because there is a steady cash flow through the business. On the other hand, you may also operate a business with a profit from the first day, but you may be out of business at the end of the first 30 days if you do not have sufficient cash flowing into the business. Insufficient capital or cash flow is one of the single, most devastating causes of small-business failures.

The Statement of Cash Flow really amounts to a calendar or schedule whereby you plot the payments that must be made within a specific time frame, and, at the same time, you try to anticipate which funds will be available to meet those obligations. Then make arrangements to offset any expected shortfalls. By doing this ahead of time to avoid any penalty assessments or interest charges, you will avoid such hidden charges which systematically eat away at your profit margins.

DON'T SPEND THE CASH TOO FAST

One of the dangers of cash-flow management in the kitchen and bath industry is the temptation to spend deposit and second-payment monies received from work in progress on expenses for marketing initiatives rather than on the actual products purchased for the project.

It is easy to have a false "snap shot" of your revenue stream, if large payments are made by clients who are not tied to account payables due to major suppliers providing product for the job. It is not unusual in our industry to be "cash rich" and "profit poor," Whether required or not, many successful kitchen and bath design firms follow a rigorous policy of paying large deposits on the products ordered for each project in tandem with client payments received. Some states require such a payment policy by law.

When planning a major expansion or marketing initiative, the expenses need to be budgeted over a period of time so the cash needed to pay for these activities comes from the profits generated by jobs under way.

DON'T USE THE CASH FLOW STATEMENT
TO YOUR DISADVANTAGE

Your cash flow statement should show salaries for owners from the start of the business. Not doing this is unrealistic, and is generally used only for showing profitability early on. This will not impress bankers, lenders and investors. They want the facts as they really are so produce your Cash Flow Statements showing a salary for you and showing the periods when you are both profitable and unprofitable. Some businesses do not become profitable for quite some time, and astute lenders and investors already know where to find that information. Prepare two statements; one reflecting your cash position that shows where it really stands before any bank loans or investments, and a second version which shows the impact of the loan(s) and your ability to repay them within the limits of your projected revenues and cash flows.

Managing cash flow includes responsibilities with respect to the management of a firm's current assets:

- **Make deposits in a timely and routine fashion.** If they are not in the bank, you will not be able to take advantage of early payment discounts, and, furthermore, you may be subjecting your business to unnecessary fines and penalties.

- **Invoice in a timely fashion.** If you employ a charge system for your clientele, you need to ensure that they are billed as quickly as possible. At this point, they are using your money, and good cash management dictates that you convert your receivables to cash as quickly as you can.

- **Work your aged receivables.** The faster you can turn your receivables into cash, the more quickly you can pay your own bills and avoid fines and penalties. You will also increase your ability to pay your bills early and thus take advantage of early payment discounts. Perhaps most important of all, you will increase the chances of collecting your money without hassle. If your customers are aware of how serious you are about collecting your money, you will no doubt be paid first. Remember, the squeaky wheel gets the grease.

- **Keep inventory levels low, but profitable.** You must have inventory on hand to sell when customers are prepared to buy, otherwise they will shop elsewhere. The problem is that, too often, a business will buy a large amount of inventory in order to get the best possible price and terms.

In order to manage the business effectively, you need as much flexibility as possible when it comes to your current assets, and, while inventory is certainly recognized as a current asset, it is the least flexible in terms of its liquidity. Be sure you maintain enough on hand to meet your requirements, but not so much that you tie up the firm's ability to meet its short-term obligations.

WHAT HAPPENS TO CASH FLOW WHEN YOU HIRE AN UNTRAINED OR INEXPERIENCED DESIGNER?

If you are the owner of the company and also the primary designer/salesperson for the firm, you might need to add an additional design specialist to your team. Adding such a person can cause havoc with your cash flow during their training period. Your sales will dip as you spend more time in your management and training mode. The new designer may make some costly mistakes if you do not watch them closely.

Most specialists suggest a new, inexperienced designer will require almost a full year of your attention before they can generate a reasonable sales volume. This expansive period is caused by the length of time consumers take to make the decisions around a new kitchen or bath, the ordering time for such projects, and the installation time. Assume a 3-month "getting to know one another" period, followed by a 3-month period of carefully supervised project planning and presentation, concluding with a 6 month trial period where you continue to have a "watchful eye" on the designs produced and the estimates prepared by this new individual. Do a careful review of client satisfaction for a new designer through this preliminary training period. Make sure you adjust your cash flow projections so you can manage a decrease in revenue, as well as budget for the non-productive start-up period required by a new employee.

CASH FLOW TEMPLATE

	JAN	FEB	MAR	APR	MAY	JUNE	JULY	AUG	SEPT	OCT	NOV	DEC
1. Cash ON HAND at the beginning of the month (equals line 15 from prior month)												
CASH IN												
2. Cash Sales												
3. Payments on open accounts (Accounts Receivable)												
4. Deposits on new sales												
5. Other cash in												
6. TOTAL CASH IN (add lines 1-5)												
CASH OUT												
7. Purchases for cash (inventory)												
8. Payment on invoices (Accounts Payable)												
9. Variable expenses												
10. Fixed expenses (Operating expenses)												
11. Other Cash Out												
12. TOTAL CASH OUT (add lines 7-11)												
13. Capital Expenditures (fixed asset purchases)												
14. Loans (+ / -)												
15. NET CASH-Month End (Line 6-Line 12) +/- Line 13 +/- Line 14 This total then carries to the first line of the next month												

Fixed Expenses are recurring items that can't easily be changed, such as rent, debt and payroll. Variable Expenses include advertising, supplies, promotion, consulting and other expenses that can easily be increased or decreased from month to month. Capital Expenditures are purchases of equipment, furniture, etc.

WEEKLY CASH FLOW REPORT

Week Ending:	Total Cash Received: $

Customer Deposits Received: $	
Customer Name:	Payment Amount:
Customer Name:	Payment Amount:
Customer Name:	Payment Amount:
Customer Name:	Payment Amount:
Customer Name:	Payment Amount:
Customer Name:	Payment Amount:

Customer Payments Received: $	
Customer Name:	Payment Amount:
Customer Name:	Payment Amount:
Customer Name:	Payment Amount:
Customer Name:	Payment Amount:
Customer Name:	Payment Amount:
Customer Name:	Payment Amount:

Total Booked Sales:	
Sales Tax Liability:	
Total Available Cash	$
Checking Account Balance	$
Money Market Account	$
Special 2% Account	$
Line of Credit Available	$

Cash Discounts Realized This Week	$
Customer Deposits Anticipated Next Week	$
Customer Payments Anticipated Next Week	$
Anticipated Payroll Next Week	$

Accounts Receivable Aging Report

Here is another tool that is invaluable. The accounts receivable aging report tells you who still owes you money and how far past due they might be with their payments.

You may or may not offer open credit accounts to your customers. For most homeowners it is not a requirement, but homebuilders and remodel contractors may require it. Regardless, in the due process of operating a kitchen and bath business, you take multiple deposits for products and services as the job progresses, but experience has shown that this does not always happen. A client falls behind in payment for any number of reasons. Your job, and an important one it is, is to stay on top of the money owed to you (accounts receivable) and be sure that you are paid in full in a timely manner. Since cash is king and you cannot operate the business without it, you have to manage it from all directions. Keep your collections in order and your need for extra cash will diminish or go away all together.

SAMPLE ACCOUNTS RECEIVABLE AGING REPORT

Customer Name	0-30 Days	31-60 Days	61-90 Days	90+ Days

FINANCIAL RATIO ANALYSIS

All the numbers in a financial ratio analysis can seem overwhelming when you are trying to see the big picture and make general conclusions about the financial performance and condition of the business.

One very useful way to interpret financial reports is to complete ratios: that is, divide a particular number in the financial report by another number.

Financial statement ratios are also useful because they enable you to compare a business' current performance with its past performance or with another business' performance; regardless of whether sales revenues or net income was bigger or smaller for the other years or the other business. Using ratios cancels out size differences.

You will not find many ratios in financial reports. Publicly owned businesses are required to report just one ratio (earnings per share or EPS) and privately owned businesses generally do not report any ratios. So why bring it up? Ratios are terrific indicators on how the business is performing. When buying a house, you or your realtor may do comparatives (or comps) on other homes in the same neighborhood. These comps might be on selling price or, more likely, on cost per square foot (total cost divided by square footage). Certainly there are other variables (condition and age of the home, quality of the kitchen and bath, etc.) but at least the square footage ratio gives you a guide.

In the kitchen and bath industry, there are several sources for guidelines, benchmarks and comparative figures.

- **The National Kitchen & Bath Association** currently offers a limited number of surveys and research findings. New initiatives are underway to expand upon these offerings in the future.

- **Trade Magazine Reports.** Several industry publications regularly report on specific and general financial ratios or business systems.

- **Cabinet Company Dealer Counsel Shared Reports.** Some manufacturers assist their dealers on business management by creating a platform where similar business models can exchange financial ratio information.

- **Buying Groups.** Similar to cabinet company networking, these groups offer a platform for firms to share information.

Estimates put the number of kitchen and bath dealers in the U.S. and Canada between 7,000 and 8,000. Some 2,000 are members of NKBA and less than 10% of these members participate in the annual Dealer Profit Report. If you are a dealer member of NKBA, you can request a copy of the latest report and then do some comparisons of your business' performance to their numbers.

Following is an income statement and balance sheet for a typical kitchen and bath business. These will serve as the example for the rest of this chapter. Notice there is no statement of cash flow here, because no ratios are calculated from data in this financial statement. These examples show and describe the most useful ratios so that you can apply your numbers to the formulas and see how your company is performing in several different areas.

The numbers in the exhibits are actual rounded off numbers from NKBA's 2004 Dealer Profit Report.

Income Statement for Year

Sales Revenue	$1,550,000
Cost of Goods Sold	$990,000
Gross Margin	$560,000
Operating Expenses	$490,000
Operating Profit	$70,000
Earnings before Tax	$70,000
Net Income	$49,000

Balance Sheet at End of Year

Assets

Cash	$75,000
Accounts Receivable	$89,000
Inventory	$25,000
Current Assets	$189,000
Fixed Assets	$93,000
Accumulative Depreciation	$38,000
Total Assets	$320,000

Liabilities

Accounts Payable	$40,000
Short-term Notes Payable	0
Current Liabilities	$85,000
Long-term Notes Payable	$20,000

Owner Equity

Capital Stock	$10,000
Retained Earning	$165,000
Total Liabilities + Retained Earnings	$320,000

Gross Profit Margin Ratio

Making bottom-line profit begins with making sales and earning sufficient gross margin from those sales. Sufficient means that your gross margin must cover the expenses of making sales, operating the business, as well as paying interest and income tax expenses, so that there is still an adequate amount left over for profit. Calculate the gross profit margin as follows:

> Gross Margin ÷ Sales Revenue = Gross Margin Ratio
>
> Gross Margin $560,000
>
> Sales Revenue $1,550,000 = 36.13% Gross Profit Ratio

In the kitchen and bath industry, the gross profit margin ranges from as low as 30% to as high as 45%. For a firm operating in a showroom environment and offering installation services, the NKBA Dealer Profit Report average of 36.13% is marginal. Most industry experts believe a (very achievable) goal for all kitchen and bath businesses should be 40% and higher. You have invested too much money, too much work and offer too many features and benefits not to achieve a higher gross profit margin. This chapter concludes with a list of ideas on how you might improve your margin.

Profit Ratio

Businesses are motivated by profit so the profit ratio is critical. The "bottom line" is not called the bottom line without good reason. The profit ratio indicates how much net income was earned on each $100 of sales revenue.

> Net Income ÷ Sales Revenue = Profit Ratio
>
> Net Income $49,000
>
> Sales Revenue $1,550,000 = 3.16% Profit Ratio

This means that for every $100 in sales the average kitchen and bath business earned $3.16. Comparatively speaking, that is poor. An average profit ratio for small business owners would be in the 5% to 10% range.

If the gross profit margin for kitchen and bath dealers had been the 40% we encouraged earlier, the profit ratio would have improved to 7% or $7.00 earned for every $100 in sales. This would have been much more respectable.

Current Ratio

A test of the short-term solvency of a business is its capability to pay the liabilities that come due in the near future (up to one year). The ratio is a rough indicator of whether cash on hand plus cash to be collected from accounts receivable and from selling inventory will be enough to pay off the liabilities that will come due in the next period.

As you can imagine, lenders (banks, credit unions, etc.) are particularly keen on punching in the numbers to calculate the current ratio. Here is how they do it:

Current Assets ÷ Current Liabilities = Current Ratio

Current Assets $189,000

Current Liabilities $85,000 = 2.22% Current Ratio

Businesses are expected to maintain a 2:1 current ratio, which means its current assets should be twice its current liabilities. In fact, some lenders may legally require a business to stay above a minimum current ratio.

Our example shows kitchen and bath businesses at a very healthy 2.22:1 current ratio, mainly because the current liabilities are relatively low.

Quick Ratio

Quick Ratio compares cash and accounts receivable to current liabilities and assesses the ability of your business to meet its current financial obligations in the event that sales decline and inventories cannot readily be converted to cash. The quick ratio is also called the **acid test** because it measures only ready assets. Here is how it works:

Cash + Accounts Receivable ÷ Current Liabilities

Cash $75,000 + Accounts Receivable $89,000

Current Liabilities $85,000 = 1.93

An acid test ratio (quick ratio) of 1 to 1 is considered acceptable, given the fact that an adequate means of collecting accounts receivables exists.

Using actual kitchen and bath industry numbers in this example shows a very respectable 1.93 to 1 acid test. The bankers would be pleased.

As you can see, using these ratios is not difficult, if you have the financial statement information and formulas for the ratios in front of you. It is logical that everyone who has invested money, sweat, love and tears into a business wants to know what their business performance is compared to the rest of the local competitors and peers in the industry. Putting these ratios to work tells you where you stand, where you are doing well and, more importantly, where you need to improve.

GROSS MARGIN

In referring back to the income statement on page 149 (known as the profit and loss statement) at the very top is "sales revenue." The next line is "cost of goods sold," followed by "gross margin" (often referred to as gross profit). A whole lot of folks get confused with exactly what gross margin is because the income statement also has a line item called net profit which is the very last line of the operating statement. (And that's why people refer to net profit as the bottom line—that's exactly what it is, the bottom line of the operating statement.)

Net profit is what the business made (or lost) after all expenses, interest and taxes have been paid.

Gross margin (or gross profit) is the profit on goods and services sold, less the cost of those goods and services, but before operating expenses. Here is a simplified example: You have sold a kitchen full of cabinets for $10,000. Your cost, including delivery of the cabinets to the jobsite, from your supplier is $6,000. By subtracting the cost of goods sold ($6,000) from the sale price of $10,000 you have a gross margin (profit) of $4,000. After this, you need to subtract the expenses related to operating the business (payroll, rent, utilities, advertising, supplies, and so forth), which will give you the operating profit. From this, subtract any interest paid on loans and taxes and you finally reach the bottom line or net profit.

Example:	
Cabinet Sale	$ 10,000
Cost of Cabinets & Delivery	$ 6,000
Gross Margin on this sale	$ 4,000

If a business is going to operate profitably, the total gross margin dollars have to be larger than the total operating expense dollars. The NKBA Dealer Profit report shows the participating businesses averaged a 36% gross profit margin and their operating expenses averaged 32%. The difference of 4% is what the profit was before taxes. The gross profit margin should be higher (40% or more) and the expenses should be lower (30% or less). Many kitchen and bath businesses currently operate at the better numbers. The challenge to you is to set goals of 40% gross profit margin and 30% on operating expenses.

The Difference Between Profit and Markup

It is amazing how many business owners and salespeople do not know the difference between profit and markup and do not know how to calculate it. Here are some examples that will clarify it.

You want to make a 40% margin on a cabinet sale.
Your cost of cabinets and delivery to you is $6,000.

Wrong Calculation:

    1.4 x $6,000 cost = $8,400 selling price or
                           $2,400 gross margin or
                           28.6% gross profit margin

Correct Calculation:

    100% minus 40% = 60%

$$\frac{\$6,000 \text{ cost}}{.60} = \$10,000 \text{ selling price or}$$

                           $4,000 gross margin or
                           40.0% gross profit margin

Putting this into words, you do not multiply the cost of goods sold times the margin you want to make. Start with 100%, subtract the margin you want to make and then divide this number into your cost of goods sold.

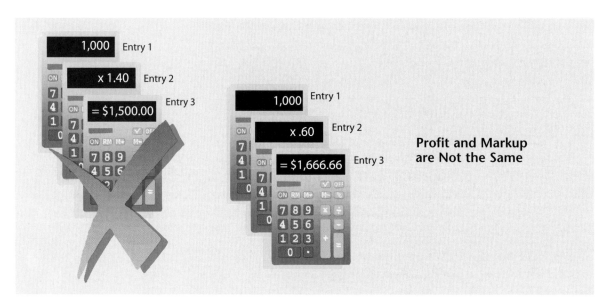

Profit and Markup are Not the Same

1,000 Entry 1
x 1.40 Entry 2
= $1,500.00 Entry 3

1,000 Entry 1
x .60 Entry 2
= $1,666.66 Entry 3

Increase markup multiplier to increase margin

1.50 multiplier	=	33.0% margin
1.60 multiplier	=	37.5% margin
1.65 multiplier	=	39.0% margin
1.72 multiplier	=	42.0% margin
2.00 multiplier	=	50.0% margin

Gross Profit Margin Adjustment

After establishing your sales goals, understand the power of percentage points.

To make more money on the sale, "raise your margins."

Once you have established your sales forecast, you will move on to gross profit. Will your margin increase, decrease or stay the same? Plug in this number.

Gross Profit Margins

What a 3% Improvement in Gross Profit Margin
Would Mean to Profit Before Taxes

	Actual	w/Improvement
Sales	$1,550,000	$1,550,000
Cost of goods sold	990,000	943,950
Gross margin dollars	560,000	606,050
Gross margin percent	36.1%	39.1%
Operating expenses	490,000	490,000
Operating profit	70,000	116,050

This is only a $46,050 increase in operating profit before taxes, and represents a 65.8% improvement in operating profit. Yes, all of this on a 3% improvement in gross profit margin. Make margin improvement a major focus of your business. Many well-run kitchen and bath businesses enjoy gross profit margins of 40%. This should be your goal. Margin is more important than sales volume.

Do not move quickly past this step. Really study your gross profit margins.

Do You Charge the Same Markup on All Parts of the Project?

There is no right answer in our industry—some industry experts will stress that once you have identified your desired profit margin within the budget, every single item receives that same markup. Others suggest that different areas of the business should operate as individual profit centers, and may carry lower margins. In the kitchen industry, the norm is for cabinets installed to carry the desired margin of the firm. Appliance sales—and sometimes countertop sales—may carry a lower margin because of competitor pressures. Large projects where you are subcontracting out major renovation costs may be another area where lower margins are appropriate.

There is no "right" answer. To determine the best business decision for your organization, you must study your competitive market, look at your business model, estimate the third stage of the budgeting process and then decide what is right for you.

IDEAS ON HOW TO IMPROVE GROSS MARGINS

A kitchen and bath business owner does a great deal. Two of the most important functions you will carry out are:

- Generating profitable sales.

- Controlling expenses.

When these are done well, the business will be profitable and worth all your hard work.

The Great Cash Hunt

STRATEGY NO. 1 – INCREASE YOUR MARGIN

Following is a list of ideas that will help you grow your margin. Not all of them will "feel good" to you but if five or more make sense for your business, try them out. Every point you bump your margin up will be money in your pocket.

> A Special Word of Encouragement from Hank:
>
> *"I have worked with businesses where these profit improvement ideas have caused margins to grow by five points or more. They work!"*

- Know what products and services are the most profitable to your business and work hard to sell them. Be sure your salespeople know what those products are.

- Always start by trying to sell the higher priced products. It is much easier to come down than it is to go up.

- If you sell from a manufacturer's suggested list price and give a discount off list, change that discount number to a smaller number, i.e., less of a discount.

- If you work from a manufacturer's cost on products and add a markup (multiplier) to it, increase the markup multiplier.

- Mix-up the discount or multiplier. Do not use the same number across the board. Make more on accessories, add-ons, and the less "shopped" items.

- Know the features and benefits of your salespeople, company and products. Then be sure to articulate them to your clients. When you add value, price becomes less important.

- Sell a nice diversity of products. Make yourself the "one-stop" shopping headquarters for kitchens, baths, libraries, entertainment centers, fireplace mantles, home offices and so on.

- Market yourself as a "design-build" firm. Price the complete project, including all products and installation. Make it difficult for the clients to "shop you" (getting alternative estimates based on the exact same specifications). Sell kitchens—not cabinets.

- Sell add-ons and always at better margins. Be sure to have one "wow" kitchen and bath display that shows every "bell and whistle" possible. Then be sure your clients are aware of the features—and make a higher margin on the "extras" and add-ons.

- Make money on freight. If freight to you averages 12% from the manufacturer, charge your clients 14% or 15%.

- Encourage (insist upon) jobsite delivery from your manufacturers. There will be less handling and less breakage.

- Negotiate better "deals" with your vendors. You do not know if you do not ask. You can make as much money on how you buy as how you sell.

- Be an important partner with your suppliers. The more important you are, the easier it will be to negotiate better deals.

- Study the advantages of being a member of a buying group.

- Price change orders at higher margins.

- Ask for "referral fees" from suppliers and subcontractors. If you are referring a lot of business to them, it should be worth something to you.

- Do not ever give out product names or numbers. Do not make it easy for the client to shop you.

- If you must warehouse products because a job is not progressing on schedule, charge a "warehousing fee." (Unless of course it is you who held up the schedule).

- Know and shop your competitors. Know what products and services they offer and at what price point.

- Add a "contingency" percentage (1%, 2% or 3%) to every quote to cover all the "things" that can and do go wrong on jobs.

- Tie your salespeople's compensation to sales and margin performance, i.e., the higher the sales and margin, the higher the compensation. Motivate them to increase margins.

- Teach salespeople how to sell in order to maximize the gross profit margin. Teach the basics, then practice, practice, practice!

Sales volume is very important, profitable sales volume driven by a good gross margin is most important.

STRATEGY NO. 2 – PAY YOURSELF FIRST

Go for the "Low Hanging" Fruit First
(Easy Profit Improvements)

Two Percent is Heaven Sent

(Source: *The Great Cash Hunt, 33 Ways to Boost Cash Flow in Your Kitchen and Bathroom Business*, by Stephen P. Vlachos, CKD, CBD and Leslie L. Vlachos, M.Ed)

The most important cash that we can boost is the cash that flows through to **you**, the business owner. After all, if there is no money for you at the end of the day then you are going to be very unhappy. It is doubtful that you will be hiring any new staff, enlarging your showroom or buying a new car. If you are not enjoying personal cash, why put up with the headaches of being a business owner? If you are not generating personal cash, it is a good bet that your growth rate will be as flat as your wallet. Remember, profits are good, and cash is paramount.

It is often difficult to understand the true profitability of a small, closely held business. Bottom-line net profit often ranges from 2% to 5%. If we generate additional profit, then we try to spend monies on goods and services that will improve our business.

Let's assume that your firm is generating 2% or more net profit. At the end of the year, are you going to look at your bottom line and wonder where the cash went? It happens to business owners all the time! The answer to that quandary is to take *your* cash up-front.

Open an interest-bearing account at the financial institution of your choice. Then every day take 2% of every dollar that your firm receives and put it into that account. Make sure that only the business owner can access the funds that accrue. In our firm, we call it the Special Account, and it appears as an entry on our balance sheet. At the end of the year you will no longer be wondering where your 2% profit went. It will be right there—earning interest!

Let's assume that your business had $800,000 in sales this year:

.02 x $800,000 = $16,000

If your business grows by 5% each year for 5 years:

.02 x $800,000 = $16,000
.02 x $840,000 = $16,800
.02 x $882,000 = $17,640
.02 x $926,100 = $18,522
.02 x $972,405 = $19,448

The total 2% saved up-front in 5 years is $88,410 plus interest!

You already *know* that you are going to generate 2% or more net profit this year. Taking the 2% up-front ensures you that cash will be there for you when you need it. Use it to plan your retirement, pay college tuition or buy your own building. Best of all, when you have a tough day, and we all have plenty of those in our business, it is gratifying to check out *your* 2% account and find that it is bigger than it was the day before.

STRATEGY NO. 3 – ONCE THE PROJECT IS SOLD, MINIMIZE PROFIT DRAIN BY CLOSELY WATCHING COST DISCREPANCY

The Great Cash Hunt

(Source: *The Great Cash Hunt, 33 Ways to Boost Cash Flow in Your Kitchen and Bathroom Business,* by Stephen P. Vlachos, CKD, CBD and Leslie L. Vlachos, M.Ed)

There is no question that your time is more valuable out on the sales floor or creating a great design. Let your office personnel handle all of the other non-income producing tasks. You do not need to open the mail, review purchase orders or log invoices for payment. You should, however, make sure that every check being sent out in the mail has your signature on it. With every check ready to be signed, insist that the gross profit made on the items being paid for be noted along with the check. If you thought that you should be grossing 40% on your stainless sinks and the note attached to the check shows 33%, then you've got a problem. If the margin is not what you think it should be, give it back to your office manager with instructions to find out why. Of course, a sharp office manger will already have determined where the problem lies.

In our business, we use "blue slips" (we print these forms on blue paper to make them stand out) for cost discrepancy reports. Our sales and design staff hate to see them coming! Our "blue slips" look like this:

COST DISCREPANCY REPORT

Job Name _____ Date _____

Item in Question _____

Item Cost on Purchase Order $ _____

Item Cost on Vendor Invoice $ _____

Difference Between Anticipated Cost
and Amount Invoiced $ _____

Explanation/Action To Be Taken _____

Signature _____

STRATEGY NO. 4 – DO NOT ALLOW SALESPEOPLE TO ALTER YOUR TARGETED MARGINS

20 Things to Do Before Cutting the Price

(Source: *How to Increase Your Kitchen & Bath Business by 25% ... Starting Next Week!* by Bob Popyk)

Price is the most common objection kitchen and bath salespeople hear. Too often, salespeople try to overcome price objections by simply lowering the price—and their profit margins along with it. Here are 20 things to do before cutting the price.

1. Do not panic. Hold the conviction that your price is right. Fear of price is the weakest point in selling. If you aren't sure your price is fair, how can you convince your customers that it is? Confidence will win their respect.

2. Know your product.

3. Discuss the products that you offer. Someone can always offer an inferior product at a lower price.

4. Get all the facts. Check the local competition. What do they sell? How much is it?

5. Look for a "catch" in a competitive price. It is nearly always there. This is especially true with Internet pricing.

6. Find out if a customer is bluffing. Does he really have a better offer elsewhere?

7. Sell your product and your service. Convince your customer that differences in product quality justify your price.

8. Be flexible. Adjust the model quoted, the materials used, etc., and then refigure your price on the reduced package.

9. Feature your exclusive brands and things you do that no local competitor can offer.

10. Cite some examples of unhappy people who bought on price alone—there are plenty.

11. Sell your dealership. Emphasize all your good points—service, stock, reputation. Salesmanship can win over price alone.

12. Be reasonable. Demonstrate the difference between price and value. Avoid arguments. Talk customer benefits.

13. Be sure to figure your own costs carefully to make sure you are on firm ground when price discussion becomes necessary.

14. Offer a concession. Work for your customers. Make them feel that you are always trying to find ways to give them better merchandise at a fair price.

15. If your service record is better than your competitor's, ask the prospective buyer to check on your reputation for service, deliveries and general character. Stand behind the products you sell as part of your dealership policy. If something goes wrong with the product, tell customers that you will take responsibility personally.

16. Offer more. Offering accessories sometimes gives you an opportunity to enhance the deal for the prospective buyer on an item you have to offer that your competitor does not.

17. Sometimes, a frank discussion of good business sense will show the prospects that your price is fair and that they'll get better service from a firm that operates on a sound financial basis with fair prices.

18. Show a different model. Then you and your competitor aren't figuring the same item.

19. Think of the future. Consider the ethics and future results of cutting a price today. Are you willing to offer that price to other prospects? Consider the problems of cutting prices too often.

20. Always remember that in any price concession, every penny comes right out of your profits.

If They Tell You They Are "Shopping"

If prospects immediately tell you that they've already been looking around at other kitchen and bath dealerships, you might want to ask them these three questions: What have you seen? What have you seen that you've really liked? Why didn't you get it? This will allow you to see their true objections.

STRATEGY NO. 5 – LOOK FOR LITTLE WAYS TO CONDUCT YOUR BUSINESS MORE EFFICIENTLY

Loose Change
A penny saved is a penny earned.

Bottom Line Boosters: 16 Ways to Cut Costs and Improve Your Profits

1. **Be a penny pincher on postage and overnight delivery.** The United States Postal Service continues to raise prices. Postage is no longer a nickel and dime item. Here are some savings ideas.

   • Sorting by zip code, zip+ 4 and printing bar codes on envelopes can net savings of almost 20%. Ask your local postmaster for details. The USPS will convert your mailing list (must be on a computer disk) to zip+4 for free. Call the USPS Address Information Center at 800-238-3150 for information.

   • If your volume is not big enough for postal discounts, see if there is a postage "pre-sort" company in your area. These firms collect mail from small businesses, do the pre-sorting and bar coding and everyone shares in the savings.

   • Get tougher on private postage. Remind employees that stamps and the postage meter are not for personal use.

   • Use postcards more. They're quick, inexpensive and convenient. Why pay more for letterhead, envelopes and postage if you do not need to?

- Use Priority Mail envelopes and boxes to take advantage of flat rate mailing charges regardless of weight and delivery address.

- Buy lighter envelopes.

- Purge your mailing lists: eliminate waste in your marketing efforts.

- Return messed up meter tapes to the USPS for refunds of up to 90%.

2. When using FedEx and UPS select the best, most cost-effective delivery schedule to take advantage of discounted shipping rates.

3. **Reduce payroll frequency.** If you pay weekly, go to every other week. Approximately 30% of small businesses still pay weekly, thus incurring higher costs.

4. **Reduce telephone costs.**

- Directory assistance calls aren't free any more! Make sure your employees use the Internet or the telephone book.

- Some long distance carriers have a service available when calling from a hotel in order to avoid multiple access charges. Contact your long distance operator to see if this service is available to you.

- Shorten long distance calls—have a checklist prepared.

- Cut unauthorized employee calls by stating your policy and enforcing it. You can also purchase a device that hooks to your phone and blocks expensive calls to 900, 976, 411 and other numbers.

- Encourage more incoming faxes from customers and vendors. "Dump" your fax cover sheet to quicken each outgoing call.

- Use e-mail in lieu of the telephone calls or faxes—it is less expensive.

5. **Stop wasting money on office supplies, equipment and printing.**

- Do not photocopy items you should be printing. Copies cost five to 15 cents each. Printing can cost as little as three cents.

- Select business forms of equal size. When printing them, have multiple forms combined in a "gang run" instead of printing them separately. This can earn you savings of up to 40%.

- Survey your office equipment service contracts. Cancel contracts for electronic typewriters, fax machines, laser printers and personal computers, because generally you will have fewer problems with these pieces of equipment. Be sure you do not have any "ghost contracts" for equipment you no longer use. Also insist on single-year contracts.

6. **Review all advertising expenses.** Could smaller Yellow Page ads and smaller media ads still get the message out? Check the performance on all advertising by tracking results. Cut from eight to four lines, etc.

7. **Manage your inventory better.** Inventory is cash sitting on the shelf. The cost of carrying excess, outdated or slow-moving inventory can eat you alive. Plus, storage space costs money. Reduce inventory and you save twice.

8. **Tighten up on legal and accounting costs.** If you are using an accounting or law firm, especially one of the big ones, put the business out to bid. You may be pleasantly surprised.

9. **Do not incur bank fees on things you can get for free.** Shop around.

10. **Refinance debts.** If interest rates are low, it may be a good time to consolidate. Ask your bank what is available.

11. **Pay down your debt with all the money you save by implementing these cost-cutting moves.** Interest on your loans is expensive; pay them off.

12. **Review your insurance coverage.** Raise deductibles. Possibly self-insure in some areas. Increase the waiting period for disability coverage. Put your insurance package out to bid. Conditions change rapidly—both yours and the insurance company's. Rates may have decreased. Do not just renew annually.

13. **Check your company job classification under workers' compensation.** Be sure you are not paying for higher risk coverage on job descriptions that have changed.

14. **Be tough on collections (accounts receivable).** The sale is not final until you have collected the money.

   - Invoice quickly.

   - Be sure your invoice contains all pertinent data and details. Eliminate questions and delays.

   - Use the phone for collections—it is much more efficient than letters.

   - Bring in a collection agency quickly if your own efforts fail.

15. **Recycle.** Options vary widely, but you may be able to turn trash into cash by collecting and recycling cardboard, newspaper, metal, aluminum and other materials. This could also cut your trash hauling costs.

16. **Set up a suggestion box.** Nobody is closer to what is happening than your employees. Ask for cost-saving ideas. Tie an incentive to it. Get their input.

STRATEGY NO. 6 – FOR EVERY CENT OR DOLLAR SAVED—YOUR PROFITS INCREASE

A Little "Industry" History from Hank

This strategy—to really search for ways to make fundamental changes in your business to be more profitable—includes a list of proven ideas developed some years ago as Ellen Cheever, Ken Rohl and I sat around the pool in Sacramento, California. As Board Members for NKBA—and colleagues who lived in California—we had agreed to get together and create a viable list of ways a business could become more profitable during a difficult time. Interest rates were soaring to near 20%, so the only people making money were stockbrokers. Clients were delaying renovation or new construction projects because of these astronomical rates.

The following list is an updated view of what we thought of that Sunday afternoon.

OPERATIONS

Elimination or reduction of profit centers, product lines and other operations having marginal profits may result in cost savings in overhead, energy, marketing and interest payments. The sale or discontinuance of low-margin product lines or second showroom or facilities may free cash for debt reduction and for expansion of more profitable operations.

Cost reduction and control are critical to maintaining profitability in economically difficult times. However, do not indiscriminately cut costs. Cut fat, not muscle. First, arm yourself with knowledge of your operations. Identify the activities and costs of providing services or fabricated products. Determine the causes of certain expenses, and what the effects of reducing or not reducing those costs will be.

- Close or sell marginal or unprofitable branches, production facilities or subsidiaries. Establish a P&L status for each stand-alone business.

- Review production and distribution of products with an eye toward reducing warehousing and transportation costs while maintaining or improving customer service.

- Consolidate job functions to reduce staffing, warehousing, administration and office support expenses.

- Share with another company the costs of certain operations, space and other overhead costs or product purchases.

- Curtail capital expenditures and expansion plans until a thorough financial analysis provides reasonable expectations.

- Sign all checks for expenses personally.

ADMINISTRATION

Many expenses are fixed. However, there are many small variable expenses that can be reduced for meaningful savings. Do not overlook anything, however small.

- Allocate administrative charges to branches, production shops and subsidiaries. Treat each distinct part of your business as a separate profit center. Eliminate unprofitable areas.

- Review all dues and subscriptions.

- Review telephone, fax and other communication costs. Compare rates and proposals of long distance communication and equipment providers. Eliminate personal telephone calls charged to the company.

- Reduce premium overnight shipment of products and documents.

- Sell or scrap excess office/warehouse furniture and equipment. Good housekeeping alone can improve employee morale and customer perceptions.

- Defer additional computer hardware and software costs unless it will achieve worthwhile payback.

- Review insurance costs. Get competitive proposals and an assessment of current coverage and insurance costs.

- Minimize professional (legal and accounting) costs.

- Review borrowing and credit card interest costs.

- Tightly control all approvals for capital expenditures.

- Reduce and eliminate excess reports and other questionable paperwork.

- Renegotiate present and future leases.

DESIGN

You cannot tolerate marginal design efforts or results. If you look at the next 10 years, you will see how important personalizing the plan for the client is to the design solution. This is far more important than specifying gadgets or creating one-of-a-kind "installation" ideas that are time consuming and difficult to execute. Additionally, you need to think of ways to employ design to increase your profits.

- Do not lower your prices on the jobs you generally do. Rather, increase your expertise in other types of projects offering higher margin opportunity.

- Consider using an outside design/drawing service in place of adding a draftsperson, or as a substitute for one full-time draftsperson.

- Keep solutions simple, based on products/craftspeople you are familiar with. This makes estimating your ideas accurately easier.

- Use products in your designs that are not easy for the client to shop.

- Increase the perceived value of your presentation by presenting better-looking plans to the client.

- Keep the showroom creative and neat.

- Look prosperous.

- Ask every client about potential cabinetry needs in other areas of the home.

- Make sure you devote your best design efforts to key accounts or repeat/referral clients.

- Talk about the increased real estate value your design will add to the client's house.

- Do not design monuments. Jobs that require a great deal of design time or installation supervision rob you of the precious time needed to design more projects and increase profit levels.

- Attend a design seminar/workshop to stay current on what's new.

- Read all the consumer magazines and trade journals to keep your designs fresh.

INSTALLATION

Most kitchen dealerships experience some "slippage" between the anticipated gross profit margin on the job and the actual amount of money made after the installation is completed. It is critical to be accurate in your estimates so that you protect every possible profit dollar coming to your company. To do this, you need to take the guess work out of the estimating process, and shorten the cycle time it takes from tear-out to job completion.

- Avoid time and material or hourly wages. Work on unit price sheets or fixed bids.

- Hold a one-hour production meeting each week, during which problem solving and tightening the cycle time is your primary focus.

- Cost-out each job thirty days after it is completed.

- Schedule a pre-installation meeting on all jobs.

- Double check jobsite dimensions and orders to eliminate errors.

- Visit the jobsite often, start the punch list early. Get the touch-up work done while the crew is still on the job.

- Improve your relationship with workers so that they focus on making money as well.

- Keep your trucks properly stocked with miscellaneous equipment so that trips to the lumber yard or warehouse are minimized.

- Insist that hourly employees track their activities by project for proper cost accounting.

- Review profitability comparisons between subcontracting installation vs. maintaining an in-house crew.

- Have installers/subcontractors attend manufacturer-sponsored training programs to insure that they are handling, installing and protecting all materials properly.

- Prepare clear and simple project documents that meet NKBA Graphics and Presentation Standards.

- Stay in touch with the client. If there is a problem, fix it immediately.

- Only represent quality products that have a guarantee mechanism that saves you time.

WAREHOUSING AND DISTRIBUTION

- Locate the most active products within the warehouse and make them the most readily accessible.

- Evaluate warehouse housekeeping and safety.

- Be familiar with your state's OSHA and Workers' Compensation law.

- Review your on-time delivery performance.

- Review vendor on-time delivery performance.

- Check vehicle maintenance programs.

- Review security and other physical controls over inventory and equipment.

- Frequently check the most critical inventory items and adjust your records accordingly. Keep accurate inventory records to reduce excess inventory.

PURCHASING

How effective is your purchasing function? It is a fact that most companies can make more money in the way they buy than in the way they sell.

- Press suppliers for the best terms.

- Consider joining a buying group.

- Consider "buy" vs. "make" items.

- Evaluate "lease" vs. "buy" items.

- Reduce rush procurement. Take time to shop the market, seek competitive bids.

- Have product delivered when needed by suppliers to jobsites to reduce your inventory.

- Evaluate all product lines. Consolidate products and/or vendors.

- Consolidate purchases for maximum discounts, freight terms, etc. (Save paperwork, telephone calls and more.)

PAYABLES

Be sure that your people are open and honest with your suppliers. At the same time, pay on the longest terms possible without penalties, loss of credit or premium prices. Make certain that your disbursement function is well managed. Unless you are taking advantage of a worthwhile discount, paying bills early costs you money (i.e., if you normally pay in 30 days, 2%/10 terms will save you 36% over 360 days).

- Pay bills when due—not before.

- Limit expense authorization to owner.

- Negotiate the longest possible terms with vendors without affecting agreed-upon pricing.

- If cash in advance is required by a vendor, discuss a discount to compensate for your loss of normal trade terms.

- Review expenditures to determine if certain payments, such as insurance premiums, can be made annually rather than quarterly. But do not be trapped into an unnecessary prepayment situation.

- Consider a short-term (30 days or less) loan to pay a vendor that offers a cash discount—you will save money.

TAKE THE DISCOUNT

Borrow to Discount

Vendor accounts payable	$50,000
2% cash terms available	$1,000
Net payable to vendors	$49,000
Cost to borrow for 30 days	$245
(6% x $49,000 ÷ 12)	
Net saved for 30 day loan	$755
($1,000 – $245 = $755	

- Taking every cash discount is easier said than done; however, making the commitment to try is a solid first step to boosting your cash. If your business purchased $500,000 worth of materials, with an average prompt-pay discount of 3%, that's a total of $15,000 of found cash. Think of all the things you could do with an extra $15,000!

MOVING CASH FASTER

Look at your order-processing and cash-collection cycles. For every day that you shorten the cycle, you improve customer service and speed up the flow of cash and profitability. Be conscientious in paying suppliers and subcontractors. Do not expect them to be your bank. Lines of credit with lending institutions are easier to arrange when you do not need the funds. If you do not know the mechanism for building a credit line, ask your banker.

- Determine how long it takes between the receipt of an order and the shipment or performance of the job. Discuss ways to streamline the process. Find out why orders are backlogged.

- Once the job is complete or the service performed, find out how long it takes to get the bill out. Invoice daily.

- When the customer makes a payment, see how long it takes to get the payment deposited. Deposit daily.

- Make certain that high-volume invoices receive priority.

- Sweep excess funds into interest-bearing accounts.

- Review compensating bank balances that are not earning interest.

MANAGING CASH FLOW

Your company's ability to manage and control its investments in receivables and inventories, while at the same time achieving the longest reasonable terms on payables, can materially offset the future of your business. Your readiest source of additional financing may be the dollars you can free from your own working capital pipeline. The investments here are substantial.

- Tap your own capital and make it work double-time. The older the receivable, the less likely you are to collect it. Less than 20% of receivables over nine months old are ever collected.

- You need timely information on your receivables and a quick follow-up process on delinquent accounts.

- Your credit policies should be tight enough to minimize bad debt losses, yet flexible enough to optimize sales and be competitive.

- Your company's gross margins may determine how conservative or liberal you need to make your credit policies.

- Receivables over 60 days are not honored by banks as assets against borrowed funds.

CREDIT AND COLLECTIONS

Good management of accounts receivable is critical to success and perhaps survival.

- Have a top-notch person responsible for credit and collections. Good communications with accounts receivable is the most important way to speed up payment. Establish standard collection procedures, including collection letters and a schedule of actions and correspondence. Call customers for delinquent payments. Calls demand answers; letters can be ignored. Set up a tickler file to follow up on payment promises made by customers. Settle customer billing disputes promptly.

- Perform credit investigations of new construction or design/build customers and obtain relevant financial information and references. Update credit information on existing new construction or multi-housing customers on an annual basis. Review current credit applications for completeness. Include a personal guarantee where warranted. Insist that this be signed if the customer is incorporated.

- Stay close to your key customers. Keep an ear to the ground for early signs of trouble. Closely monitor key customer accounts receivable balances. Contact customers immediately when their average collection period increases.

- Renegotiate long-overdue accounts to get immediate cash flow. Consider partial but immediate payments with a realistic schedule for future payments. Obtain a signed payment agreement note that is secured by "real" property.

- Link sales commissions to final payment. Involve designers/salespeople in collection efforts.

- Offer cash discounts to encourage earlier payments, rebill customers for discounts taken but not earned. Charge interest on past due accounts.

- Develop and stick to your own deposit/collection schedule. (Many kitchen/bathroom dealers use a 50% deposit, 40% on delivery and 10% on completion schedule.)

- Use your deposit/collection schedule on all change orders. If necessary, hand carry payments on change orders.

- Exercise lien rights, as applicable in your state.

- Make certain your invoices are clear and understandable.

- Get special credit card equipment to reduce processing charges for credit card sales; and negotiate with your bank for two-day turnaround on your payables at no more than a 1.5% service charge.

- Utilize all legal means to collect your money—including Small Claims Court, mechanics liens and collection attorneys. You worked hard to deliver your products and services and you deserve to be paid for them.

CHAPTER 6: Protecting Your Business

Just what does "protecting your business" really mean? Protection includes those steps we take to ensure continuity of business operations in the event of unforeseen problems. It also includes protecting your personal assets from business creditors in the event of a business problem.

Part of owning and operating a business includes being fully aware of the potential liabilities that may result from any number of situations, such as selling a product that somehow injures someone. Would a refrigerator falling over on someone be an example? Probably not, but other events may occur.

- Your showroom could be damaged or a company-owned vehicle could be involved in an accident.

- Your installation specialist may hook up a gas stove incorrectly resulting in an explosion and injuring someone. Or, you could be sued by a customer or employee for a number of reasons.

- Designers who "sell" plans are in jeopardy of being sued for a design error that costs the client money or harm in someway because of a planning, construction or code violation.

The list is endless and the key word is "awareness." Once you are aware of the potential problems, you can take steps to limit your liability and business disruption in the event of unforeseen circumstances. Keep in mind that as a practical matter you can only limit your liability, not reduce it to zero. You must take steps to keep your potential liability at acceptable limits. That is, how much can you afford to lose without becoming "insurance poor" (i.e., buying too much insurance)?

PROTECTION INCLUDES SOME OF THE FOLLOWING:

- Choose the most suitable business legal structure.

- Obtain professional advice when required.

- Fully understand contracts and personal guarantees.

- Use credit bureaus to help scrutinize clients for open accounts.

- Develop an insurance program.

- Build in systems and procedures to help protect you from theft.

Business Legal Structure

The various business legal structures are explained in Chapter 3. They range from the sole proprietorship to various forms of corporations. Take the time necessary to understand the various advantages and disadvantages of each business legal structure. The legal structure you choose relates directly to your potential personal liability and therefore to your insurance program. Always consider your personal exposure when selecting your legal structure.

Professional Advice

Protection starts with appropriate financial and legal advice on all tax, contractual, and human resource matters relating to your business.

Do not take chances, especially in the legal world. "After the fact" is too late. With legal, financial and human resource matters, do not be "penny-wise and pound-foolish." Business legal problems can sneak up on you and you must be ready. You do that by having your attorney review contracts and other business documents before signing them. Do not be pressured by time constraints or the excitement of the moment.

Likewise, you should have a human resource attorney review all of your various "people" forms: everything from the job application form to your employee handbook to termination paperwork.

Your accounting professional needs to help you make sure that all taxes are paid on time and that any other forms and payments due the various governmental agencies are handled properly.

Contractual Agreements and Personal Guarantees

Many of your larger suppliers, and some smaller ones too, will ask you to complete a detailed credit application in order to do business on terms rather than cash. Additionally, they will also want to see current financial information and will ask you to sign a personal guarantee. With a signed personal guarantee, you are liable for the guaranteed amount of money owed regardless of your business' legal structure. Personal guarantees are usually executed when business is going well so one tends not to think of the potential downside.

As recommended before, consult with your business advisors. Do not ever sign a personal guarantee on the spot.

Review the guarantee considering the worst-case scenario. For example, assume your business has gotten off to a great start. You started out in a small retail space and now you want to move to a larger space in an even greater location. The owner of the property insists that, along with the standard commercial space lease contract, you sign a personal guarantee. You sign, you move and two years later disaster strikes. You file for bankruptcy and close the doors. You still had three more years to go on the lease. Since you signed the personal guarantee, you will personally be responsible for the final three years of the lease—and the fine print in the personal guarantee may state that you must also pay for tenant improvements as the new tenant.

With personal guarantees, and indeed anything you are considering signing, recall the advice of H. Jackson Brown, Jr. In his *Life's Little Instruction Book* he notes, "Read carefully anything that requires your signature—because the big print giveth and the small print taketh away."

Be careful and cautious when it comes to signing a personal guarantee. And require a personal guarantee to you on any open accounts that you choose to work with—if the business is a corporation. If they are a sole proprietorship or partnership, the individual's signature on the credit application will suffice as this states they will be responsible for all payments.

Extension of Credit to Your Customers

Your suppliers will be demanding and they will insist on signed commitments from you. You need to treat your customers in the same good business fashion. If you offer an open account to any client, and many kitchen and bath businesses do, have a legally approved credit application and personal guarantee approval system in place. Insist the application be completely filled out and signed. Ask for credit references. Check them out. Use credit bureaus to help you. They are not expensive and are reliable. If the client is a corporation, you might consider using Dunn and Bradstreet's (D&B) services for checking past payment history and related information. You can find them on the Internet at www.dnb.com or call 866-314-6335 (United States) or 800-463-6362 (Canada).

Virtually every state/province has Mechanics Lien/Builder's Lien laws that are in place to protect homeowners, contractors and suppliers. The regulations vary by state/province, so learn how the Mechanics Lien/Builder's Lien regulations work in your state/province and use them. They are a great tool to help ensure that you are paid.

DEVELOPING AN INSURANCE PROGRAM

The importance of insurance cannot be over emphasized and neither can the danger of paying for insurance you do not need. Solicit the advice of an independent business insurance agent. Do not forget to shop. Talk to three or four agents and compare recommendations and prices. Some agents may suggest some coverage that you just do not need. This after all, is how they make their living. To learn more about this important piece of your business puzzle, visit the Independent Insurance Agents of America website at www.iiaa.org.

In some cases, you can obtain insurance coverage at favorable group rates through various professional associations such as NKBA or your local Chamber of Commerce.

Whatever your final insurance program looks like, revisit it at least every six months. Your business can change rapidly, especially in the first several years of operation and your insurance needs will change with it. Keep in touch with your insurance agent, using him/her as a mentor in this important aspect of your business. Do not be afraid to make changes when necessary.

Business Interruption Insurance

This protects against loss of revenue because of property damage. For instance, this insurance would be used if you could not operate your business during the time repairs were being made because of a fire or in the event of the loss of a key supplier. The coverage can pay for salaries, taxes and lost profits.

Burglary, Robbery and Theft Insurance

Comprehensive policies protect against loss from these perils, including those crimes committed by your own employees. Be certain that you understand what is excluded from this coverage.

Disability Insurance

Cover yourself by disability insurance whether or not you decide on "key person" insurance. This insurance, along with business interruption insurance described above, ensures your business will continue to operate in the unfortunate situation that you are unable to work. Pay particular attention to the definition of "disability," the delay time until payments start, when coverage terminates and the adjustments for inflation.

Errors and Omissions

Regardless of what kind of business you own, customers can claim that something you did on their behalf was done incorrectly, and this error cost them money or caused them harm in some way.

In the litigious world we live in today, many business owners protect themselves with errors and omissions insurance (E&O). This type of insurance may be appropriate for anyone who gives advice, makes educated recommendations, designs solutions or represents the needs of others, such as teachers, consultants, software developers, ad copywriters, web page designers, placement services, telecommunication carriers or inspectors. It is essential if you "sell" plans as part of your product offering.

Although formalizing a contract with your clients and listing the proper disclaimers on your plans can help limit your liability, the big expenses in an errors and omissions claim is the legal defense needed to prove liability or innocence. Errors & Omissions policies are designed to cover many of these defense costs and ultimately the final judgment, if the business owner does not win the case.

Copyrighting Your Drawings

It is the industry standard that the copyright ownership of drawings belong to the firm (not the designer). Your plans should include a copyright notice. Additionally, plans should have a disclaimer detailing what purpose your drawings are intended for. Next, your final plans should be dated and signed by the consumers so there is little opportunity for preliminary plans to be mistaken for final ones. It is recommended by the National Kitchen & Bath Association that all of this information appear in a drawing title block (Samples follow).

COPYRIGHT STATEMENT FOR DRAWINGS

Copyright© 2005

Design plans are provided for the fair use by the client or his agent in completing the project as listed within this contract. Design plans remain the property of ABC Design Studio and cannot be used or reused without permission.

Example of Drawing Title Block

INTENDED USE OF PLANS DISCLAIMER

These design plans are not provided for architectural or engineering use. It is the respective trades' responsibility to verify that all information listed is in accordance with equipment use, applicable codes and actual jobsite dimensions.

FINAL PLAN ACCEPTED BY: *Missey Smith C.K.D*

DATE: *2/29/05*

PRELIMINARY PLAN ONLY: *Missey Smith C.K.D*

DATE: *1/4/05*

Fire Insurance

Fire insurance, like all insurance, is complicated and you should understand what is and is not covered. For example, a typical fire insurance policy covers the loss of contents but does not cover your losses from the fact that you may be out of business for several months while the rebuilding takes place. Do not forget to check whether the contents are insured for their replacement value or for actual value at the time of loss.

Consider a co-insurance clause that reduces the policy cost considerably. This means that the insurance carrier will require you to carry insurance equal to some percentage of the value of the property, usually around 85%. With this type of clause, it is very important that you review coverage frequently so that you will always meet the minimum percentage required. If this is not met, a loss will not be paid no matter what its value.

Health Insurance

Most employees need, want and expect to receive this as one of their benefits. For employers it has become a major issue due to spiraling costs. There are a number of economically attractive packages offered to small businesses. Small groups are usually defined as 25 or fewer employees. Most of the kitchen and bath businesses in the USA and Canada would fall into this category.

Two questions small business owners face when considering health insurance are: "What kind of benefits should I buy?" and "How much can I afford to pay?" Regarding the first, buy the benefits that will protect you, your employees and your families in case of emergency. Regarding the second, it depends on your age and the age of your employees, gender and whether families will be covered.

Be sure to explore the wide range of options available in health care coverage today, including:

- **Fee-For-Service:** Provides the eligible employee with services of a doctor or hospital with partial or total reimbursement depending on the insurance company.

- **Health Maintenance Organization (HMO):** Provides a range of benefits to employees at a fixed price with a minimal contribution; or sometimes no contribution from the employee, as long as the employees use the doctors or hospitals specified in the plan. Many HMO's have their own managed care facilities.

- **Preferred Provider Organization (PPO):** Considered managed fee-for-service plans because some restrictions are put in place to control the frequency and cost of health care. Under a PPO, arrangements are made among the providers, hospitals and doctors to offer services at an alternative, usually lower, price. Most of the time there would be a co-pay amount for each visit.

- **Health Savings Account (HSA):** Combines a high deductible health insurance plan (HDHP) with a tax-free savings account that works like an IRA, except the money is intended to be used for qualified health care costs. The primary advantage of this plan is lower premiums while providing protection from big medical bills.

- **A Flexible Benefit Plan:** Allows employees to choose from different fringe benefits. This is sometimes referred to as a "cafeteria plan." Check with your insurance agent for more details on the wide variety of health plans that are available.

Key Person Insurance

This type of insurance is particularly important for small "mom and pop" businesses where the loss of the owner/manager or lead design/sales person, from illness, accident or death could render the business inoperable or severely limit its operations. This insurance, although expensive, can provide protection for this situation.

Liability Insurance

This is probably the most important element of your insurance program. Liability insurance provides protection from potential losses resulting from injury or damage to others or their property. Think about some of the big cash awards you have read about that have resulted from lawsuits concerning liability of one kind or another and you will understand the importance of this insurance. If your agent recommends a comprehensive general policy, make certain that it does not include items you do not need. Pay only for insurance you really need. Do not confuse business liability coverage with your personal liability coverage. They are both recommended. Your personal coverage will not cover a business-generated liability. Check to be certain.

Compare the costs of different levels of coverage. In some cases a $2 million policy costs only slightly more than a $1 million policy. The economy of scale is true with most forms of insurance coverage. That is, after a certain value, additional insurance becomes very economical.

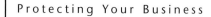

Life Insurance

This is one of the lowest cost benefits you can offer your employees. For a small additional fee, health insurance providers allow you to purchase a life insurance plan either from them or from another company.

Owner's Disability Insurance

The disability insurance discussed earlier is for the business. If something happened to you, the owner, then the money would go to the business because you are not there to run it. Personal disability covers you in the event you were disabled and unable to work. Normally the amount paid is slightly less than your current salary. Cost for this coverage varies considerably depending on your profession, salary level, how quickly the benefits start, and when they end. Benefits paid are tax free only if you, not the company, pay the premium.

Workers' Compensation Insurance

If you have employees, you will be required in most states/provinces to cover them under workers' compensation. The cost of this insurance varies widely and depends on the kind of work performed and your accident history. It is important that you classify your employees properly to secure the lowest insurance rates.

Guidelines for Developing Your Insurance Coverage Package

This list could continue since it is possible to purchase insurance for just about any peril you can imagine, if you can afford to pay the premiums. When considering your insurance coverage—use the following guidelines:

- Before speaking with an insurance representative write down a clear statement of what your expectations are.

- Do not withhold important information from your insurance representative about your business and its exposure to loss.

- Get at least three competitive bids using brokers, direct agents, and independent agents. Note the interest that he or she takes in loss prevention and suggestions for specialty coverage.

- Avoid duplication and overlap in policies; do not pay for insurance you do not need.

- Complete insurance packages for small businesses do exist in some areas. Ask for a BOP (Business Opportunity Plan.)

- Ask whether the insurance firm is "licensed to transact business in your state." If so make sure it has a solvency fund should a catastrophe put the insurance company in danger of going under.

- Reassess insurance coverage on an annual basis. As your firm grows, so do your needs and potential liabilities. Being under-insured is one of the major problems growing businesses face. Get competitive bids on your total package every two or three years.

- Keep copies of your insurance policies and complete records of premiums paid, itemized losses, and loss recoveries. This information can help you get better coverage at lower costs in the future.

Following is a Business Insurance Planning Worksheet that lists every type of insurance to help you put together the insurance program that is right for your business.

BUSINESS INSURANCE PLANNING WORKSHEET

Type of Insurance	Required	Yearly Cost	Cost Per Payment
General Liability Insurance			
Product Liability Insurance			
Errors & Omissions Liability Insurance			
Malpractice Liability Insurance			
General Liability Insurance			
Automotive Liability Insurance			
Fire & Theft Insurance			
Business Interruption Insurance			
Overhead Expense Insurance			
Personal Disability Insurance			
Key Employee Insurance			
Shareholders' or Partners' Insurance			
Credit Extension Insurance			
Term Life Insurance			
Health Insurance			
Group Insurance			
Workers' Compensation Insurance			
Survivor – Income Life Insurance			
Care, Custody and Control Insurance			
Consequential Losses Insurance			
Boiler & Machinery Insurance			
Profit Insurance			
Money & Securities Insurance			
Glass Insurance			
Electrician Equipment Insurance			
Power Interruption Insurance			
Rain Insurance			
Temperature Damage Insurance			
Transportation Insurance			
Fidelity Bonds			
Surety Bonds			
Title Insurance			
Water Damage Insurance			
Natural Disaster Insurance			
TOTAL ANNUAL COSTS			

PROTECTING YOUR BUSINESS FROM THEFT

This is not a pleasant subject to talk about, but it is a necessary one. Every business is subject to theft, ranging from a handfull of paperclips to hundreds of thousands of dollars. The theft can be someone unknown to you breaking into your business and stealing product, cash, computers—anything of value. Or it could be a long time and "trusted" employee.

Employee Theft

Employee theft is one of the most emotionally devastating problems that can occur in a business. It can cast a shadow of doubt over everyone working for the company until the person who is responsible for the theft is caught. You should be alert to the following:

- Office supplies and equipment missing.

- Inventory disappearing.

- Cash missing from the cash box.

- Accounting books that do not balance.

- Checks written to people and/or companies that you do not recognize.

- Purchases made for products and services that are never delivered.

- Employees who do not charge friends or relatives for products they receive.

- Overtime exaggerated.

- Vacation and sick days taken advantage of.

Protect Yourself

To help limit your losses from employee theft, check the background of all prospective hires. Get to know your employees to the extent that you can detect signs of financial or personal problems. If they trust and respect you, they may ask for help before they take their problems out on the business.

Here is a random list of several things you can do to limit both internal and external theft:

- Install a security system. This should include alarms on all doors and windows, sound and motion sensors, and the system should be tied into a central "listening" station. Put signage on windows and doors to tell people you are protected. Be prudent in who you give the access code to.

- Have outside lights that automatically come on at dusk and go off at dawn. Keep the property well lit.

- Balance the cash box every night.

- Have someone you know come into the business and purchase something for cash. Then track the cash and paperwork all the way through your system and into the bank. Let everyone know you have done this and that you will continue to do it on a random basis.

- Conduct a surprise check of products loaded on a truck ready for delivery. Make sure there is not more product leaving the building than the paperwork calls for.

- Be alert to employees leaving the premise with boxes, bundles, and bags that they did not come in with.

- If employees park their cars right next to the storage areas, be alert to unscheduled trips to their cars during working hours.

- You, the owner, should open every bank statement. Review every check written to be sure you know to whom it was written and what it was for.

- Require two-signature checks—you being one of the signers.

- Check all time cards on hourly employees.

- Review each pay register to be sure people are being paid the correct amount.

- Review your financial statements monthly. Be on the lookout for unusual expenditures or changes in cash flow.

- Let employees know that theft is a major concern of yours and even though you trust them you will continually be doing prudent exercises to make sure that theft does not happen.

- Lock cash and all valuable documents in a fire safe each and every night.

This is a delicate and sensitive subject but being wise, alert, prudent and smart, you can avoid some of the possibilities.

Protecting your business is no easy assignment. This guide should help you in getting started. As in several other areas of the business, take advantage of all the professional help you can.

CHAPTER 7: Basic Tax Management

Almost every entrepreneur hates dealing with taxes. Even so, spend a bit of time learning the basics so taxes are as painless as possible, and, hopefully, save you money in the process. Here is what you need to know about taxes if you run a small business.

The amount you or your business pays in annual taxes depends on several factors:

- The legal form of your business.

- How much money it made that year.

- What your expenses were.

- How sharp your accountant is.

- How much you personally know about the tax system.

Deductions

You already know that you can deduct "ordinary and necessary" business expenses to reduce your taxable income. Travel, supplies, inventory, labor costs—all are deductible from your Federal income taxes. The real question is, "Are there any loopholes you can use?"

AUTOMOBILE

There are two methods for calculating your vehicle deduction.

- The "standard mileage" method allows you to deduct 48.5 cents per mile (2005) when you drive the car for business, as well as business-related tolls and parking expenses.

- The "actual expense" method allows you to deduct your total expenses for gas and repairs, plus depreciation for business travel. For example, if your total auto expenses for the year are $10,000 and the usage was 60% business and 40% personal, you can deduct $6,000. You will have to keep a detailed written log of the mileage in order to determine the business vs. personal usage.

CHARITIES

Sole proprietors, partnerships, LLCs and S-Corporations can have charitable contributions passed through and deducted on the owner's personal tax return. C-Corporations claim charitable contributions as expenses.

ENTERTAINMENT

In the past businesses were able to deduct up to 80% of all legitimate entertainment expenses—the limit is now 50%. The good news is that almost any entertainment activity that relates to business can be deducted: a round of golf, important lunches/dinners, taking a client fishing, to a game or a concert, or even a weekend in the mountains. Keep records, all receipts, and be able to prove that the expense is related to business. Write on the receipt whom you were with before filing it away.

If you throw a party, picnic or some other entertainment event for your staff and their families—these expenses are 100% deductible.

LOANS AND CREDIT CARDS

Deduct interest on loans, purchases or advances.

TRAVEL

Travel expenses you incur for your business are 100% deductible. However, if your family joins you on a business trip, their expenses are not deductible. If you stay over for a night or two in order to get a discounted airfare—your extra hotel and meals are deductible.

MISCELLANEOUS TAXES

Sales taxes on items you buy for the business are deductible. Fuel and excise taxes are often overlooked deductions. Property tax and local assessments are deductible. Employment taxes you pay are deductible although the self-employment tax paid by individuals is not deductible, and neither is Federal income tax paid.

OTHER TAX BASICS

Employee Taxes

Employees and taxes go hand-in-hand. When hired, your employees need to fill out a Federal W-4 Form and an Immigration and Naturalization Service Form I-9. As you begin to pay the employee, you deduct a variety of taxes from their payrolls.

- Social Security (FICA)

- Medicare

- Unemployment Tax

- State/province Income Taxes

With the first three, you must also make a matching payment.

Because payroll and employee withholding is such a complicated area, it is advisable to hire an outside payroll service such as ADP, Paychex, or someone similar.

Sales Taxes

Unless you live in a state/province or territory that has no state/province or territory tax, if you sell a product, you are required to collect and pay your state/province tax money. What you owe varies greatly; not only do amounts vary by state/province, but some states/provinces tax services as well as products. Check with your State/Province Tax Board to see whether the rules apply to you.

There are exceptions to the sales tax rules (which essentially amount to paying taxes on anything sold to anyone). The first is resellers—such as wholesalers and retailers with a resale license—who do not owe sales tax. Also, you owe no sales tax on sales to tax-exempt organizations like public schools and churches.

Deadlines

When you own a small business, be aware of tax deadlines beyond April 15.

- Corporations must file their tax returns within 2-1/2 months after the end of their fiscal year.

- Quarterly estimated taxes are due four times a year: April 15, June 15, September 15 and January 15.

- Sales taxes are due quarterly or monthly, depending upon which state/province you are in.

- Employee taxes may be due weekly, monthly or quarterly—depending upon the number of employees you have.

- If your business owns real estate, it will owe property taxes.

TAX TIPS

All business owners want to save money on taxes. Many different strategies help to reduce your tax bite. Do not wait until December 31 to decide to take action. Preplanning can go a long way in reducing the government's share when tax time arrives.

Set Up a Retirement Plan

The self-employed have the opportunity to divert pretax dollars into different types of retirement savings accounts and thereby reduce their yearly tax liability. Most retirement plans have catch-up provisions for those over 50.

One last bonus for creating a business retirement plan: you can get a tax credit of up to $500 for the first three years of the plan if you have less than 100 employees.

RETIREMENT PLAN COMPARISON CHART

(Source: 401khelpcenter.com, LLC)

A Retirement Plan Comparison Chart, which will assist you in identifying the various plans available, follows on the next three pages. Note: You should consult with an employee benefits professional before setting up any type of retirement plan for you and your employees.

Retirement Plan Comparison Chart

Feature	Basic plan type	Who generally adopts	Can employer sponsor other qualified retire-ment plans	Who can contribute	Maximum employee deferral contribution
401(k)	Defined Contribution	Corporations, partnerships, limited liability companies	Yes	Employee; employer contributions are optional	The lesser of $14,000 for 2005 (indexed for inflation each year) or 100% of compensation
Solo 401(k)	Defined Contribution	Sole proprietorships, partnerships, limited liability companies and corporations with no common law employees	Yes	Employee: employer contri-butions are optional	The lesser of $14,000 for 2005 (indexed for inflation each year) or 100% of compensation
Safe Harbor 401(k)	Defined Contribution	Sole proprietorships, partnerships, limited liability companies and corporations	Yes	Employee and employer	The lesser of $14,000 for 2005 (indexed for inflation each year) or 100% of compensation
SIMPLE 401(k)	Defined Contribution	Sole proprietorships, partnerships, limited liability companies and corporations with 100 or fewer eligible employees	No	Employee and employer	The lesser of $14,000 for 2005 (indexed for inflation each year) or 100% of compensation
Profit Sharing	Defined Contribution	Sole proprietorships, partnerships, limited liability companies and corporations	Yes	Employer	None
SEP IRA	IRA based	Sole proprietorships, partnerships, and small businesses	Yes	Employer	None, contributions are generally by employer only
SIMPLE IRA	IRA based	Sole proprietorships, partnerships, limited liability companies and corporations with 100 or fewer employees	No	Employee and employer	The lesser of $14,000 for 2005 (indexed for inflation each year) or 100% of compensation

Retirement Plan Comparison Chart

Feature	Employer Contributions	Catch-up contributions for those age 50 and older	Employee eligibility	IRS reporting by employer
401(k)	Discretionary; maximum tax-deductible employer contribution is 25% of eligible payroll; overall maximum contribution per eligible employee is 100% of compensation not to exceed $42,000	$4,000 for 2005 (indexed for inflation each year)	Age requirement cannot exceed 21; service requirement can't exceed one year: may exclude union employees	Form 5500
Solo 401(k)	Discretionary:maximum tax-deductible employer contribution is 25%	$4,000 for 2005 (indexed for inflation each year)	Age requirements cannot exceed 21; service requirements can't exceed one year	Form 5500-EZ when plan assets reach $100,000
Safe Harbor 401(k)	Required match of 100% on the first 3% of employee deferral plus 50% on the next 2% of employee deferral **OR** 3% of compensation to all eligible employees	$4,000 for 2005 (indexed for inflation each year)	Age requirement cannot exceed 21; service requirement can't exceed one year; may exclude union employees	Form 5500
SIMPLE 401(k)	Required match of 100% up to 3% of employee's compensation **OR** 2% of compensation to all eligible employees	$2,000 for 2005 (indexed for inflation each year)	Age requirement cannot exceed 21; service require-ment can't exceed one year; two years if 100% vested; may exclude union employees	Form 5500
Profit Sharing	Discretionary; maximum tax-deductible employer contribution is 25% of eligible payroll; overall maximum contribution per eligible employee is 100% of compensation not to exceed $42,000	N/A	Age requirement cannot exceed 21; service requirement can't exceed one year; two years if 100% vested; may exclude union employees	Form 5500
SEP IRA	Discretionary; cannot exceed the lesser of 25% of the employee's compensation or $42,000	N/A	Age requirement cannot exceed 21; have earned compensation in three of the past five years; received compensation of at least $450; may exclude union employees	None
SIMPLE IRA	Required match of 100% up to 3% of employee's compensation (may be reduced to 1% in 2 of of any 5 years) **OR** 2% of compensation to all eligible employees	$2,000 for 2005 (indexed for inflation for each year)	All employees earning $5,000 for any past two years and expected to do so in current year; no age limit permitted; may exclude union employees	None

Retirement Plan Comparison Chart

Feature	Establishment deadline	Funding deadline	Minimum vesting
401(k)	By the last day of the plan year for which the plan is effective	Employee contributions must be deposited as soon as administratively possible, but no later than 15 business days after the month in which the deferrals were made; employer contributions must be deposited by the time the corporate tax return (with extensions) is filed for the tax year in which the deduction is being taken	Immediate on Employee Contributions; Employer contributions can be subject to vesting schedule
Solo 401(k)	By the last day of the plan year for which the plan is effective	Unincorporated businesses – employer/employee contributions: by the time the corporate tax return (with extensions, is filed for the tax year in which the deduction is being taken; Incorporated businesses – employer contribution by tax-filing date plus extensions and employee contributions must be deposited as soon as administratively possible, but no later than 15 business days after the month in which the deferrals were made	Immediate
Safe Harbor 401(k)	Any date between January 1 and October 1; may not have an effective date that is before the date plan is actually adopted	Employee contributions must be deposited as soon as administratively possible, but no later than 15 business days after the month in which the deferrals were made; employer contributions must be deposited by the time the corporate tax return (with extensions) is filed for the tax year in which the deduction is being taken	Immediate
SIMPLE 401(k)	Any date between January 1 and October 1; as soon as administratively feasible for businesses established after October 1st	Employee contributions must be deposited as soon as administratively possible, but no later than 15 business days after the month in which the deferrals were made, employer contributions must be deposited by the time the corporate tax return (with extensions) is filed for the tax year in which the deduction is being taken	Immediate
Profit Sharing	By the last day of the plan year for which the plan is effective	Contributions must be deposited by the time the corporate tax return (with extensions) is filed for the tax year in which the deduction is being taken	Employer contributions can be subject to vesting schedule
SEP IRA	Established by the time the corporate tax return (with extensions) is filed for the tax year in which the deduction is being taken	Funded by the time the corporate tax return (with extensions) is filed for the tax year in which the deduction is being taken	Immediate
SIMPLE IRA	Any date between January 1 and October 1; as soon as administratively feasible for businesses established after October 1st	Employee contributions must be deposited within 30 days after the end of the month in which the amounts would otherwise have been payable to the employee in cash; employer contributions must be deposited by the time the corporate tax return (with extensions) is filed for the tax year in which the deduction is being taken	Immediate

Lease Your Property to Your Business

If your business uses property that you personally own, you can save on business taxes by leasing the property to the business. The lease expense to the business is tax-deductible, and the income you generate personally from the lease income is not subject to Social Security tax. You can then take any applicable depreciation allowance for the leased property.

> The Internal Revenue Service/Canada Revenue Agency has an excellent site devoted to small businesses, with industry-specific information, audit guides, links and more. Go to www.irs.gov/business/small/ (United States).

Tax Laws

The Jobs and Growth Tax Relief Reconciliation Act of 2003 offered plenty of help for the small business owner. The best part of the bill is the generous change in the rules for depreciating business expenditures.

Previously, equipment and business assets had to be depreciated over a five to seven-year time frame. Under the new rules, however, you can now depreciate and deduct 100% of the cost of almost all new and used assets in the year you buy them. In addition, the deduction topped-out at $25,000, but you can depreciate up to $100,000 for any asset acquired after May 5, 2003.

There is more to the area of taxes. Seek the advice of a professional.

CHAPTER 8: The Basics of Human Resource (People) Management

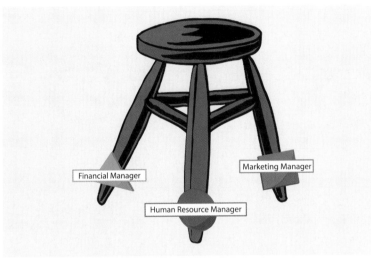

Earlier, we mentioned that every business is comprised of three major management areas: Financial Management, Marketing Management and Human Resource Management. The owners and managers of today's kitchen and bath businesses must be equally strong in all three areas. We know that is asking and expecting a lot, but you do not have a choice.

Being a good people manager is a learned art and skill.

Large companies have separate departments, helped by professional human resource managers, who are dedicated to handling this part of running a successful business. The kitchen and bath industry, made up of several thousand small (20 or fewer employees) companies, does not have the luxury of hiring specialists to manage the different segments of the business. So the owner ends up doing everything. Owners, who recognize they must become well-rounded professional managers, will be the survivors in this increasingly competitive market.

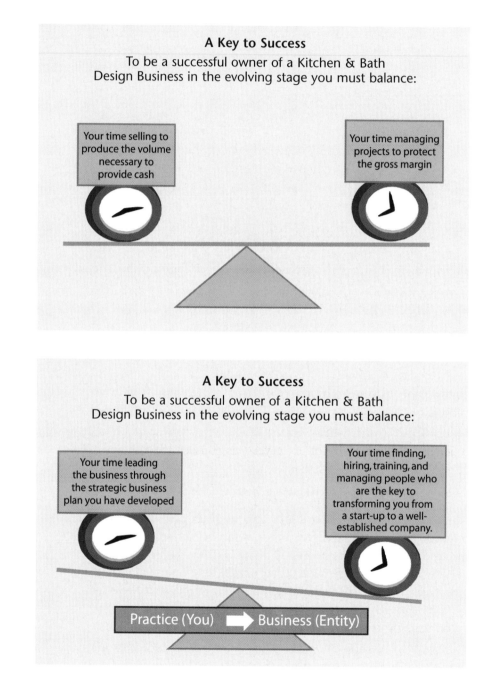

Employees represent the intellectual capital that can make or break a firm's ability to remain competitive. People are your most important asset. But if they are not well managed, they can also be a liability.

As business becomes more complex, so does the human resource function now encompassing everything from addressing staffing needs more strategically to launching effective training initiatives, interpreting federal and state/provincial codes, and implementing policies and benefits that safeguard workers while protecting company interests. The stakes are high. The legal and economic consequences of a major human resources misstep can be enormous.

For many kitchen and bath business owners, human resource management is an intimidating prospect. The next two chapters cover this important subject: Chapter 8 covers the basics, and Chapter 9 is directed to the owner/manager of the business or the head of human resources, if the business has one.

THE BROAD PICTURE OF HUMAN RESOURCES

Most people in business agree that being sensitive to, and doing your best to meet the "people needs" of your employees, is in your best interest as an employer. However, debate exists concerning just how much responsibility a company must assume with respect to those people needs, and how much time and money a company must devote to the needs and priorities of employees, as opposed to those of its business operations and customers.

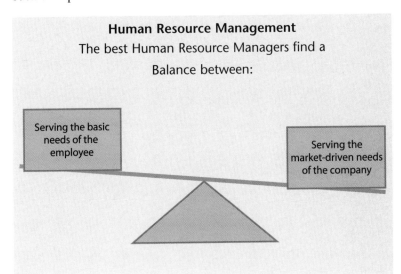

Human Resource Management
The best Human Resource Managers find a
Balance between:

Serving the basic needs of the employee

Serving the market-driven needs of the company

That is where you come in. As the owner, and probably the human resource manager, your job is to focus on the practices and policies in your company that directly affect the welfare and morale of your most important asset—employees. It is up to you to help your company to strike the optimum balance between the strategic needs of your business and the basic needs of your employees. Most kitchen and bath business owners would agree that the task is not only harder than ever before, it is more important than ever before.

For one thing, the market for employees with the skills and knowledge that growing technology-driven businesses require is extremely competitive today. Consequently, your ability to attract good employees relates more closely than ever to the "human" side of the day-to-day working experience (i.e., the general atmosphere that prevails in the workplace), and the extent to which your company practices help people balance the pressure of work and home.

Whether called "human resources management" or "personnel administration," this important facet of business is generally described as "the decisions, activities, and processes that must meet the basic needs and support the work performance of employees."

Human Resource Managers
Are Responsible for:

- Staffing
- Basic workplace policies
- Compensation and benefits
- Regulatory issues

The most common areas that fall under human resource management include:

- **Staffing:** Strategically determining, recruiting and hiring the people to help operate your business.

- **Basic Work Place Policies:** Orienting your staff on policies and procedures such as schedules, safety and security.

- **Compensation and Benefits:** The salary and company services which ensure your staff stays with you and grows in knowledge and experience to help your company grow and expand.

- **Regulatory Issues:** What your company must do to stay in compliance with the ever-increasing number of federal, state/provincial and local regulations.

HUMAN RESOURCE MANAGEMENT IS ALL ABOUT:

Human Resource Management Is Really About People:
- Finding and recruiting them
- Training and developing them
- Creating a safe/healthy/productive place for them to work
- Communicating with them
- Motivating them
- Compensating them

As it happens, every company, regardless of size, location and purpose, must deal with human resource issues in one way or another. The only exception would be a work-at-home, self-employed designer.

You Are the Human Resource Manager

Most small business owners function as the human resource manager. You will be/are responsible for personally overseeing and conducting all human resource functions at your company: hiring/firing employees, researching compensation and benefit packages, writing paychecks and keeping appropriate records, training and developing employees and communicating with employees.

You need to become a good human resources manager if you hope to thrive and survive in the business world. However, when and how will this ever happen while you are still the number one salesperson and marketing person in the business? Tough questions to answer, but they need answering nevertheless. Reading these chapters will be a good start. Putting various methods, policies, procedures and forms to work for you would be the next step, and buying some books and CDs on the subject and attending seminars or community college classes is always recommended.

Out-sourcing May be the Answer

Fortunately, outsourcing is a growing trend in human resource management that can help the owners of small businesses. Engage an outsider to help administrate operational functions, such as the payroll and the benefits package. They can give advice on almost every human resource issue that may arise. There are several out-sourcing companies that specialize in small business human resource needs. Speak with your accounting and legal advisors for a reference.

HUMAN RESOURCE TRENDS FOR THE FUTURE

There have been more changes in human resource management in the past fifteen years than in the hundred years before that, and the changes in the next ten years will be just as dramatic. What might the future hold?

Managing the Human Side of Change

The number one challenge that you face in the decade ahead will be managing change, and the number one contribution you can make in the human resource area is to become a true catalyst for change in your organization. You may be a one-person management team, but it will be up to you to envision the kinds of change that take place and to adapt those changes in a timely manner.

Adapting to the Changing Nature of Jobs

The most significant change in the organizational structure of most companies has less to do with the fundamental structure of companies and more to do with the fundamental nature of jobs and the working arrangements of the people who hold these jobs.

Today's workplace is not necessarily an office or showroom where employees perform their jobs. Today is the age of the telecommuting and the "virtual office." More and more employees are performing some or all of their work from home.

Moreover, today is the age of flextime, with many companies providing some or all of their employees with an opportunity to modify the normal nine-to-five schedule in ways that suit their lifestyle. When you have a showroom that needs to be "covered" and only one or two salespeople on staff, building in flextime can be difficult, but being aware of the trend and trying to "work with" your employees is important.

Some working moms and dads want to spend more time with their children. This has opened part-time positions for qualified professionals. Part-time positions can be difficult because of customer availability and continuity.

A trend that is favorable to our industry is that people are working longer, past the normal retirement age of 65. They are living longer and want to stay active. Do not overlook this growing source.

Workforce Diversity

The demographics of the American workforce have changed dramatically in just the past fifty years. White males dominated the workforce in the past. Today, the workforce consists of females and males, of all ethnic backgrounds.

These changes in demographics have forced human resource managers and business owners to alter the structure and administration of their benefit packages. There is no longer a "one-size-fits-all" benefits package. The trend today and for the future is "cafeteria-style" offerings, where employees receive an "allowance" and have the opportunity to select which benefits give them the biggest bang for their buck.

The biggest challenge that diversity poses involves how to manage this mixture of genders, cultural backgrounds, ages and life styles at a time when companies are moving away from the old-style way of management, and replacing it with a more open, empowered and team-oriented approach to decision making.

The challenge to companies in general, and human resource professionals in particular, is not to simply adapt to diversity, but to capitalize on it. Many kitchen and bath businesses are discovering that they are competing in a much different marketplace than they were twenty years ago. Customers and workforces are better educated and more diverse. Be smart and use this to your competitive advantage.

Using Technology to Help Manage Human Resources

Computers streamline almost all aspects of the human resource function. There is some excellent human resource software available and some terrific outside sources available to help you manage your human resource department, even if you are the whole department.

Rules and Regulations

A workforce that is free of hazards, sexual harassment, and discrimination is no longer considered a "benefit" in today's environment; it is something that employees have every right to expect from the company they work for. It is also something that federal, state/provincial, and local government agencies are using their enforcement muscle to ensure.

Many rules and regulations have been introduced in the past 25 years and there is no reason to believe that this trend will not continue.

If you do not have a human resource background, perhaps your biggest challenge will be familiarizing yourself with all the various government-mandated regulations and programs with which your company must comply.

The government-mandated regulations that most companies need to remain closely aware of today involve almost every aspect of the human resource function, including safety and health, equal employment opportunity, sexual harassment, pension reform and work environmental issues. Someone in your company must make sure that everybody is following the rules and regulations; probably you.

Becoming "Family Friendly"

Is your company "family friendly?" It better be if you want to attract and retain top performers. Being "family friendly" means that your company's scheduling and general operating policies take into reasonable account the personal needs of the employees—in particular, their desire to balance job responsibilities with family responsibilities.

It has become increasingly apparent in the past ten years that family-oriented policies do more than simply enhance a company's recruiting initiatives. They also produce a number of bottom-line benefits, such as reduced absenteeism, fewer disability claims, and fewer workplace accidents. Chief among the practices and policies that are typically found in companies actively pursuing work and family initiatives are flexible scheduling (a.k.a. flextime), telecommuting, individual arrangements, employees assistance programs (EPAs), and benefit programs that enable employees to select those benefits that are relevant to their particular needs.

**FIGURING OUT
YOUR NEEDS**

Hiring is a multi-step process. The first and most important step is to form a clear understanding of your staffing needs. You must not only identify what position to fill, but when to fill it and what the costs will be.

Too often, owners/managers of kitchen and bath businesses operate using "seat-of-the-pants" decisions regarding who, what and when to hire. They do not have well thought-out strategies, written job descriptions, or documented compensation plans to guide them in the process. You should not simply be "filling jobs." You should constantly be seeking to bring to your company the skills, experience and attributes that it needs to meet whichever challenge it may face.

DOCUMENT THE JOB

Once you've determined need and affordability, establish the following:

- A written job description for the position which outlines, in detail, all aspects of the job

- Minimum and maximum compensation to be paid, including fringe benefits

- Type of compensation program you will be using

    (Straight salary, straight commission or salary plus commission)

- Performance goals for sales, gross profit, number of jobs, etc. This should be done for a 12-month period

- Qualifications and experience required to perform the job (i.e., CKD/CBD, computer skills, selling experience, etc.)

DOCUMENT THE HIRING PLAN

Once you've done this, then develop your plan for hiring:

- Identify where and how to find new people—local or regional ads, word of mouth, etc.

- Set a timeline for advertising, interviewing, checking references, hiring and training

- Determine if part-time, backup or a subcontractor will fill the need.

Hank warns the reader:

"Stop! Do not skip this because the term may sound complicated. The concept itself is actually quite simple."

Building Competency Models

Competency modeling is determining what particular mix of skills, attributes and attitudes will produce superior performance at your business. This strategy not only applies to hiring decisions, but also to training and development strategies.

For example, the core of your business is designing and selling kitchen and bath projects. Many owners put design skills ahead of the skill of selling. Certainly, producing winning designs is important, but selling the products and services is even more important. Everything starts with the sale. This is what pays the bills. Great designs are important to helping consummate the sale, but selling skills are even more important.

Therefore, the competency model for a design/sales position should take into account the skills, attributes, and attitudes of both the design and selling side of the position.

You may not always be able to fill every position with people who meet the total competency model, but at least you can identify with greater precision any "skill deficits" (i.e., gaps between the requirements of the job and the qualifications of the candidate). From this understanding, work to close these gaps through training and coaching.

Developing an Employee's "Skill Inventory"

Once you gain a general sense of the competencies that will produce superior performance, you are nearly ready to take the next step in a strategically driven hiring process, which is developing an employee skill inventory.

This is exactly what the name implies: a portfolio of the human capital in your company—a catalog of the individual skills, attributes, credentials and areas of knowledge that currently exist. The focus should be on any skills and attributes that have led to successes and accomplishments (i.e., the better-performing employees) in the past.

Segments of the Employee's "Skills Inventory"

The key to developing a practical, user-friendly employee skills inventory lies in how you organize various categories of information.

A typical list of employee skills inventory should include some of the following fields:

- **Skills/Knowledge Areas.** Business-related functions or activities in which the employee has either special knowledge or a proven record of proficiency.

- **Special Preferences.** Requests that the employees have made about their own career aspirations or other jobs in the company they would like to pursue.

- **Educational Background.** Schools, degrees, credentials, and subjects that the employee has been exposed to.

- **Job History at Your Company.** Details about work history and performance.

- **Previous Job History.** Experience, skills and performance at previous jobs.

- **Training Courses and Seminars.** List of programs with topics covered which identifies knowledge/skill set the employee has previously developed.

- **Test Results.** If applicable.

- **Licenses, Credentials and Affiliations.** These should be work-related and limited to the tasks and responsibilities of the job. NKBA certifications are meaningful, and if you offer installation, a contractor's license will also be important.

The Job Description
- Spells out—IN DETAIL—what the job entails
- Is the basis for key hiring criteria
- Ensures the candidate has a clear understanding of what to expect if hired
- Becomes a reference tool during evaluation process
- Acts as the benchmark for performance after you hire the candidate
- Establishes a minimum-maximum compensation range

Developing a Job Description

The job description has long been the tool of hiring for well-managed businesses. Unfortunately, most kitchen and bath businesses do not have detailed written descriptions for each position in the company. This is unfortunate because job descriptions are important in the hiring process and to the employee when hired, as well as during job performance evaluations.

Executed correctly, a well thought-out job description delivers the following benefits:

- Spells out in detail what the job entails, ensuring that the "boss" and all involved in the hiring process will be on the same page.

- Serves as a basis for hiring criteria.

- Ensures that candidates have a clear idea of what to expect if you hire them.

- Serves as a reference tool during the evaluation process.

- Serves as a benchmark for performance after you hire the candidate.

- Establishes a compensation range.

Think of a job description as a "snapshot" of the job. It should communicate clearly and concisely what responsibilities and tasks the job entails, indicate the key qualifications for the job, the basic requirements, and, if possible, the attributes that underline superior performance.

CATEGORIES THAT MAKE UP A WELL-WRITTEN JOB DESCRIPTION

- Title of the position

- Department (if applicable)

- Direct report (to whom the person reports)

- Responsibilities

- Necessary skills

- Experience necessary

SAMPLE JOB DESCRIPTION

Position/Title: _____
(i.e., Designer/Salesperson)

Department: _____
(i.e., Sales)

Reports to: _____
(i.e., Owner)

Overall Responsibility: _____
(i.e., Design/sell kitchen and bath projects)

Key Areas of Responsibility

- Meet and greet clients coming into the showroom.

- Articulate features and benefits of yourself, the company and the products and services throughout the selling process.

- Qualify the client: Who are they? Why are they there? What is their time frame? Have they been shopping? What is their budget? Do they need design services? What products (styles finishes, wood species, etc.) are they interested in? Do they have a contractor? Are they looking for a turnkey job? And any other information that allows the salesperson to proceed.

- Help the client in the selection of products.

- Complete designs that meet and exceed the client's needs.

- Develop a complete list of all products.

- Quote prices on products and services.

- Follow up all project quotes until client accepts or rejects.

- Manage the project through completion.

- Work with the installation team to coordinate the project (if applicable).

- Communicate with clients, vendors, subcontractors and all others involved with the project in a regular timely manner.

- Collect deposits and money as the project progresses.

SAMPLE JOB DESCRIPTION -continued-

Key Areas of Responsibility (continued)

- Maintain detailed and complete files on each client and project.

- Use CAD system for designs.

- Participate in an ongoing training program to maintain a high level of skills in design, sales, product knowledge, computer, company policies and procedures, and industry styles and trends.

- Achieve mutually agreed upon sales and profit goals.

- Be active in industry associations (NKBA, ASID, etc.).

- Be professional in dress, language, and all personal aspects.

- Be a good team member and help others when called upon.

Skills and Attributes

- Strong product knowledge.

- Strong design skills.

- Strong sales skills.

- Strong people skills.

- Detail-oriented.

- Good organization skills.

- Good time-management skills.

- Good team player.

- Good knowledge of installation.

Experience/Ability Requirements

- Minimum of 3 years design and sales of kitchens and baths.

- High school graduate.

- NKBA Certification a plus.

- Minimum of 3 years CAD experience.

Alternatives to Full-time Employees

Kitchen and bath dealers frequently use independent contractors to provide legitimate help for their businesses. It is important, however, to be aware of proper payroll deductions because U.S. Internal Revenue Service and Revenue Canada keep a close watch on how small businesses classify independent contractors vs. employees.

PROS AND CONS OF INDEPENDENTS

Independent contractors are essentially self-employed individuals who provide services using their expertise and their equipment to accomplish the job. They may or may not work on your premises. An independent contractor is neither a consultant, nor a vendor. A consultant generally advises management, while an independent contractor performs specific tasks. A vendor typically provides goods and services and operates at a separate established location, while an independent contractor works in your showroom environment.

Dealers use independent contractors as a way to control hours and expenses, and to manage the ebb and flow of day-to-day business. Since many independent contractors have worked for a variety of businesses, they bring a depth of experience and knowledge. They are more likely than employees to provide you with unbiased opinions and input.

On the downside, it can be tougher to earn loyalty from independent contractors. Maintaining focus can also be a problem, as can confidentiality.

The best use of independent contractors is for filling in gaps, rather than handling everyday functions. They can also manage pilot programs or test markets.

MEETING TAX LAWS

The United States Internal Revenue Service has been keeping particularly close tabs on small businesses to make sure they appropriately classify independent contractors vs. employees. In the event of an IRS audit, your firm could be liable for back employment taxes if the IRS determines that one of your independent contractors does not meet their definition of an independent contractor. Discuss your job description with your legal and accounting advisors to determine if they meet the IRS definition of an independent contractor.

Both the IRS and individual states often use the "20 Common Law Factor" test in determining whether or not to reclassify the tax treatment of a worker. For a detailed discussion of these factors, consult your business attorney and your CPA.

EMPLOYEE VS. INDEPENDENT CONTRACTOR

1. Is the individual providing services required to comply with instruction on when, where, and how the work is done?

2. Is the individual provided with training to enable him or her to perform the job in a particular manner?

3. Are the services performed by the individual a part of the contractor's business operations?

4. Must services be rendered personally?

5. Does the contractor hire, supervise, or pay assistants to help the individual performing under the contract?

6. Is the relationship between parties a continuing one?

7. Who sets the hours of work?

8. Is the individual required to devote full time to the party for whom the services are performed?

9. Does the individual perform work on another's business premises?

10. Who directs the sequence in which the work must be done?

11. Are regular oral or written reports required?

12. What is the method of payment – hourly, weekly, commission, or by the job?

13. Are business or traveling expenses reimbursed?

14. Who furnishes the tools and materials necessary for the provision of services?

15. Does the individual have significant investment in the tools or facilities used to perform his or her services?

16. Can the individual providing services realize profit or loss?

17. Can the individual providing services work for a number of firms at the same time?

18. Does the individual make his or her services available to the general public?

19. Can the individual be dismissed for reasons other than non-performance of contract specifications?

20. Can the individual providing services terminate his or her relationship at any time without incurring a liability for failure to complete a job?

Following are some helpful points offered by D. S. Berenson, the managing partner of Johanson, Berenson LLP, a Washington, D.C.-based national law firm specializing in the home improvement industry. His comments are reprinted from *Remodeling* Magazine's February, 2004 issue, and should be considered for informational purposes only and not construed as legal advice.

> *"Having a detailed written agreement with your installer . A word of warning: State audits are usually triggered by a disgruntled individual, often filing for workers' comp. On occasion, it may be faster and less expensive to pay a small claim rather than assert that the worker was an independent contractor and face a full examination."*
>
> *"If an examination takes place, the IRS and some State tax agencies may request that an employer or worker complete a 'Form SS-8'. This is a heavily biased form designed to support reclassification, and completing it almost always subjects the business to a reclassification examination. Disgruntled workers often provide the most damaging statements on these forms (which are hard to refute because the identity of the worker is not disclosed). Any business should first consult legal counsel before completing an SS-8."*

Is the New Position Exempt or Non-exempt?

An exempt employee normally is an executive, managerial or professional. Other types of exempt employees are those who are "learned" or "artistic" professionals. All others are non-exempt employees who are subject to the wage and hour laws of your state. Merely placing an employee on salary or straight commission does not exempt that person from wage and hour laws. Salaried workers who are non-exempt employees earn overtime the same as hourly wage earners. Only qualified exempt employees do not earn overtime or any other right enumerated in the Industrial Welfare Commission (IWC) orders.

Many kitchen and bath dealers, as well as other small business owners, do not comply with the Federal and state/provincial laws that apply to this subject.

The line between exempt and non-exempt employees can be a difficult one to draw. Many owners and managers have difficulty distinguishing between the two. Seek guidance from your financial or legal consultants to learn what Federal and state/provincial laws affect your business. The laws vary and, in some instances, the state laws supersede federal laws.

Before meeting with your counselor, have written and detailed job descriptions for all employees. If you know exactly what responsibilities are to be performed, you will have an excellent starting point to help you classify your employees correctly.

The kinds of job responsibilities performed will help define an exempt employee. The Fair Labor Standards Act (FLSA) of 1938 (and amended many times since then) regulates methods of wage payments and hours of work for your employees. The FLSA also recites laws concerning child labor, minimum wage and overtime pay.

Human Resource Forecasting

Do you normally wait until someone quits or you terminate them to start looking for a replacement? Do you wait until everyone is overloaded, complaining, or about to quit because the workload is bigger than the current staff can handle? These situations put pressure on how to fill the slot. And too often then the slot is filled with the first warm body to come along. Pressure makes it difficult to hire properly.

Chapter 2 explored the importance of a business plan, and Chapter 4 discussed the annual budget. Both of these are important business management tools to help forecast employees' needs. They will tell you when you should be starting the next hiring process. Do not wait until everyone's plate is so full that service levels suffer and morale goes "in the tank." Anticipate, as closely as possible, when the next salesperson should be brought on board. Track sales, expenses, and profits—and know what is happening on a day-to-day basis—so you know when to start looking.

When you build in time to look for, interview, hire and train staff, you will have a much smoother transition and will do a better job because you have not been rushed or pressured.

With sophisticated computers and software, it is much easier to track workload than before. Sure, sales numbers are important, but numbers of projects (in process and forthcoming), numbers of work orders, invoices, purchase orders, etc., are guides, as well. Use this information to help forecast for future human resource needs.

Important Questions to Ask Before Hiring

- Is the business profitable? (Don't add expenses if it's not.)

- Are projections for continued growth positive?
  (Do some market research.)

- Can the business support an additional person?

- How will adding an additional design/sales person affect
  the current staff? (Will it take business away from them?)

- Does continued good customer service dictate hiring
  the additional person? (This is very important.)

DECIDING ON THE RIGHT COMPENSATION SYSTEM FOR YOUR SALES TEAM

The compensation package for employees is one of the main engines that drives your business. And if your company is like most companies, it is an expensive engine to maintain—probably your number one expense.

For all small businesses in America, people costs are between 50% and 60% of their total operating expenses. According to NKBA's most recent Dealer Profit Report, total payroll expenses were 56.4% of the total operating expense (right in line with national small business averages.) What is yours? Be sure to add in all related people costs (salary, all taxes, benefits, perks, commissions, bonuses, etc.), including the owner's.

Payroll is more than simply an "expense." How much you pay your employees and the factors that you use to establish pay scales and award bonuses and other incentives can profoundly affect the quality of your work force. And, equally important, it can affect your ability to attract and retain productive, reliable employees.

At industry business management workshops, one of the liveliest topics is always compensation. "What pay structure do you use?" (Salary, straight commission, or combination.) If commission, "Is it on sales, gross profit, or both?" "How much should you pay a sales/design person?" (Productivity has a lot to do with this.)

There is no one right answer to each of these questions. There are too many variables. But there are some guidelines and parameters. Some of the basics:

The Basic Language of Employee Compensation

The basic language of employee compensation (unless you specialize in human resources and, more specifically, employee compensation) can get confusing. Start with a list of terms in the field.

- **Compensation.** This term is used to define all the "rewards" that employees receive in exchange for their work, including base pay, commissions, bonuses, and other incentives.

- **Base Wage and Salary.** The salary or wage that employees receive before deductions and other incentives.

- **Incentives.** These are special rewards such as commissions, bonuses, spiffs, profit sharing, etc., that you offer employees in addition to base wage or salary.

- **Benefits.** Benefits are all special rewards that you offer to employees in addition to base wage or salary. Examples include health insurance, stock options, 401(k) retirement plans, vacation, sick days and so forth.

- **Exempt Workers.** Employees who receive salaries (those paid on a flat weekly, bi-weekly or monthly, as opposed to an hourly, basis) and who are ineligible, in most cases, for overtime pay.

- **Non-exempt Workers.** These are full-time and part-time workers to whom you pay an hourly wage. The provisions of the Fair Labor Standards Act (FLSA) and comparable state/ provincial laws, particularly with respect to minimum hourly wage and overtime pay, cover non-exempt employees. Be sure to check your state/province on the criteria that constitutes and clarifies the difference between exempt and non-exempt employees. It varies from state to state/province to province.

- **Commission.** A percentage of a price or gross margin earned on the sale of products and/or services. A commission can be the total wage or can be combined with salary or hourly wages.

Setting the Foundation for an Effective Compensation System

First, think system. And then think strategy—that is, with a constant eye toward the needs and goals of your business. An effective compensation system is a well thought out set of practices that helps to ensure the following results.

- Your employees receive a fair and equitable wage (from both the owner and employee's perspective) for the work they perform.

- Your payroll costs are in line with the overall financial health of your business.

- Your employees clearly understand your basic philosophy of compensation, which has strong support of managers and employees alike.

- The pay scale for the various jobs in the company reflects the relative importance of the job and the skills that performing these jobs require.

- Pay scales are competitive enough with others in your region so that you are able to retain and attract employees (you do not want to be losing key people to competitors).

- Your compensation policies (and levels) are in line with state/province and federal laws involving minimum wage and job classification.

- Your compensation policies keep pace with the changing nature of today's labor market—particularly in recruiting and retaining the "knowledge workers" who are in strong demand.

Establishing a Compensation Philosophy

Do you just try to meet the minimum compensation it will take to bring a new employee on board, and then react to wage increases as employees put the heat on? Or, do you really have a well thought out strategy that becomes the basis for your wage and salary decisions?

> *Hank comments: "If you fall into the former category you have a lot of kitchen and bath business owner experience. If you fall into the latter group you may not be the 'lone ranger', but you are unique."*

Some of the questions you may want to ask yourself if you want to develop an acceptable compensation strategy might be:

- Will you make your pay scales simply competitive with the going rate in your area, or will you try to pay just a little more?

- Will you try to determine how much each position in the company is worth to the business? Or will you set up salaries on an individual basis, based on the qualities and potential (and demand) of the person filling the position?

- To what extent are the monetary rewards you offer your employees going to take the form of salary, commissions, performance incentives or benefits?

- Will you base the salaries on how well people perform or on other factors, such as how long they stay with you or what credentials (certifications) they brought to the job?

- Are you going to award incentives based on individual performance, tie them to company results, or use a combination thereof?

Keep in mind, there are no right or wrong answers to these questions. Every situation is different. What is important is that your compensation philosophy takes into account your company's mission and strategic goals. If your goal is to be the biggest and best kitchen and bath business in your area, you will probably have to pay just a little more in order to attract and retain the best people. If your goal is to improve—increase—productivity and performance, you may want to build in incentives to reward employees for their individual and/or collective efforts.

223

The Most Common Compensation Plans

In the kitchen and bath industry there are almost as many compensation plans as there are businesses. This is okay as long as your plan works for you. Here is a brief look at the four most popular plans and their various pros and cons.

REGULAR (STRAIGHT) SALARY PLAN

This plan pays the employee a set amount of salary (exempt employees) or hourly (non-exempt employees) on a regular (weekly, bi-weekly, monthly) basis.

Employee	
Pros	**Cons**
• Security	• Lacks incentive
• Guaranteed same $ each month	
• Easy to budget	
• Makes the same regardless of productivity or performance	

Management	
Pros	**Cons**
• Easy to plan and budget	• Lacks incentive
• Easy to administer	• Employee makes the same regardless of production
• Total control	

COMMISSION ONLY PLAN

This usually only applies to salespeople. Pays a certain percentage on monthly (most often time period used) sales, gross margin, or a combination of both.

Employee	
Pros	**Cons**
• Big incentive to sell more or increase margins or both • No limit on how much can be made	• Can have variance in income • Cannot plan or budget

Management	
Pros	**Cons**
• Only pay for productivity (Pay for what you get) • May attract very productive salespeople	• Harder to administer • Cannot plan/budget as well • Lose "team player" (more individualistic) • Employee can be too aggressive • Lose control of employee • If on sales–no incentive to achieve margins

COMBINATION SALARY – COMMISSION PLAN

The compensation is made up of a percentage of salary (guaranteed) and commission (driven by productivity). Management sets both with a goal that the total will offer both security and incentive.

Employee	
Pros	**Cons**
• Partial guarantee • Partial incentive • More security than straight commission	• Only account for part of total comp • Incentive may not be big enough

Management	
Pros	**Cons**
• Partial incentive • Employee has to be productive for part of it	• Harder to administrate • Incentive may not be big enough • Can only plan or budget for part of it

GUARANTEED DRAW AGAINST COMMISSION

A straight commission plan (can be on sales, margin, or both), but instead of waiting for sales/margin results the employee gets a guaranteed amount in advance that is then subtracted from the commissions when results are in.

Employee	
Pros	**Cons**
• Does not have to wait for commissions • Big incentive to sell more, increase margins, or both • No limit on how much they can make • Can plan and budget	• Can fall behind and have to owe company

Management	
Pros	**Cons**
• Same amount every month (+/- commissions) • Easy to plan and budget • Big incentive to employee • Only pay for productivity • May attract big sellers	• Employee falls behind, may be hard to collect • Harder to administrate • Harder to plan/budget • Employee can be aggressive • Can lose some control • If commission on sales or margin only, could lose incentive

EXAMPLES OF
COMPENSATION PLANS

How much do you want/have to pay a design/salesperson to produce "x" amount of sales and/or gross margin. You can make any one of the previously described plans work. Simply plug in the numbers or percentages to make that happen.

Here is how you do it:

Assumption				
Monthly Sales	$80,000		Yearly Sales	$960,000
Monthly GP %	40%		Yearly GP %	40%
Monthly GP $	$32,000		Yearly GP $	$384,000
Monthly Comp	$5,000		Yearly Comp	$60,000
(Less Benefits)			(Less Benefits)	

- *Example 1 – Straight Salary Plan: Regardless of Sales or Gross Margin*

$5,000 per month = $60,000 per year.

It is important to note that in the kitchen and bath business, the sales professional is rarely paid a straight salary. Salaries are typically an entry-level compensation plan when a designer is starting. A salary is often paid during the training period, and is normally modest. Individuals then, typically, move to a split salary and commission and then onto a draw against commission or straight commission as detailed below.

- *Example 2 – Straight Commission on Sales Plan*

Monthly Sales	$80,000	Yearly Sales	$960,000
Commission %	6.25%	Yearly Comm %	6.25%
Mo. Commission	$5,000	Yearly Comp	$60,000

- *Example 3 – Straight Commission on Gross Margin ($)*

Monthly GP ($)	$32,000	Yearly GP	$384,000
Commission %	15.625%	Yearly Comm %	15.625%
Mo. Commission	$5,000	Yearly Comp.	$60,000

- *Example 4 – Combination Salary-Commission Plan
  (You pick the salary portion)*

This example is commission on sales.

Mo. Base Pay	$2,500	Year Base Pay	30,000
Mo. Sales	$80,000	Yearly Sales	960,000
Mo. Comm. %	3.125%	Yearly Comm %	3.125%
Mo. Comm. $	$2,500	Yearly Comm $	$30,000
Total Mo. Comp	$5,000	Yearly Comp	$60,000

- *Example 5 – Combination Salary – Commission Plan
  (You pick the salary portion)*

This example is commission on gross margin.

Mo. Base Pay	$2,500	Yearly Base Pay	$30,000
Mo. G.P. %	40%	Yearly GP%	40%
Mo. G.P.	$32,000	Yearly GP	$384,000
Mo. Comm %	7.8125%	Yearly Comm %	7.8125%
Mo. Comm $	$2,504	Yearly Comm $	$30,048
Total Mo. Comp	$5,004	Yearly Comp	$60,048

You decide how much you want to pay, what plan will work best for you, how much productivity (sales and G.P. margin) you expect to achieve for the dollars paid and then plug in the numbers.

Examples 4 and 5 offer some guaranteed compensation ($2,500 per month) and build in an incentive that encourages more sales and gross margin. You can even "sweeten" that incentive to benefit the company by building in a sliding scale commission based on monthly gross margin. When the margin goes up—so does the commission percentage. When the GP dollars go down, so does the commission percentage.

Here is an example: (Again, make the numbers work for you.)

> Example of a sliding scale commission plan that is driven by both sales and gross margin productivity. You decide what the monthly base pay should be in order to achieve your goals.
>
> | Mo. Commission Percentage | Mo. Gross Margin Percentage (Commission % x Mo. G.P.$) |
> |---|---|
> | 44% and over | 10% |
> | 42 - 43.99% | 9% |
> | 40 - 41.99% | 8% |
> | 38 - 39.99% | 7% |
> | 36 - 37.99% | 6% |
> | 34 - 35.99% | 5% |
> | 32 - 33.99% | 4% |
> | Less than 32% | 0% |

For example, if monthly sales were $100,000 and the gross margin percent was 40%, the gross margin dollars are $40,000. You would pay a commission of $3,200 (8% x $40,000).

Running the Numbers

Straight salary is easy to budget, but here are some examples of how you might approach commission structures.

Assumption: You want/expect the salesperson to achieve $50,000 sales per month at 40% gross profit. You can either pay 10% commission on total sales or 25% commission on gross profit dollars.

- *Commission-only: Per Month*

    10% Commission on $50,000 = $5,000

    Total Compensation, with No Benefits $5,000

    – or –

    40% Gross Profit on $50,000 Sales = $20,000

    20% Commission on $20,000 = $5,000

    Total Compensation, with No Benefits $5,000

- *Combination Plan: Per Month*

    Base Salary of $1,500

    7% Commission on $50,000 = $3,500

    Total Compensation, with No Benefits $5,000

    – or –

    Base Salary of $2,500

    40% Gross Profit on $50,000 Sales = $20,000

    12.5% Commission on $20,000 = $2,500

    Total Compensation, with No Benefits $5,000

Or, pay commission on a sliding scale based on performance, rather than on a fixed rate. Here is an example of what that might be, paying commission on gross profit.

Monthly Average Gross Profit Margin Percent	Monthly Gross Profit Commission Rate
44% +	14%
42% to 44%	13%
40% to 42%	12%
38% to 40%	11%
36% to 38%	10%
34% to 36%	9%
42% to 34%	8%
30% to 32%	7%
25% to 30%	5%
Below 25%	0%

Set goals and communicate those goals to your employees at the start. If the employees exceed the goal, consider a special bonus.

Employment Contracts

Regardless of what payment method is used, make up a contract with each salesperson that contains the following points:

1. How is the salesperson to be paid?

A. Salary + Commission

B. Commission on Sales

C. Commission against Draw

D. Commission on Gross Profit

E. Earned Commission

2. What is the commission paid on?

A. Commission is based on sales volume.

B. Commission is based on profit margin of each project.

3. What forms the basis for the payment calculations?

A. Sales amount without taxes.

B. Gross profit, including overhead calculations or only job-related costs?

C. How do company and salesperson share design fees?

D. Will the commission rate be the same for all products and services (i.e., cabinets, appliances, countertops, plumbing, installation, etc.)?

4. When does the salesperson get paid?

For a salary or draw:

A. Weekly, bi-weekly, etc.

B. When are commissions due and payable?

C. When does the draw stop?

D. What relationship is there between contract payments and commission payments?

For example, one company has the following policy for a Straight Commission Program based on gross profit.

Straight Commission: Straight commission salespeople are the most productive and profitable when paid on a percentage of the gross profit earned on the job. Straight commissions are based on the following formulas:

- Commission rates are a minimum of 30% and a maximum of 40% of the gross profit generated on a job.

- Minimum gross profit required is 30%. Maximum acceptable gross profit is 50%. Gross profit under 30% receives no commission.

- Company overhead, gifts or other charges may be included in the gross profit calculations as a cost to the job.

- 60% of the estimated gross commission is paid to the salesperson in the next pay period providing they provide the following to the company's satisfaction:

  A. A signed contract.

  B. The required deposit.

  C. The plans and elevations required.

  D. A job cost estimate sheet.

  E. Other appropriate materials identified by the company.

- The 40% balance of the commission is paid in the next pay period when:

  A. The job is completed.

  B. All costs are entered.

  C. All costs are reconciled.

  D. The actual gross profit can be determined.

  E. The job is fully paid.

5. What happens when the company terminates the salesperson?

    A. To their draw.

    B. To commissions earned.

    C. To future commissions.

    D. To their overdraw.

    E. To the jobs in progress.

    F. To the jobs almost sold.

    G. To the jobs that must still be completed.

    H. To the jobs that run over cost.

    I. To the leads generated while employed.

6. What happens if the salesperson leaves the company?

    A. To their draw.

    B. To commissions earned.

    C. To future commissions.

    D. To their overdraw.

    E. To the jobs in progress.

    F. To the jobs almost sold.

    G. To the jobs that must still be completed.

    H. To the jobs that run over cost.

    I. To the leads generated while employed.

In Summary

One of the keys to successful human resource management is compensating the best. When you do, you should also expect the best productivity. You should also expect to see good morale and good employee retention.

RESOURCEFUL RECRUITING

The recruiting stage of the hiring process is a lot like fishing. Success depends on not only how well you do it, but where you do it and what "bait" you use.

There are numerous ways to go "fishing" for qualified candidates. Some strategies require more time, effort, and cost than others. The key to effective recruiting, however, is to make sure that whatever options you select are logically and strategically aligned with your priorities.

The number one question is, "Where can I find good people?" There is no one set pattern or easy answer. If you are operating a highly successful business, where the environment is professional and fun, and the people are happy, motivated, and well compensated, you will have prospects knocking on your door looking for opportunity. Good news travels, and word will get out that your business is a good company to work for.

Another option is to develop your own good employees. Hire bright, well-educated, motivated, hard-working people who will be a good cultural fit to your company. The long-term benefits usually outweigh the short-term effects.

For example, hire for "Job A" (a less responsible job requiring less experience), then train and move employees to "Job B." A receptionist can meet and greet clients, answer phones, do back-up paperwork and chores and so on. They learn your system and procedures, attend all staff meetings for product knowledge and selling skills, and in the course of a year or two, are ready to move into the sales department. It is a good practice to promote from within. It builds morale, motivates, and allows you, the boss, to build your own team.

Recruiting is More Than a Numbers Game

When preparing to hire a new person, it is a common belief you should interview as many prospects as possible. However, more important than quantity is quality. You want to attract the highest quality of candidates possible. When you advertise or visit local colleges during a "Job Fair," you will be making a statement about your company. It is important that the statement is positive. To recruit the best talent, establish a positive and professional image and reputation for your company. This challenge carries through to the interview stage, as well (i.e., being warm and courteous helps your image).

Getting Started

Recruiting—finding qualified candidates—is probably the most challenging part of hiring. The obvious sources are:

- Classified advertisements (trade journals and/or newspapers).

- Ask vendor reps for names.

- The NKBA job posting website.

- The Internet.

- Personnel agencies (that specialize in the kitchen and bath industry).

- Industry meetings and events.

- Job Fairs/Open Houses).

- Colleges with either interior design or kitchen/bath design curriculums.

- Ask family and friends.

Hank shares his experience:

"I have had experiences with all of the above and cannot really say one proved better than the other. I was using all of them—at one time or another—to help me achieve my recruiting goals. The best was always prospects knocking on our door because they heard we paid well and were a 'great place to work'."

Make Recruitment an On-going Process

Companies known for their ability to attract and hire good employees are always recruiting, even if they do not have any current openings. If recruiting is part of your responsibility as the owner, always be on the lookout for people who can contribute to your organization's success, even if they are working somewhere else at the time and you have no immediate need for them. At the very least, keep an active file of names and resumes of individuals who have the experience and qualities you are looking for.

Create a Strategy

You need a plan. What sources do you plan to use? When will you start? When do you hope to have all the resumes in to start reviewing? How long will the interviewing process take? When do you want to have someone on board? If you set timeframes and deadlines for each of these, you will have a better chance of achieving your goals. Do not set it in concrete; allow for flexibility.

Keeps Tabs on Your Progress

Monitor your efforts on a regular basis; not just the quantity of inquiries, but also the quality. Depending on internal needs and how the response is going, you may have to change gears, "kicking it up a notch," or, perhaps, slowing it down somewhat. Thus, being flexible will be important.

Recruiting from Within

As mentioned previously, there are several advantages to recruiting from within. It helps keep morale and motivation levels high. In addition, you do not need to worry about the employee fitting into your culture; they will already "know the territory."

There are two possible drawbacks to promoting from within. First, you may have a limited range of candidates to look at. Might there be someone even more qualified on the outside? Second, will promoting one person upset another? Usually, in our small businesses, this is not a problem.

Classified Advertisements

These may be the most widely used method to recruit people in the kitchen and bath industry, especially the trade magazines. This does not mean that it is necessarily the best.

The main advantage of using classified ads is that after writing and placing the advertisement, you can sit back and let the ad do all of the work. You can be reasonably sure that people looking for jobs in the kitchen and bath field will be reading the ad. That is also a negative aspect—folks who are happy in their present positions probably are not reading the advertisements.

HOW TO WRITE A CLASSIFIED AD

Do not start with the idea that you are going to win the literary prize. You are trying to attract qualified candidates. Keep in mind the following considerations when writing a job ad:

- The goal of a classified advertisement is not only to generate responses from qualified candidates, but also to screen out candidates who are clearly unqualified. You are better off getting 10 responses from people who clearly deserve an interview than getting 100 responses from people you would never dream of hiring.

- Think "sell." You are advertising a product, your company. Every aspect of your advertisement must seek to foster a favorable impression of the position and the organization.

- If you have done a good job writing a detailed job description, a good portion of the advertisement is already written. In fact, you should think of the advertisement as a synopsis of the existing job description.

As for the advertisement itself, the following list describes the elements you need to think about as you compose it:

- **Headline:** This will usually be the job title.

- **Job Information:** Put in a line or two about the general duties and responsibilities of the job.

- **Company Information:** Always include a few words on what your company does.

- **Qualifications and Hiring Criteria:** Specify the level of education and experience needed to do the job.

- **How to Respond:** Let applicants know the best way to get in touch with you (phone, fax, e-mail, "regular" mail, and so on).

Bear in mind the following key components, as well:

- You want to convey some sense of your organizational cultural values with a few phrases ("family-oriented," "team-driven," "client focused," and so on).

- Use active voice and action words throughout the ad. Make the ad move—not just sit there passively on the page ("very successful," "fast growing," "well respected," and so on).

- Create a buzz, a sense of enthusiasm, arousing the applicant's interest. A dull advertisement will draw dull candidates.

- If there is something special about the job or company, spell it out ("award winning," "live in California," "the playground of America," and so on.)

Following is an advertisement for a designer/sales position.

CLASSIFIED ADVERTISING

KITCHEN-BATH DESIGN SALES PROFESSIONAL

A successful, growing and award-winning kitchen and bath business seeks an experienced, well-organized person to work in its newly remodeled showroom. This opportunity offers living in beautiful Northern California and working in a family, team-oriented business. The successful candidate will work with clients in designing and selling high-end, quality kitchen and bath products. The business offers one-stop shopping and turnkey projects to a growing list of clients. The company offers above-average compensation. A minimum of five years experience, strong sales record and NKBA certification is highly desired. Respond via email.

JOB APPLICATIONS, RESUMÉS, TESTING, AND NARROWING DOWN THE LIST OF CANDIDATES

Just about everyone would agree that the job interview is the most important element of the hiring process. However, another important key is effective screening. If you do not do efficient screening, two things may happen—both bad. First, you may inadvertently "weed out" candidates who should have received a second look. Second, you could waste valuable time on candidates who are clearly unqualified.

Job Applications

This was the primary method of screening. However, thanks to the resume, applications do not figure as prominently with the hiring process. There are probably two reasons for this. The resume contains all or most of the information and, Equal Employment Opportunity (EEO) legislation now prohibits the interviewer from asking many of the questions that were standard. Items relating to age, marital status—even birthplace—are illegal to ask.

A comprehensive legal application form does provide a uniform means of reviewing the information and it may force the candidates to furnish facts that they might otherwise omit.

Office supply stores offer inexpensive and basic preprinted applications. These are okay, but you may elect to create your own. If you do your own, think about how much information you really need. As a general rule, less is more. And, very important, if you do your own, have it reviewed by a human resource attorney.

Here are questions you should stay away from:

- Race

- Religion

- Sex or sexual orientation

- Age

- Ancestry or national origin (although you can ask if a candidate is eligible to work in the U.S.A.)

- Military service

- Height/weight

- Political preference

- Handicaps/disabilities

- Whether the candidate owns or rents a house

- High school/college graduation dates (allows you to figure age)

And if that is not enough, here are some other "things" that you should not do, or ask about:

- No pictures before they are hired

- No maiden names

Final Rule: If you do not need it (specific information), do not ask it.

A well-designed application form should provide you with the following four different types of information:

- Vital statistics—name, address, and so on

- Educational background

- Detailed work history

- Background information

Always have the applicants sign the form and affirm the accuracy of the information they furnish. This does not guarantee that all of the information is true, but it gives you some protection if, after you hire an applicant, they do not work out and you discover that they made misrepresentations on the application.

241

A Screening System

There are no set rules for screening, other than common sense. Here is a system that works well:

- **Scan for the basics.** These could be core qualifications for the position you are seeking to fill.

- **Screen for criteria.** Using the written job description as your guide, start to focus on the more specific hiring criteria. Start with a "high standard" of evaluation, with only those applications meeting most or all of your criteria placed in a "follow-up" file. This eliminates those that obviously do not meet the criteria.

- **Set up a separate file for the "finalists."** At this point, you probably want to establish a separate file for each of the candidates who pass the initial screening process. Attach a "flow" sheet to the front of each file to keep up-to-date with each candidate. The flow sheet lists the steps in the screening process with spaces for the date and initials of the person completing the step.

- **Extend an invitation.** Depending on how many "finalists" you have, take it to the next step. If you are fortunate and have quite a few finalists, you can make telephone calls to help expand or clarify information. Or, if you have not received a completed copy of your application form, invite them to come in to complete it.

Analyzing Resumés

This can be a difficult process. Most candidates have learned how to write a resumé that makes them look like the perfect candidate; those that cannot write one, hire someone to do it for them.

Resumés come in two different forms:

- **Chronological:** All the work related information appears in a chronological sequence.

- **Functional:** The information appears in various categories (skills, achievements, qualifications, and so on).

Both serve the purpose and one should not be favored over the other. Some candidates may use a combination of the two.

Here are some observations to consider:

- Many resumés are professionally prepared and designed to create a winning, but not necessarily accurate, impression.

- Resumé screening is tedious—you may have to sift through the stack several times (keep the aspirin handy).

- Do not delegate the screening.

READING BETWEEN THE LINES

Because people get help in creating their resumés, it is more difficult than ever to get an accurate reading but here are some characteristics worth looking for:

- Lots of details—the more details a candidate furnishes, the more reliable (as a rule) the information is.

- A history of stability and achievement. Look out for people who have traveled job-to-job, regardless of the reasons they give. The work history should show steady progression into greater responsibility. Do not go by job titles alone. Look at what the candidate did.

- A strong, well-written cover letter. Assuming the candidate wrote it, it is generally a good indication of their overall communication skills.

RED FLAGS

Sometimes what is not in a resumé or what is done through carelessness or mistake can reveal quite a bit about a candidate. Here are some of the things to look for:

- Sloppy overall appearance

- Unexplained chronological gaps

- Static career pattern

- Typos and misspellings

- Vaguely worded job descriptions

- Job "hopping"

- Over emphasis on hobbies or outside interests

243

Testing

Pre-employment testing is probably the most controversial of all the screening options in use today. Most people agree with the basic rationale that test results can often alert you to attributes and potential problems that you will not pick up from the resume, and that might not surface during an interview. There is, however, no conclusive proof that testing results will equate to a better hire. They are a guide with more positives than negatives.

Tests are simply tools—that's all. Each type measures a specific aspect or quality of an applicant's skills, knowledge, experience, or—more controversial—personality (or psychological makeup).

There are literally hundreds of tests available. In our industry, it is easy to test design skills, both done by hand and a CAD system. It is more difficult to test selling skills. Some personality tests will help tell you if the candidate would be a good fit for the corporate culture.

Hiring the right person the first time is so important (and cost effective), so try some testing. Why not use all the tools you can to help you make the right hiring decisions? You can find information on testing potential employees on the Internet.

THE ART OF INTERVIEWING

Conducting an interview is an art—a learned skill—and it looks easier than it is. Therein lies the problem. Too many kitchen and bath owners/managers take interviewing for granted. They do not invest the time, effort and concentration that effective job interviewing requires. Unfortunately, too many interviewers "wing it." They do not prepare enough in advance. It is a proven fact that good, well thought-out, organized interviews equate to better, more productive, longer-lasting employees.

- **Look out for the "professional" interviewee.** They are more schooled and practiced at putting on a good "performance." They know how to give the answers you want to hear. Do not be fooled!

- **Who is conducting the interview anyway?** More and more applicants approach the interview with the attitude that they are here to check out your company and the position, rather than the other way around. If you find the candidate asking all of the questions, you have lost control.

Hank remembers:

"There was an interview where the man brought his wife with him. This was fine, except for the fact that she answered all of my questions and asked all of his. He did not get the job, but should I have hired her?"

- **Sour grapes, legal issues.** Now that more candidates are well versed in anti-discrimination legislation, candidates who do not get the job are more likely than ever to claim, justifiably or not, that your company's interviewing practices are discriminatory. The answer to this is to "stay legal."

The Basics of Interviewing

Job interviews enable you to perform the following four tasks that, when combined with other steps you take, are essential to making a sound hiring decision:

- Elicit firsthand information about the candidate's background and work experience that augments or clarifies what you have already learned from their resume, application form, or previous interview.

- Get a general sense of the candidate's overall intelligence, aptitudes, enthusiasm, and attitude, with particular attention to how these attributes match up to the requirements of the job.

- Gain some insight, to the highest extent possible, into the candidate's basic personality traits.

- Estimate the candidate's ability to adapt to your company's work environment.

The Five Deadly Sins of Job Interviewing

These are all too common practices that are surefire recipes for hiring mistakes:

1. **Not taking enough time.** Failing to give the interviewing process the time and effort it deserves. With all the "hats" that kitchen and bath owners have to wear, it is easy to understand why they neglect to take the time to do a good job. On the other hand, considering the cost of making poor decisions and the effect on the company and other employees, can you afford not to take the time to do a good job?

245

2. **Getting bored with the repetition of the interview.** The most successful interviews have a plan and a routine. You need structure so you do not miss or overlook anything, so you can make comparisons.

3. **Talking too much.** Let the candidate do all of the talking. If you are talking more than 20% of the time, you are talking too much. If you do the majority of the talking, the only thing that you will learn is that the candidate is a good listener.

4. **Placing too much emphasis on one particular aspect of the candidate's overall presentation** (credentials, interests and so forth).

5. **Trying to be like Dr. Freud.** Being able to "read" people can be an enormously valuable skill for anyone who interviews candidates. However, unless you are formally trained as a psychologist or psychiatrist, leave the couch at home and try not to seek out the subconscious meaning behind everything the candidate says or does.

Setting the Stage

Being well prepared for an interview is one of the keys for success. Here are a few things you can do to prepare yourself for the interview process:

- Thoroughly familiarize yourself with the written job description, especially the hiring criteria.

- Review everything the candidate has submitted to date: a job application, resume, cover letter, etc. Make notes on anything (positive and negative) that jumps out at you.

- Set up a general structure for the interview.

- Write out the questions you intend to ask and keep the list in front of you.

- Set up a timetable, always allowing yourself plenty of time.

- Conduct the interview in a room that is quiet, private, and reasonably comfortable. Clear your desk, close the door, put calls on hold, and avoid interruptions.

The Introduction (Warming Up)

Your first priority is to put the candidate at ease. If you are seated when the candidate comes in, stand, shake their hand, smile and let them know you are pleased to see them. Start with some small talk (keeping it to a minimum), giving the candidate an overview of what you are expecting to get out of the interview. Let them know approximately how long the interview will take (45-60 minutes), unless you determine early on that this is not the right candidate. If that is the case, end the meeting sooner in a polite way.

The Art of Asking Questions
- Have a focus, know what information or insights you are looking for
- Make every question count
- Pay attention. DO NOT "think ahead"... listen
- Do not hesitate to probe
- Give the candidate plenty of time to answer
- Hold your judgments
- Take notes

The Art of Questions and Answers

How you phrase questions and how you follow up on everything makes usable the answers you receive.

The following are guidelines for this process:

- **Have a focus.** Even before you start to ask questions, you want to have a reasonably specific idea of what information or insights you are expecting to gain from the interview. Research the hiring criteria you developed in your job description.

- **Make every question count.** Every question should have a specific purpose.

- **Pay attention.** Be a good listener; ask, then listen (remember the 80% listening guideline). Fight the tendency to think ahead.

- **Do not hesitate to probe.** If you ask a specific question and receive a general answer, come back and ask another question that will give you the specific information you are seeking. For example, when the candidate for a sales job says they were the number one salesperson that does not mean as much as getting a specific sales number.

- **Give the candidate plenty of time to respond.** A bit of silence while the candidate thinks about the answer to your question is fine. If the silence hits 10 seconds or more, you may want to consider reformatting your question to make it more understandable.

- **Hold your judgments.** This may sound easy, but try to keep your attention on the answers you are getting instead of making interpretations or judgments. Be careful not to prejudice yourself in the beginning of the interview so that you fail to accurately process information that comes later.

- **Take notes.** If you are interviewing more than two candidates, you will have a difficult time keeping the facts straight and remembering everything you should, unless you take notes. Try to be unobtrusive in the note taking so the candidate does not feel like they have to slow down and wait for you. Use a clean sheet of paper rather than the resume to make your notes.

15 Great Interview Questions You Can Ask

1. Can you tell me a little about yourself?

2. What do you know about our company and why do you want to work here?

3. What interests you about this job, and what skills and strengths can you bring to it?

4. Can you tell me a little about your current job?

5. I see that you have been unemployed for the past _____ months. Why did you leave your last job, and what have you been doing since then?

6. What would you describe as your greatest strengths as an employee? Your greatest weaknesses?

7. Who was your best boss ever and why? Who was the worst, and, looking back, what could you have done to make that relationship better?

8. How do you think your best boss would describe you?
The worst boss?

9. What do you think was/is your greatest achievement at your prior/current job? What was/is your greatest failure?

10. What sort of things do you think your prior/current/last company could do to become more successful?

11. Can you describe a typical day at work in your prior/current job?

12. What sort of work environment do you prefer? What brings out your best performance?

13. Where do you see yourself and your career in three years? Five years?

14. Can you tell me a bit about an important decision you made at work and how you arrived at it?

15. How do you handle conflict? Can you give me an example of how you handled a workplace conflict in the past?

Closing on the Right Note

If you have managed your time well during the interview process, you should have enough time left for the candidate to ask you questions. These can be important because they will give you an idea of the candidate's interests and how much preparation they did for the interview. Questions about the job itself versus questions about salary, perks, etc., would be more revealing.

Finally, in ending the interview, you can:

- Offer the candidate a broad summary of the interview.

- Let the candidate know what comes next.

- End the interview on a formal note.

Then, as soon as possible after the candidate's departure, take a little time to collect your thoughts and summarize your views of the interview and your notes. It will help you when going back to review the finalists.

MAKING THE FINAL
HIRING DECISION

The decision-making process in the final stages of hiring is no different than the process of making any complex decision—whether it is buying a new computer system for the business, changing your cabinet supplier, or changing the showroom location. Look at your options, weigh the pros and cons of each, and, unless you are one of those people who gets paralyzed at the thought of making a decision, you make a choice.

Some base decisions on intuition or "a gut feeling," while others are highly systematic. Some people rely entirely on their own judgment, while others may seek input from other sources. You can never be certain the decision you make is going to yield the desired result. The only thing of which you can be certain is that you manage the decision-making process in a reasonably disciplined, intelligent way. To do this you should perform the following tasks:

- Early on in the hiring process, do a thorough job of identifying your needs and of putting together a job description that pinpoints the combination of skills, attributes and credentials that a particular job requires.

- Gather enough information about each candidate through interviewing, testing and observation that you have a reasonably good idea of the candidates' capabilities, personalities, strengths and weaknesses.

- Remain reasonably objective (no easy task) in evaluating candidates. Do not allow your personal biases to steer focus away from your hiring criteria.

- "Sell" the candidates you favor on the job and make sure they are enthusiastic about the position.

Much of the process involves guesswork, but by doing the things listed above, it should be educated guesswork. And, the more educated you are about the hiring process as a whole, the more accurate your "guesses" are likely to become.

What to be Looking For

The resources available to make hiring decisions are limited. There is only a handful of information available. Here are a few sources you might be able to use:

PAST EXPERIENCE

The best indicator of a candidate's future performance is past performance.

INTERVIEW IMPRESSIONS

The impressions you pickup during an interview will usually carry a great deal of weight in the hiring decision. The problem with interview impressions is that they are just that—only impressions.

TEST RESULTS

Arguments for and against testing exist. Some candidates are great testers and others totally freeze. If you do decide to use test results in your decision-making process, make sure of these two things: the validity of the tests (whether they do, indeed, predict the quality of future job performance) and their legality (whether their use complies with all state and federal laws and does not result in discrimination).

REFERENCES AND OTHER THIRD-PARTY OBSERVATIONS

Reference data is a useful and necessary component of the hiring process. But in today's litigious environment, most former employers are reluctant to say anything even remotely negative about an employee for fear of a lawsuit. Use reference information as a secondary source—to verify impressions and other information.

FIRST-HAND OBSERVATION

Watching candidates actually perform some of the tasks they would be doing if hired is clearly the most reliable way to judge their competence. That is why many companies have instituted combination training and probationary periods. Ask a sales/design candidate to both sit at a board and the computer to do a simple kitchen or bath design. How fast is he or she? How accurate?

Still another trend in hiring today is the practice of starting out a new employee as a temporary, with the understanding if the person works out, the job will become full-time.

"A" RATING SCALE

Here it gets a little tricky. Instead of simply looking at the candidate as a whole, you look at each of the criteria you set down, and rate the candidate based on how he/she measures up in that particular area.

By weighing each performance category, you show which is more important to the success of the job.

- Using this weighted scale to compare one candidate to another requires both subjective and objective opinions from you.

- Constructing a weighted scale by category may be difficult, but breaking out different parts of the job should help in the selection process.

A Note from Hank's Experience:

"To explain the concept of a 'weighted scale': individual business needs will establish priorities. Therefore, by having two employee rating systems you are able to evaluate each point on its own merit. Then rank the importance of the skill, talent or ability according to your needs."

WEIGHTED EVALUATION SCALE

The following is a sample weighted evaluation scale. (Note: One column is the weight of importance you assign to each category, and the other is how you rate the candidate.)

Candidate's Name:

Position:

Performance Category	Weighted Importance 1 (Low) - 5 (High)	X	Candidate Rating 1 (Low)-5 (High)	=	Total Score
Design Skills (hand)	3		5		15
Design Skills (CAD)	4		3		12
Selling Skills	5		1		5
Design Skills (hand)					
Design Skills (CAD)					
Selling Skills					
Time Management Skills					
Organizational Skills					
Communication Skills					
Previous Employment					
Reliability-Work Ethics					
Team Player					
Past Work History					
Professionalism					
Product Knowledge					
Follow-through					
Motivated					
Enthusiastic					
Cultural Fit					
TOTAL					

Note: Make this work for you by adding or deleting any categories and by changing any of the assigned weights. What may be the most important categories for one may not be for the other.

FACTORING IN THE INTANGIBLES

The tough part of any evaluation procedure is attaching numerical ratings to the "intangibles"—those attributes you can only measure through your observations. Following is a list of several of the intangible factors that you most commonly find in the criteria for most jobs, along with some suggestions on how to tell whether the candidate measures up.

- **Industriousness and motivation.**

  Definition: The candidate's work ethic—how hard they are willing to work and how important it is to them that they perform to the best of their ability.

  Possible ways of measuring: Verify accomplishments in their last jobs.

- **Intelligence**

  Definition: Mental alertness, thinking ability, capability to process abstract information.

  Possible ways of measuring: Testing. Evidence of good decision-making ability in previous jobs.

- **Temperament and Ability to Cope with Stress**

  Definition: General demeanor—whether the candidate is calm and levelheaded, hyperactive, or hotheaded.

  Possible ways of measuring: Personality testing. Examine stress levels in previous jobs.

- **Creativity and Resourcefulness**

  Definition: The ability to think "outside the box"—to come up with innovative solutions to problems.

  Possible ways of measuring: Examples of previous work (portfolio of designs). Previous accomplishments or awards.

- **Orientation to Teamwork**

  Definition: Whether the candidate can work harmoniously with others and share responsibility for achieving the same goal.

  Possible ways of measuring: Previous work experience (did they work on their own, or in groups), leisure preferences (are they solitary or group-oriented).

Making the Offer

You have done all of your homework and have made your final choice on whom you want to hire. It is not time to relax. You must make the offer and convince the candidate to come to work for you. Without the proper execution, you might lose the candidate, or they come to work, but do not feel as good about the offer as they should.

- **Do not delay.** Once you have made up your mind, put the offer out as soon as possible.

- **Put everything on the table.** No games. Give the person all of the details about pay, benefits, hours, and any extras. Never put something on the table and then pull it away. You should have a standard job offer letter that you can customize for this candidate. Always put the job offer in writing.

- **Set a reasonable acceptance deadline.** The candidate may need a reasonable amount of time to make his or her decision—but no more than a week.

- **Employment contracts (yes or no).** There is no need for long, formal legal documents. Use a one-page letter that specifies the job title, duties, responsibilities and obligations, conditions of employment, and severance arrangements if things do not work out. This eliminates questions, surprises, and misunderstandings.

- **"Selling" the candidate.** If this is someone you really want to come to work for you and they are showing some reluctance, you will have to find out (via questions and answers) what is causing the reluctance. Here is a list of factors that have the most bearing on how excited your offer is likely to make the candidate:

  1. The nature of the job, its responsibilities and obligations.

  2. Advancement opportunities.

  3. Salary (commission) structure and frequency of reviews.

  4. Benefits package—especially how it compares to the candidate's previous job.

  5. Culture and company working style.

  6. Policies toward work/family balance issues such as flexible scheduling, telecommuting, childcare, etc.

255

7. Commuting considerations—how long will it take them to get to work?

8. Reporting relationships in the job; personality of the immediate supervisor.

9. Self-development opportunities (company training, participate in NKBA courses, certification, etc.).

10. Relocation of the candidate and family.

11. Perceived strength, solvency and market competitiveness of the company.

How far you are willing to go to accommodate a reluctant candidate generally depends on two factors:

A. How badly you want the candidate; and

B. The policies and precedents of the company.

Three questions to ask yourself:

1. Are there any other equally qualified candidates available?

2. How long would it take to pursue them?

3. Has the position been particularly hard to fill?

If your initial attempts to woo a reluctant candidate fail, the best thing to do, in many cases, is to cut your losses and move on. Sometimes you just have to walk away. The goal at this point should be to end the process so the candidate leaves with a feeling of fair treatment.

CHAPTER 9: Human Resource Management— After the Decision is Made

I hope by now that you agree that people are your most important asset—your real key to success. The whole human resource topic is a full book unto itself. In this one, we are concentrating on the basics and the areas of human resources that we believe will be of the most help to kitchen and bath business owners and managers.

> Hank Comments:
>
> *Based on my experience, here are five areas of human resource that, if done well, will almost guarantee the success of your business.*
>
> - Hire the best
>
> - Train the best
>
> - Communicate the best
>
> - Motivate the best
>
> - Compensate the best
>
> *Do each of these the best, and the odds are very good that you will be the best.*

THE ORIENTATION PERIOD

Almost every new hire will be a bit apprehensive and unsure of what to expect and what to do in those first few days on the job. They need a period of acclimation to your company and teammates. This is commonly known as the "orientation period." Large companies tend to have formal programs, but small businesses have less formal ways of welcoming new employees.

Regardless of its form, the basic goal of every orientation process is that, after a reasonable amount of time, your new "partners" know their responsibilities, are productive, and feel like they are part of the team.

Here are a few things not to do:

- Leave the employee alone to learn the ropes simply by observing and asking questions.

- Letting the new person just follow a more experienced person around.

- Showing them a ten-minute video on your orientation program.

Now, here are some things you should do:

- Ease the anxieties. The main purpose of an orientation plan is to accelerate the process of making employees feel at home. Here are a few suggestions on how to help make that happen:

  1. Let all the other employees know that a new person will be starting. Let them know who, what, when, and why.

  2. You, the owner, should meet the new employee and take them to his/her workstation.

  3. You, the owner, should take him or her around and introduce all other employees.

  4. You, the owner, should give him or her a tour of the facility pointing out restrooms, coffee pot, lunchroom, etc.

  5. Give the new person a company roster with names and phone numbers, along with job titles.

  6. Take the newcomer to lunch on the first day—maybe with one or two other teammates.

  7. Give a clear sense of tasks and expectations, including:

     A. A written copy of their job description.

     B. Review of the job description in detail, item by item.

     C. Explanation of expectations.

     D. Explanation of the performance evaluation system you use and the standards you will use to measure them.

     E. Explanation of your compensation review policy.

- Review the company mission statement, and what the company goals are. Review, in detail, exactly what the company does.

- Give the new hire the company policy and procedures manual or employee handbook. Ask him or her to review it in detail. Answer any questions and clear up any misunderstandings. Have the new employee sign a form acknowledging he or she received, read and understood the content of the policy manual and/or employee handbook.

A word of caution: Do not throw too much information at a new hire too quickly. Try to space things out. Think of the orientation as a process, not an event. Set priorities. Stay in close touch. Be proactive.

Mentoring: The Secret to Success

What employees see happening around them affects them as much as what they hear and see during a formal orientation program. The best way to make sure that this factor works in your favor is through the use of mentors. That is, other employees who act as a "big brother" or "big sister" for the first few days or weeks. Mentors can show the new person the ropes and be available to answer questions and give whatever support the individual might need.

In small kitchen and bath businesses, the mentor may very well be the owner. In this case, the owner or manager has to make the time and effort to help the new employee get started in a positive way. First impressions are important.

TRAINING AND DEVELOPMENT

You are off to a good start. You have hired the best. You have done a great job with the orientation program and the new employee is settling in nicely. Now the real work begins—training. Training starts with the employee's first day of work—and never ends. Training is one of the five components of good human resource management. (Hiring, motivating, communicating, and compensation are the other four.)

Unfortunately, most kitchen and bath owners do not have formal training and development programs. Most of the training would be on-the-job training with the owner or co-workers helping when they can. Sometimes you are lucky and you're able to hire well-trained, productive people—sometimes not. In either case, almost every employee can improve. It is your job to help them do that. It is good for the employee (the more productive they are, the more they can earn), and it is good for you (the more productive they become, the more you will earn)—a "win-win" for all.

Larger, more sophisticated companies do something called "needs assessment." They actually develop a means to evaluate their "needs" in terms of training. Because you are a small business with ten or fewer employees, you will know who needs training and in what areas, and how much they need. Your challenge is making it happen.

Training can be fun, inexpensive and rewarding. It becomes part of the employee's job description, and it becomes one of your main management focuses.

There are really only a few areas to concentrate on:

- Product Knowledge

- Sales Skills

- Design Skills

- Communications Skills

- Time Management and Organizational Skills

- Compensation

- Computer/Technology Skills

You cannot do everything all at once. Identify priorities (it will probably vary by employee). Establish timeframes and budgets. And, look at training and development as a long-term, never-ending process.

An important part of building your training program is to know what your company's long-term goals and objectives are. Your training program is then designed to meet these goals and objectives. For instance, if you want to grow sales from $1 million to $2 million over the next three years you will need sales/design people. Your annual and three-year budgets, coupled with cash-flow projections, will tell you when to add people.

In our industry, there are several good means of training. Some of these are:

- In-house. You or someone else acts as the coach and mentor, spending as much time as necessary to "grow" each employee. Hold weekly staff meetings on the same day, at the same time, every week, with mandatory attendance. Use a percentage of these for product knowledge training (either by you or a manufacturer's representative). Some would be for sales training (again, by you or an outside professional). Some would be for internal policies and procedures. Others might be state-of-the-company communication. And still others might be open topic brainstorming.

- Manufacturer rep or factory product training. Some of this would happen at your place of business and some at the factory.

- NKBA and other organization schools and seminars.

- Books, audio and visual CDs on a variety of topics. Build your own library and offer an incentive to encourage use. (Or make it a mandatory part of the job.)

- CAD system training (in-house or out of house).

- The Internet. There are more and more good training programs becoming available this way.

- Local community colleges—depending on the courses offered and training needed.

For employees other than sales/design (installers, bookkeeping, general office, warehouse, etc.) there would be different programs. However, training is for all people—all of the time.

Because your goal is to help employees increase their productivity and enjoy their work more, it is good if you can tie in some rewards. Most people react favorably to "carrots"—especially if they "taste" good.

Training does not just apply to employees. It is as (or even more) important for you—the boss—to continually work to improve yourself. The better you are, the better the employees will be.

Be proactive. Do not wait for someone else to do it for you. Take the training bull by the horns and make it happen.

NKBA Professional Development

When you enroll in the National Kitchen & Bath Association's Professional Development Courses, you take the first steps toward becoming one of the finest professionals in the kitchen and bath industry. Whether you simply want to improve your professional development one course at a time, or you want to work toward NKBA Certification using the recommended Certification Track, you will come away from all courses with real solutions that will enhance the level of service you provide to your clients.

261

WHAT IS NKBA PROFESSIONAL DEVELOPMENT?

In order to meet the increasing need for qualified professionals in the kitchen and bath industry, NKBA created a series of Professional Development Courses through its planning guidelines, course offerings, technical resource and reference manuals, books, learning tools, and multi-level certification program.

NKBA Professional Development Courses are an invaluable opportunity for kitchen and bath professionals to enhance their careers through the industry's premier professional development courses. NKBA provides focused training and unique networking opportunities to discuss industry-related issues in classroom settings throughout North America. For more convenient learning, you may choose to participate in an NKBA Distance Learning Program.

NKBA Professional Development Courses are designed to assist you in achieving your professional goals, and support you and the way you choose to conduct business in today's changing industry.

For students entering the industry, NKBA offers Supported and Endorsed Programs throughout North America, where an NKBA-approved curriculum is offered at two- and four-year learning institutions. From there, it is a smooth leap into the industry, and a quick spring to becoming an NKBA Certified Designer.

WHO ATTENDS NKBA PROFESSIONAL DEVELOPMENT?

All levels of professionals in the kitchen and bath industry, as well as individuals in the construction, remodeling and design fields, attend these courses. Kitchen and bath professionals attend courses to enhance their careers by staying up-to-date on the latest trends and techniques, to obtain further Continuing Education Units (CEUs) toward their industry certifications, or to gain experience in a new aspect of the industry.

NKBA CAREER PATHS

NKBA offers two career paths—Professional Development and Professional Certification—to assist you in making the choices that will fit your career in the kitchen and bath industry. The benefits of each path are outlined below.

- **Path One – Professional Development**: As you choose NKBA courses that fit your goals, you are continually improving yourself and your business—giving you a clear competitive advantage. NKBA courses keep you in tune with the latest industry techniques, trends, products and building code requirements. Path One gives attendees the flexibility to study the topics that fit their needs, and the face-to-face courses and distance learning programs allow students to choose the most convenient process to achieve their specific career goals.

- **Path Two – Professional Certification**: NKBA provides a career path in kitchen and bath design that recognizes education and experience progression through testing and achievement. NKBA developed its two recommended Certification Tracks as a way for kitchen and bath professionals to enhance their careers and market themselves as experts in the specific competencies related to their business. NKBA provides the tools you need to promote yourself as an NKBA Certified Designer to your clients, and puts you on the fast track to success.

Path Two includes a curriculum of educational programs and experience designed to meet the needs of the kitchen and bath professional at each stage of his or her career. The three levels of recognition for professional achievement through NKBA Certification are created to provide options for professionals from all segments of the industry. These levels are:

1. **Associate Kitchen & Bath Designer (AKBD):** This entry-level certification program is for individuals who have entered into the industry, graduated from an NKBA-Endorsed Program or whose position does not encompass all of the design competencies required of the CKD/CBD. This certification level recognizes achievement as one continues along a logical career path as a professional designer to the next level.

2. **Certified Kitchen Designer (CKD) and Certified Bath Designer (CBD):** These certifications are for individuals who have had a minimum of seven years of industry experience and education within the industry. The CKD/CBD has been established as the benchmark certification level for the kitchen and bath industry, indicative of education and design experience.

3. **Certified Master Kitchen and Bath Designer (CMKBD):**
This master level is synonymous with advanced achievement and experience. The CMKBD is awarded to designers who have 10 years of full-time experience since their first certification. Holding an advanced level of certification recognizes industry professionals for their achievement and dedication to continuing their education.

To be NKBA Certified as a kitchen or bath designer, you must acquire NKBA Educational Hours (or equivalent). NKBA considers equivalents to be any college courses specific to kitchen and/or bath design (drafting, CAD, kitchen design, bathroom design, building systems, lighting, construction, etc.) and some training courses serving as required curriculum for related certification.

POLICY AND PROCEDURES MANUAL

A policy and procedures manual that incorporates an employee handbook is an invaluable tool for you and your employees.

- It spells out everything about how your business is run.

- It puts everyone on the same level.

- Everyone works according to the same rules, policies and procedures.

- It allows the boss and all supervisors to manage in a fair, firm and consistent manner.

The manual covers everything from unlocking the doors in the morning to turning off the alarm to making the coffee—how the coffee is to be served to clients, and every detail about your business. Yes, a manual is a great deal of work to put together, but start with one section at a time and build from there.

The policy and procedures manual informs all employees exactly how the business operates. It enforces a consistency that most small businesses do not enjoy. And, most importantly, it adds value—sometimes substantial value to the business if you ever want to sell it. Why? Because it is the systematic, timesaving "how to" manual for the new owner.

There is some excellent software available to help you in the process of writing a manual. If you want to be one of the successful owners/managers in our industry, make writing a formal, detailed policy and procedures manual a high priority.

OUTLINE FOR A POLICY AND PROCEDURES MANUAL

ABC Kitchen and Bath Company
Main Street
Anywhere, USA or Canada
Table of Contents

1. All About ABC Kitchen and Bath Company
   A. Where do I work?
   B. What are the house rules?
   C. Company Mission Statement
   D. Organization Chart
      (1) Job Descriptions
         a. Sales/Design Consultant
         b. Sales/Design Assistant
         c. Office Manager
         d. Office Support
         e. Installation Supervisor
         f. Installer
      (2) Job Performance Evaluations
         a. How They Work
         b. Employer's Responsibility
         c. Timing

2. Products and Services
   A. Products We Sell
   B. Services We Offer
      (1) Company Brochures
   C. Working with Clients
      (1) Kitchen and Bath Retainers
   D. Showroom Etiquette

3. Design, Estimating and Sales Presentations
   A. Company Pricing Worksheet
   B. Requesting Supplier Quotations
   C. Setting Margins
   D. Figuring Freight Costs
   E. Learning and Practicing Selling Skills
   F. Protocol for Presenting Projects

4. Project Paper Flow
   A. Sales Agreements
   B. Deposits
   C. Creating a Job File
   D. Invoices
   E. Purchase Orders

OUTLINE FOR A POLICY AND PROCEDURES MANUAL -continued-

   F. Change Orders
   G. Order and Purchase Order Editing
   H. Margin-buster Report
   I. Delivery Information
     (1) Jobsite Directions
     (2) Final Plans for Delivery

5. Equipment Use and Etiquette
   A. Using the Telephone
   B. Understanding the Alarm System
   C. Using the Copy Machine
   D. Computer Usage
   E. Processing Credit Card Transactions
   F. Using the Fax Machine
   G. E-mail Protocol

6. Installation Services
   A. Installation Estimate Procedure
   B. Installation Payment Schedules
   C. Referral Programs
   D. Installer Performance Agreement

7. Office Follow-up Services
   A. Shipping and Receiving Documents
   B. Product Expediting
   C. Billings and Collections
   D. Job Costing
   E. Product and Service Warranties
   F. Service Calls
   G. Customer Service Surveys
     (1) Sixty-Day Follow-up
     (2) One-year Anniversary Follow-up
   H. Customer Thank Yous
     (1) Notes
     (2) Gifts
   I. Referral Cards/Gifts

8. Being a Staff Member
   A. Commission Procedure
   B. Retirement Plan
   C. Professional Growth Plan
   D. Employee Handbook

OUTLINE FOR A POLICY AND PROCEDURES MANUAL -continued-

9. Personal
   A. AIDS
   B. Americans with Disabilities Act
   C. Attendance and Punctuality
   D. Compensation Practices and Pay Schedule
   E. Discipline and Offense Descriptions
   F. Dress
   G. Drug and Alcohol Abuse
   H. Employee Assistance Programs
   I. Employee Discipline
   J. Employee Relatives
   K. Equal Employment Opportunity
   L. Ethics and Personal Conduct
   M. Family and Medical Leave Act
   N. Grievance Procedures
   O. Holidays
   P. Housekeeping
   Q. Jury Duty
   R. Leaves of Absence
   S. Management Rights
   T. Manual Development Guide
   U. Maternity Leave
   V. Military Leave
   W. Orientation
   X. Overtime Availability
   Y. Peer Review
   AA. Performance Reviews
   BB. Personnel Records Access
   CC. Probationary Period for New Employees
   DD. Reporting Improper Behavior
   EE. Safety and Health
   FF. Safety Rules
   GG. Sexual Harassment
   HH. Sick Leave
   II. Smoking
   JJ. Telephone Usage
   KK. Termination of Employment
   LL. Time Cards
   MM. Transfer and Relocation
   NN. Vacation
   OO. Wage Garnishment

CREATING AN EMPLOYEE-FRIENDLY WORK ENVIRONMENT

According to a Robert Half International, Inc. (the world's largest specialized staffing firm) survey, nearly two-thirds of Americans said they would be willing to reduce both their work hours and their compensation in exchange for more "family or personal time." That is why it is important for every kitchen and bath business owner to recognize this and try to promote "quality of life" human resource policies as both a recruitment and an employee retention tool. Some might consider this a "new" concept, but for a number of kitchen and bath businesses being both customer and employee "friendly" has been one of their major keys to success.

The Basics of an Employee-Friendly Workplace

There are six main areas of consideration (in no particular order):

- Pay and benefits

- Opportunities

- Job security

- Pride in work and company

- Openness and fairness

- Camaraderie and friendliness

EMPLOYEE WELL-BEING AS A CORE VALUE

If you treat your employees as a cherished asset you are well on your way to creating that friendly workplace. Employee-friendly businesses routinely take the welfare of their employees into consideration when making bottom-line decisions.

MAKE A REASONABLE COMMITMENT TO JOB SECURITY WHENEVER POSSIBLE

In the event of a market downturn, the owner and top management should take the first and biggest cuts. Then an across-the-board 5% decrease in salary is better than letting someone go.

CREATE A "PEOPLE-FRIENDLY" FACILITY

State/provincial and federal laws dictate that a workplace must be safe. Above and beyond this, having a comfortable break room, clean restrooms and convenient parking all help.

BE SENSITIVE TO WORK/FAMILY BALANCE ISSUES

Being sensitive to work/family balance issues is more important than ever before. It can be difficult for people today—especially parents with young children—to juggle family responsibilities with work responsibilities. Owners of small businesses have the flexibility to support their employees whenever there is a medical emergency or—on a more pleasant note—some special event at their children's school. It is not just the permission given—it is the manager/owner's attitude that goes with it.

EMPOWER YOUR EMPLOYEES

The more you empower your employees to make decisions and do things "their way" (as long as you get the results you are looking for), the happier they will be. You will find that they will work harder and do a better job when they are accountable for their own decisions and actions as opposed to simply "following orders."

OPEN COMMUNICATION

Secrecy breeds suspicion. So the old notion of not sharing financial information or being involved in important decisions is finally disappearing (well, at least decreasing.) Keep folks informed of what is happening—during both good times and bad times.

CREATE A SENSE OF "OWNERSHIP"

Create a sense of "ownership" with your employees. You may not choose to share any part of actual ownership, but you can create a "profit sharing" program that allows all employees to share in the fruits of their labors.

ALTERNATE WORKING ARRANGEMENTS MAY ATTRACT GOOD CANDIDATES

Alternative work arrangements are those that deviate from the traditional Monday to Friday, 9:00 a.m. to 5:00 p.m. workweek. (Many kitchen and bath owners are open on Saturdays and some evenings.) Alternate working arrangements are here (some 84% of American companies offer some form of flexible work arrangement) and they are growing.

The basic idea behind this is that you give employees some measure of control over their work schedules, thereby making it easier (more friendly) for them to manage personal or non-business responsibilities. The hope would be that happier employees would be more productive and loyal. These situations should be handled on a case-by-case basis—just so they do not start to favor certain employees over others.

Options For Alternate Work Arrangements

- **Flex Time.** Someone may choose to work 8:00 to 3:00 because they want to be home when their children get home from school; someone else may opt for 10:00 to 5:30 because they need to get the spouse and children off to work/school.

- **Compressed Work Week.** Instead of working five 8-hour days, the employee could work four 10-hour days or six 6.5-hour days. (Check your state/provincial wage and hour laws on the over 8-hour day. You do not want to pay overtime.)

- **Job Sharing.** This means that two part-time employees "share" the same full-time job. This could save you money on the benefits package, but the skills of a design/sales person and the continuity of client service would make sharing this position hard. However, there may be other positions (receptionist, warehouse) where this might work.

- **Telecommuting.** This refers to any work arrangement in which employees—on a regular, pre-determined basis—spend all or a portion of their workweek working from home or another company location. Once again, if we are talking showroom design/sales person and you need showroom coverage, this can be difficult. Unless, of course, you have three or more salespeople—then, this could work.

- **Permanent Part-time Arrangement.** The hours would usually be in the 20 to 30 per week range. If possible, the employee could pick the days and times. In smaller kitchen and bath businesses, where a bookkeeper would be a great addition—but there is not a full week's work—the part-time arrangement could work very well.

You can usually tell, simply by the general atmosphere in the workplace and by the manner in which employees interact with one another, whether morale is high or suffering. Good, open communication (up or down) and diligent observation are the tools for judging employee morale.

Meetings Are Good

Holding productive meetings will support your communication efforts. Professionally conducted meetings set goals, clarify responsibilities and create future leaders for your company. Meetings are not gripe sessions fostering negativity. They should not bore the attendees to death, nor distract them from the real work that needs to be done.

An article, "Calling a Meeting" by Linda Case, CAR (Remodelers Advantage Inc.—Fullton, Maryland) in the May, 2004, issue of *Remodeling* Magazine offers excellent guidelines for a well-run meeting.

"Planned and conducted properly, meetings are not a waste of time and money. Well-run meetings help your team achieve goals and be accountable for results in their day-to-day roles." Here are some important points:

- Schedule weekly meetings—if the manager or owner is on vacation, have the meeting run by a key team member.

- Have an agenda, collect information via e-mail from the entire team before the meeting. Prioritize the issues (just in case there is too much on the agenda) and circulate the agenda before the meeting.

SALES MEETINGS

- Many companies have a sales meeting once a week, others find it more useful to have a meeting every month.

- Sales meetings might be reserved just for the sales staff, or might be for the entire organization. (This is particularly effective if it is a monthly meeting and scheduled late in the day.)

- Should be a forum for reporting goal achievement, assistance, encouragement, problem solving, training, sharing and general communication.

- Sales meetings are also an excellent time to have supplier partners or other specialists address the group.

- Make meetings more fun, educational and productive.

    1. Avoid individual problems.

    2. Stick to the agenda.

    3. Concentrate on group concerns and opportunities.

    4. Avoid an over-emphasis on the negative.

    5. Avoid "product information" drone.

    6. Stress the best methods of getting clients to buy new products.

> Remember: Salespeople need and want encouragement, challenge, training, incentive, respect, answers, positive environment and rewards. Focus your sales meetings on providing these motivations.

If your sales meetings are floundering, make them productive using these tools:

- Have a clear purpose.

- Review guidelines for behavior at the meeting.

- Develop a written agenda.

- Stay within a defined period.

- Consider hiring a facilitator.

- Prepare and disseminate minutes.

- Present a weekly "flash report" of sales performance accomplishments.

A SUCCESSFUL MEETING

- Run it like clockwork. Start on time, end on time.

- Do not allow interruptions unless it's an actual emergency.

- Hold it weekly (If the manager or owner is on vacation, the meeting is run by a key team member.)

- Have an agenda based on info from the entire team before the meeting, which is prioritized and circulated before the meeting is conducted.

- Have a "flash report"—a concise one-page report with key data for each attendee: leads taken in, sales made, jobs closed, client evaluation scores received.

- Take minutes. E-mail to all attendees after the meeting with a clear note who is responsible for which tasks or projects identified or assigned during that meeting. At the beginning of the next meeting, follow-up on these items.

A STATE OF THE COMPANY ADDRESS

Employees like to be part of "The Big Picture." One California kitchen/bath dealer makes a "State of the Company" presentation to employees at least once a year (usually at year-end)—more often if the situation dictates. All company employees are called together and the owner makes a 45- to 60-minute presentation. General financial information is shared (i.e., sales up, margins down, expenses holding, etc.).

If you choose to do likewise, keep in mind that successful presentations require planning and rehearsal. Remember, communication is only effective if your message is clearly understood. Plan ahead—determine the points you want to make and what visual aids and handouts you want to use.

"State of the Company"
Preparing the Address

- Outline the various points you want to make, and the order in which to present them.

- Determine how much time you will need (keeping the presentation as concise and to the point as possible).

- Practice your presentation several times until it comes out naturally.

- Prepare for different responses so that as you and the employees interact you are able to "go with the flow."

- Be sure to allow for questions and answers. Good communication is a two-way street.

MEASURING EMPLOYEE PERFORMANCE

Few management practices are more basic or more widespread than performance evaluations (appraisals). That is, of course, when we are not talking about small "mom and pop" businesses like the majority of kitchen and bath dealers. Few kitchen and bath businesses have formal performance evaluation programs or, in fact, do performance reviews with their employees. This is unfortunate because evaluations are extremely helpful for both the owner and the company as a whole, and the employee in particular.

Performance evaluations are a vital management function, and it is up to you to implement a structured, meaningful and well-administered (and delivered) appraisal system, which has tremendous value to all concerned. Performance evaluations are an employee's report card on how they are doing. Everyone needs to know and deserves to know exactly where they stand. Do the evaluations at least once a year, though twice a year is better.

An Overview of the Process

Creating and implementing a structured performance evaluation process takes time and work. But a formal evaluation forces you to establish goals and to identify the behaviors necessary to achieve them. The very nature of an appraisal system puts both the employee and the supervisor into situations that many people find uncomfortable. Some supervisors find it difficult to be both candid and constructive when they are conducting an appraisal session that involves negative issues.

So why should you go to the trouble to create and implement this process? Simply put—the benefits of an effectively structured and administered performance evaluation process far outweigh the time and effort the process requires. Here is a list of things that a well-designed, well-implemented performance evaluation system can do for your company.

The Benefits of a Performance Evaluation System

- Enhance the impact of the coaching that should be taking place between employees and their supervisors.

- Motivate employees to improve their job performance.

- Provide an objective—and legally defensible—basis for key human resources decisions, including merit pay increases, promotions—or terminations.

- Establish a reasonably uniform set of performance standards that are in accord with company values.

- Confirm that employees possess the skills and attributes needed to successfully fulfill a particular job.

- Verify that existing reward mechanisms are logically tied to outstanding performance.

- Iron out difficulties in the employee/supervisor relationship.

- Give employees who are underperforming the guidance that can lead to better performance.

- Keep employees focused on business goals and objectives.

- Validate hiring strategies and practices.

275

- Reinforce company values.

- Assess training and staff development needs.

- Motivate employees to update their skills and job knowledge so that they can make a more meaningful contribution to your company's success.

- Provide the forum for open communication.

Conducting the Performance Evaluation

Before the Interview

- Make sure supervisor and employee understand the purpose of the evaluation

- Both parties review the job description

- Both parties review previous documentation

- Both parties prepare comments that are concise with back-up examples

- Employee knows the format of the interviewing process

- A date and time is set for the interview

Preparing for the Evaluation

- The first step is making sure that both the supervisor and the employee understand the purpose of the evaluation process— i.e., to set goals, provide constructive feedback, and to analyze strengths and weaknesses.

- **Review the job description.** (This is just another reason why they are so important.) Both parties need to review the job description so that when they sit down they both know what the specific job expectations are. The supervisor must focus on the job as it was described and performed, and not on the employee's personality or personal issues. He or she must also be evaluating the whole past 12 months and not just the recent past (month or two). This is also a good time to revise and update the job description to be sure it reflects current duties and responsibilities.

- **Review previous documentation.** During the course of the year, you should accumulate the necessary information to prepare the evaluation. This information would include the prior year's appraisal, sales and margin goals (if a sales person), all notes and information, both positive and negative—everything that will help you evaluate the past twelve months performance.

- **Be concise, but precise.** Use bullet points, not paragraphs. Give examples to back up comments. Be as specific as possible. Do not draw generalized conclusions.

- **Involve the employee in the evaluation.** Ask the employee to do a self-evaluation using the same basic form you will be using. This helps keep the lines of communication open and gives you valuable insight as to how the employee perceives himself or herself. Many times the employee will be tougher on himself or herself than you are. Also, for more employee involvement, ask the employee to be prepared to answer questions like:

  1. What do you feel your major accomplishments have been during the year?

  2. What could you have done better?

  3. What can I do to help you do a better job?

  4. Is there anything you would like to see changed in your job?

- **Set goals and objectives.** Once the current year's performance is evaluated, establish the goals and objectives for the following year. All the goals and objectives must be achievable. They should be easy to understand and measure. After deciding the goals, the manager and employee must:

  1. Agree on the steps the employee must take to achieve the goals.

  2. Agree on the method to measure achievement of the goals.

  3. Agree on benchmarks throughout the year to monitor progress toward achieving the goals.

- **Set the date and time for the review.** Give both yourself and the employee at least two weeks to prepare—especially if you use the employee self-appraisal system.

- **Rehearse what you are going to say.** Because reviews can be highly emotional, especially for the employee, it is a good idea for you to have a written agenda. Plus, you should know in advance what you are going to say during each part of the review. Be sure you are successful in delivering the message you intend regardless of the employee's response.

Conducting the Performance Evaluation
During The Interview

- Make sure the room is comfortable and well lit

- The setting should be private with no interruptions

- Plan a relaxing greeting

- Present an overall summary

- Start with strengths

- Identify areas to improve

- Ask for feedback

- If required discuss salary

- Close on a positive note

Conducting the Performance Evaluation

Now that you and the employee are well prepared, it is time to have the sit-down.

- **Be sure the meeting room is comfortable and well lit.** Alert everyone that you do not want to be disturbed. No interruptions.

- **The Greeting.** Start with a warm greeting and perhaps some brief small talk to help the employee relax and to create an atmosphere conducive to the review.

- **Overall Summary.** Explain where the employee's overall performance ranks—starting with the more general comments and leading into specifics.

- **Strengths.** Unless the employee's performance is totally unsatisfactory, you will be able to identify some strong points. Compliment him or her on both major and minor strengths as they relate to the job. You are trying to start out on a positive side. You can be either specific or general in covering the strengths.

- **Weaknesses.** Unless you have the perfect employee with a truly exceptional performance, you will have identified some areas that need improvement. In reviewing weaknesses, be as specific as possible. Instead of saying you are always late, recite the exact dates and how late. If there is a big list of weak points, do not go through all of them. Prioritize them and cover just two, three or four. One goal for you will be to maintain the employee's self-esteem throughout. A browbeating will not accomplish your goal.

- **Feedback.** When—and hopefully if—you both agree on the areas that need improvement, you need to establish a system/method that will cause improvement to take place. Both the employee and you should be part of putting together the "plan" to improve. (When they have been part of helping build the plan they will be more apt to want to see it succeed.) Both of you must reach agreement on the steps to be taken and the timeframe. (You create a mini-contract.) Part of feedback is giving the employee the opportunity to air his/her thoughts. Listen politely. Do not interrupt. Good feedback will be helpful to all parties concerned.

- **Salary.** Most companies tie a salary review to the performance review. But this may not be the best strategy. Why? If the employee knows that salary is covered at the end of the review, it is what he/she is going to be thinking about and so may miss all the important things you have been talking about. Do the compensation review at a different time—one to two months after the performance review. This also acts as a motivator for the employee to follow through and really try to improve the weak areas.

- **Closing.** Unless the employee's review is bad, end on a positive note. Thank them for the effort they put into preparing for the review, and for being a good, open-minded listener. Tell them that you appreciate them as an employee and are glad they work for you.

Performance Evaluation Legal Issues

The most frequent job-related legal problems are often a direct result of unrealistic employment reviews. Managers too often avoid conflict by failing to appraise a poor employee's performance accurately and truthfully. Later, if the employee is fired, it is easier for the employee to claim discrimination and offer their performance reviews as evidence of adequacy to carry out the job requirements.

- **The first step.** Make sure all supervisors give each employee an honest and realistic review. Additionally, all reviews should be issued in writing—including all "agreements" and/or "disagreements" that come out of the review. The reviewed employee should receive a copy of his or her review and they should sign a copy acknowledging that this is what took place. If the employee were to refuse to sign a negative review, ask a witness to verify that you tried and the employee refused.

- **Develop a consistent review criteria.** Have a written performance evaluation procedure. Be sure all supervisors and employees are familiar with it. Be sure your attorney has reviewed it and the evaluation forms. A key point is that reviews must be much more specific than general.

- **Other steps you can take to avoid legal issues over reviews are:**

  1. Establish grievance procedures.

  2. Have more than one person determine each employee's overall performance rating, or at least provide input during the pre-appraisal period.

  3. Give employees feedback during the year, as appropriate, to avoid performance review surprises.

  4. Work closely with employees who have received poor performance ratings to help them improve.

In Summary

- **Evaluate all year long.** Have frequent conversations about how the employee is doing, even if they are informal. It makes the employee feel good to know that his or her manager is interested in their work.

- **Handle more important "issues" immediately.** Do not wait for the evaluation "sit down."

- **Do not make the evaluation a surprise.** If you evaluate performance on a regular basis, you have the opportunity to catch mistakes before they evolve into big problems.

- **Document, document, document.** Keep notes about performance issues, both good and bad. Do not rely on your memory to write the review. It will also help keep you legal, especially if you forsee a termination.

- **Get the employee involved.** Ask the employee for feedback during the year. At review time, have them do a self-appraisal. Also, get them involved in establishing strategies to improve.

- **Evaluate performance—not the person.** Measure behavior or output against prearranged, agreed upon standards.

- **Maintain the employee's self-esteem.**

- **End on an upbeat note.**

DEVELOPING DISCIPLINARY PROCEDURES

Not that many years ago, if an employee was not performing up to standard or had done something wrong, you could just fire them without worrying about a possible law suit. Not so today. All termination decisions must be reviewed carefully and objectively to assure that they are not improper or could be argued as improper before a jury or government agency. Unfortunately, in employment litigation, what the jury believes is what matters, irrespective of the actual facts surrounding the discharge. Some employers elect to adopt a formalized disciplinary process, one that reasonably and systematically warns employees when performance falls short of expectations. Consistency in following the process is a key. The owner/manager, all supervisors, and the employees need to know what the process is—and that it is followed carefully.

The specifics of the process can vary, but most disciplinary procedures are structured along the same lines.

- **Initial Notification.** The first step in a typical progressive disciplinary process is informing employees that their job performance or workplace conduct is not measuring up to the company's expectations and standards. This initial communication is typically delivered verbally in a one-on-one meeting between the employee and his or her manager. A written form signed by the employee is put in the employee's file.

- **Second Warning.** This phase applies if the performance or conduct problems raised in the initial phase worsen or fail to improve. The recommended practice is for the manager to have yet another one-on-one meeting with the employee and accompany that oral warning with a memo that spells out job performance areas that need improvement. It is important at this stage in the process that the employee be made aware of how his or her behavior is affecting the business. The manager should try to work with the employee to come up with a plan of action that gives the employee the opportunity to improve. You should also advise the employee that failure to improve/ change could lead to a termination. This requires another form, signature, and filing.

- **"Last Chance" Warning.** The "last chance" phase of discipline usually takes the form of a written notice from a senior manager or, in the case of the kitchen and bath businesses, from the owner. The notice informs the employee that if the job performance or workplace conduct problems continue, the employee will be subject to either disciplinary action or termination. What is happening here is you are applying the heat and covering yourself from legal repercussions. This requires another form, a signature, and filing.

- **Termination.** This is the last step in the process—the step taken when all other corrective or disciplinary actions have failed to solve the problem. These progressive disciplinary steps are meant to serve as general guidelines for legal counsel. However you decide to structure your disciplinary plan, the process itself should meet the following criteria:

  1. Have clearly defined expectations and consequences.

  2. Have early intervention.

  3. Be sure the discipline is appropriate for the offense.

  4. Be consistent—always.

  5. Have rigorous documentation.

DEFINING AT-WILL EMPLOYMENT

For a long time, employers in the United States have operated under a doctrine generally known as At-Will employment. This simply means that in the absence of any contractual agreement that guarantees employees certain job protections, you have the right as an employer in the private sector to fire any of your employees at any time and for any (or no) reason. In other words, you may terminate an employee without cause and with or without notice. At the same time, your employees have the right to leave at any time, for any (or no) reason, even without giving notice.

There is more to this subject than can be adequately covered here. Learn more about this before deciding if it is appropriate for your business. If it is appropriate, make "firing at-will" an item in your policy and procedures manual. However, seek legal or professional advice before implementing.

TERMINATING AN EMPLOYEE

Even when you have ample cause for doing so, terminating an employee is always a cause for stomach knots and heartache—not only for the employee who is losing his or her job, but also for the manager who has to make the decision and perform the action. It is also hard on co-workers who may have established close relationships with the dismissed employee.

As the owner or manager of your company, you can do a great deal to help ensure that your company's approach to firing meets two critical criteria:

- First: Maintain the dignity and the rights of the terminated employee.

- Second: Protect the company from retaliatory action by a disgruntled former employee.

Who Should Do It and Where

The immediate supervisor should deliver the termination notice. The supervisor should have been doing the performance evaluations and warnings, and, as a result, should be more familiar with the facts. Deliver the message in person and in a private location. Depending on the circumstances, it might be advisable to have a third person present. However, co-workers should not be involved.

Preparation

Regardless of why an employee may be leaving your company, it is essential that the termination meeting be as conclusive as possible, which means you need to have many things ready before the meeting takes place. Here are some things to consider when you prepare your list of to-dos:

- **Final Payment.** Ideally, the dismissed employee (regardless of the reason) should walk out of the termination meeting with a check that covers everything he or she is entitled to—including severance. Depending on your company's policy—and on the circumstances that led to the employee's departure—the amount of the check will probably include money from some or all of the following:

  1. Salary obligation (pro-rated through the day of dismissal).

2. Severance pay (if applicable).

3. Any outstanding expense reimbursements due the employee.

4. Money due by virtue of accrued vacation, sick days, or personal day benefits.

- **Security Issues.** You should go into the meeting with a prepared list of all items related to company security, including keys, access cards and company credit cards. It is also a good idea to change locks and alarm codes after the dismissal.

- **Company-owned Property.** If the employee is still in possession of any company-owned property, the property should be turned over immediately. If the property is off-site (computer, uniforms, etc.), arrangements for pick up should be made immediately. (You may want to hold part of the final check if there is a lot of money involved.)

- **Extended Benefit Information.** If your company is subject to COBRA regulations—and most are—you are obligated to extend the employee's medical coverage—with no changes—for 18 months. Who pays for it—the company or the employee—is your call, though you are under no legal obligation to pickup the tab. Just be sure the employee leaves with all the information they will need to keep the coverage going. Make sure, also, that all questions regarding an employee's 401k or pension plan are resolved during the meeting, including up-to-date information on what options, if any, the employee has with regard to these benefits.

- **Notification of Out-placement or Other Support Mechanisms.** If your company has set up out-placement arrangements (or any other services designed to help terminated employees find another job), make sure that you have all of that information available.

- **Delivering the News.** There is no perfect script for letting employees know that they are being discharged, but come right to the point. Be direct, be firm, and do not allow yourself to get into an argument. The decision has been made. End of conversation.

- **Spelling Out Reasons—or Not.** If you have a legally approved terminate at-will clause, you do not want to give any reasons for the termination. If you have done a good job with performance evaluations, it will not come as a surprise to the employee. If you do decide it is appropriate to give reasons—no more than two or three short, factual sentences will do. There is no need for drawn out explanations. Tact and sensitivity are important, but so is total honesty. Be very careful what you say, and how you say it. You do not want legal problems to come back at you because of mistakes you made during the termination meeting. You should have a termination form. It should be completely filled out—including final payments. You need to ask the employee to sign it. If they refuse, ask a third person to witness that you asked the employee to sign, but they refused. Then the witness signs the form attesting to the facts.

- **Post Termination Protocol.** This is what happens immediately following the termination meeting. The "break" should be as clean as possible—albeit with due respect to the feelings and the dignity of the fired person. Harsh and humiliating as it may seem, the manager (terminator) should accompany the dismissed employee back to the workstation, give the employee the opportunity to collect personal belongings, and escort the employee out the door. If the company has confidentiality agreements, employees should be reminded—in writing—of their legal obligations. Advise the terminated employee that they are no longer authorized to access the company's computer system and any on-line accounts.

TERMINATION FOR
"JUST CAUSE"

There really is not a "best" time to conduct a termination meeting. Experience shows that late in the day (5:00 p.m.) and early in the week (Monday, Tuesday, Wednesday) are the best. Late in the day spares the dismissed employee the embarrassment of having to clear out their work area in the presence of others. Early in the week gives the employee a chance to get started on a job search.

There are certain employee infractions and misdeeds that are so blatant that you can generally terminate the employee without going through the normal disciplinary channels. Your employee handbook or policy procedures manual should spell out these offenses that lead to immediate dismissal. Here are some you might consider including in your manual:

- Stealing from the company or from other employees.

- Possession or use of drugs or alcohol on the job.

- Distribution or selling of illegal drugs.

- Blatant negligence that results in the damage to or loss of machinery or equipment.

- Falsifying company records.

- Violation of confidentiality agreements.

- Misappropriation of company assets.

- Making threatening remarks to other employees or managers.

- Engaging in activities that represent a clear case of conflict of interest.

- Lying about credentials.

IN CONCLUSION

Are You a Candidate for a Top 10 CEO Award?

Having a great company is possible if you become a great leader. Running a small business is as challenging as leading a large corporation. You can learn from the leadership strengths of big company CEOs.

- "In today's world, a CEO must focus on a number of elements to be effective. However, there are three critical areas on which he or she must concentrate. First, a CEO must establish the highest ethical standards for the organization and implement them through written and verbal communication, as well as through personal example. Second, a CEO must establish a strategic vision that creates a competitive advantage for the organization and significantly enhances profitability. Finally, a CEO must MOTIVATE and enthuse employees by empowering them, and must communicate the company's goals."

- "While a company's leaders need to be knowledgeable, intelligent, approachable, hard-working and effective communicators, I believe the single most important attribute of all truly good leaders is HONESTY. A leader must be honest in all they do in order to secure and maintain employee, consumer, investor and partner trust, and in return they need honest people surrounding them in order to effectively lead their organizations. Without honesty, the rest is meaningless."

- "The most important attributes of a good CEO, president or chairman are honesty, integrity, consistency and a strong sense of FAIR PLAY. Additionally, a good CEO needs to be a good communicator and delegator."

- "A good CEO is a goal-setter; a coach and a cheerleader for his people. He/she has got to be a person that keeps everybody's eye on the ball, whether it is manufacturing, marketing, sales or systems. People should be FOCUSED on the ultimate goal of the company."

- "A leader must have wisdom, authority, courage and a BENEVOLENCE to achieve long-term success. In some cases, right and wrong is not easy to decide. Always err on the side of being overly fair. Treat people like they are important and they will help make you successful."

In a recent article *Home Furnishings News* magazine asked home goods executives to weigh in on the attributes a chairman, president or CEO needs to possess in order to succeed in the wake of recent corporate scandals. Here is what various executives said:

Based on these industry executives' comments, the top six attributes of the "ideal" CEO are:

1. **Honesty.** Ideal CEOs should not only be honest with their management team and employees, but also with themselves when devising and executing a business strategy.

2. **Integrity.** It may sound like a no-brainer, but it is a character attribute that is sorely missed in corporate leadership.

3. **Effective Communication.** The CEO who effectively communicates possesses a skill that can boost worker morale, improve business relationships and bolster a company's market position.

4. **Long-term Vision.** The ills affecting a poorly performing company can be cured by a visionary CEO who has the dedication to execute a long-term strategic plan.

5. **Leadership by Example.** Ideal CEOs are not afraid to roll up their sleeves and lead their management teams by example.

6. **Fair, Firm and Consistent**—at all times.

SAMPLE FORMS

The following forms are provided as samples only. You are encouraged to consult with a human resource specialist and other legal advisors as to their appropriate use. NKBA accepts or provides no warranties for the use of these materials.

- Job Description Form

- Employment Application

- Weighted Evaluation Scale

- Rate Schedule for Sales Commission Plan

- Health Insurance Payroll Deduction Authorization

- Employment Status Form

- Employee Performance Evaluation

- Employee Self-Evaluation

- Time Sheet

- Leave Request

- Employee Conference Summary

- Termination Notice

JOB DESCRIPTION FORM

Job Title:	Location:
Supervisor:	Date Needed:
Estimated Starting Pay: $	Budgeted: [ ] Yes [ ] No

REASON FOR HIRE

[ ] New Position	
[ ] Replacement For:	Date Vacated:

TYPE OF EMPLOYMENT (Check one in each column)

[ ] Regular, Full Time	[ ] Exempt	[ ] Commission	[ ] Class A Truck Driver
[ ] Regular, Part Time	[ ] Non-Exempt	[ ] Non-Commission	[ ] Class B Truck Driver
[ ] Temp, Full Time			[ ] Forklift Driver
[ ] Temp, Part Time			[ ] Other [ ] N/A

WORK EXPERIENCE / SKILLS	PHYSICAL REQUIREMENTS	EDUCATIONAL QUALIFICATIONS
Required:	Required:	Required:
Desired:	Desired:	Desired:

PRIMARY RESPONSIBILITY OF POSITION (Essential Job Functions)

ADDITIONAL COMMENTS

APPROVALS

Submitted by:	Title:	Date:
Approved by:	Title: General Manager	Date:
Approved by:	Title: President	Date:
Received by:	Human Resources	Date:

THIS SECTION TO BE COMPLETED BY HUMAN RESOURCES

Sources Contacted:	
Date Filled:	Name of Candidate Selected:
Source:	
Hired By:	Position:
Starting Date:	Rate:

EMPLOYMENT APPLICATION

An Equal Opportunity Employer	FOR COMPANY USE ONLY	
Please Print in Ink	To Start (Date):	Emp. #
	Pay Rate:	
Date:	$ per	Commission Yes or No
Position applying for:	Location:	
	Position:	Job #
	Supervisor:	
Location applying to:	Hired By:	
	Hire Source:	
	Pay Rate:	

Check	[ ] Full Time	[ ] Part Time	[ ] Regular	[ ] Temporary

Name:	First Middle Last	Social Security #
		Telephone #
Address:		

How were you referred to our company?	[ ] Ad	[ ] Agency	[ ] Relative	[ ] Friend	[ ] Walk-in	[ ] Other
Have you been employed by us before?	[ ] No	[ ] Yes	Dates:	Locations:		
Have you ever been convicted of a criminal act?	[ ] No	[ ] Yes	If yes, please explain: (Conviction will not automatically exclude you from employment)			
Are you legally allowed in the U.S.?	[ ] No	[ ] Yes	If hired, federal law requires documentation to work verifying your identity and legal authorization to work in the U.S.			

EDUCATION

	NAME	CITY / STATE	# of YRS	GRADUATED	DEGREE/MAJOR
High School:					
College/University:					
Trade School:					
Other:					

List any other education, training, special skills or certificates that you possess related to the job for which you are applying:

List any machines or equipment that you are qualified and experienced at operating:

List all computer software programs and systems with which you are experienced:

Salary Desired:			
May we contact your present employer?	[ ] No	[ ] Yes	(if yes) Phone #:

291

EMPLOYMENT APPLICATION -continued-

| WORK HISTORY |
| Start with your most recent employment, including self employment, military and volunteer experience. |
| This section must be completed even if submitting a resume. |

Employer:			Telephone:		
Address:					
Employed From (Mo/Yr):	To (Mo/Yr):	Income Starting:	Income Ending:	Title:	
Job Duties:					
Reason for Leaving:					

Employer:			Telephone:		
Address:					
Employed From (Mo/Yr):	To (Mo/Yr):	Income Starting:	Income Ending:	Title:	
Job Duties:					
Reason for Leaving:					

Employer:			Telephone:		
Address:					
Employed From (Mo/Yr):	To (Mo/Yr):	Income Starting:	Income Ending:	Title:	
Job Duties:					
Reason for Leaving:					

Employer:			Telephone:		
Address:					
Employed From (Mo/Yr):	To (Mo/Yr):	Income Starting:	Income Ending:	Title:	
Job Duties:					
Reason for Leaving:					

IMPORTANT–READ BEFORE SIGNING

I certify that the information in this application is true and complete. Any false statements, concealments or omissions are grounds for refusal to hire or immediate dismissal, if hired.

I authorize (YOUR COMPANY NAME) to investigate and verify the information contained in this application which may include contacting my schools and former employers, and for (YOUR COMPANY NAME) to keep and preserve such records. I understand that, if hired, my employment is at will and may be terminated without cause and without notification by either the Company or me. THIS APPLICATION DOES NOT CONSTITUTE A CONTRACT FOR EMPLOYMENT, EXPRESS OR IMPLIED. If employed, I agree to adhere to the Company's rules and regulations.

Signature _____   Date _____

WEIGHTED EVALUATION SCALE

The following is a sample weighted evaluation scale. (Note: One column is the weight of importance you assign to each category and the other is how you rate the candidate.)

Candidate's Name:

Position:

Performance Category	Weighted Importance 1 (Low) – 5 (High)	X	Candidate Rating 1 (Low) – 5 (High)	=	Total Score
Design Skills (hand)	3		5		15
Design Skills (CAD)	4		3		12
Selling Skills	5		1		5
Design Skills (hand)					
Design Skills (CAD)					
Selling Skills					
Time Management Skills					
Organizational Skills					
Communication Skills					
Previous Employment					
Reliability-Work Ethics					
Team Player					
Past Work History					
Professionalism					
Product Knowledge					
Follow-through					
Motivated					
Enthusiastic					
Cultural Fit					
TOTAL					

Note: Make this work for you by adding or deleting any categories and by changing any of the assigned weights. What may be the most important categories for one may not be for the other.

RATE SCHEDULE FOR COMMISSION PLAN

Employee:	Location:
Effective Date:	Date of Previous Schedule:

Design Fees	Gross Profit %	Commission Rate (% paid)
Appliances and Countertops		

Design Fees	Gross Profit %	Commission Rate (% paid)
Plumbing products, kitchen and bathroom cabinets, door and cabinet hardware.	42.00 and over	13
	40.00-41.99	12
	38.00-39.99	11
	36.00-37.99	10
	34.99-35.99	9
	32.00-33.99	8
	30.00-31.99	6
	25.00-29.99	4
	Less than 25.00	0
Appliances and Countertops	20.00 and over	12
	17.00-19.99	10
	14.00-16.99	8
	10.00-13.99	5
	Less than 10.00	0

Commission Payment Schedule	
Design Fee	
Project Deposit	
Project 2nd Payment	
Project 3rd Payment	
Project Final Payment	
Project costing completed	

I understand that this Commission Rate Schedule is subject to change without notice.

Employee's Signature:	Date:
Manager's Signature	Date:

Copy Distribution:

Personnel File (original); Employee; Branch Manager; General Manager; President; Accounting

HEALTH INSURANCE
PAYROLL DEDUCTION AUTHORIZATION

I. Instructions

Complete Sections II, III and IV.

Complete the applicable enrollment forms in Section II.

Return ALL forms to HUMAN RESOURCES within five days.

II. Election of Coverage	
[ ] No	I waive health insurance. I understand that if I initially waive health coverage, I may be subject to enrollment limitations. For more information, please call the Human Resources Department.
[ ] Yes	I elect health insurance coverage. Health insurance is effective the first of the month following 90 days of employment.
	INSERT HEALTH PLAN NAME HERE Complete Enrollment Application – including signature and date
	INSERT DENTAL PLAN NAME HERE Complete Enrollment Application – including signature and date

III. Covered Individuals		
I elect coverage for:		
[ ] Employee Only	[ ] Employee + One	[ ] Employee + Family

IV. Authorization (sign and date)
I hereby request coverage for the group health insurance for which I am or may become eligible. I certify that the individuals I have enrolled are eligible dependents. I authorize my employer to make the necessary payroll deductions required for this insurance.
This payroll deduction authorization supersedes and cancels any health insurance deduction authorization I currently have on file.

Employee's Name:
Employee's Signature:
Date Signed:
Location:
COMPANY USE ONLY: Effective

295

EMPLOYMENT STATUS FORM

Employee #:	Employee Name:

CURRENT POSITION/ WAGE

Job Title:		Branch / Department:	
Pay Rate:	Per:		Since:

NEW POSITION/ WAGE / STATUS

Changes checked below are to be effective:

[ ] Status Change	From:	To:		
[ ] Exempt [ ] Non-Exempt	[ ] Commission	[ ] Non-Commission	[ ] Part Time [ ] Full Time	
[ ] Transfer	From:	To:		
[ ] Job #:				
[ ] Job Title:				
[ ] Wage Rate: Per:				

APPROVALS (Route in the following order)

Manager:	Date:
General Manager:	Date:
Human Resources Manager:	Date:
President:	Date:

SUPPORTING INFORMATION

Duties to be added or deleted:

Comments on Performance:

Other:

NOTE: Once approved, two copies of this form will be returned to the requesting Manager for appropriate distribution.

TO BE COMPLETED BY HUMAN RESOURCES

Copies Sent:	HRIS Updated:

EMPLOYEE PERFORMANCE EVALUATION

Name:		Title:	
Location / Department:		Due Date:	Period Covered:

APPRAISAL TYPE	[ ] Introductory	[ ] Promotion / Transfer	[ ] Annual	[ ] Other

EVALUATION CODE

E = Excellent	Performance consistently above standards with minimal supervision
C = Competent	Performance fully meets Company's standards
U = Unsatisfactory	Performance falls below minimum standard
NA = Not Applicable	

SUPERVISOR RATING OF EMPLOYEE

Rate the Following:	Eval. Code	Comments
1. Proficiency in Field / Specialty Degree of competence. Professional manner.		
2. Administrative Effectiveness Skill in planning, organization and implementing work assignments or projects.		
3. Leadership Skill in getting work done through formal or informal direction of others.		
4. Judgment / Decision Making Degree of analysis, objectivity and foresight used to make decisions.		
5. Relationships Ability to work effectively with subordinates, peers and superiors.		
6. Initiative and Resourcefulness Amount of drive and creativity. Ability to start and accomplish work. Degree of supervision needed.		
7. Supervisor Skill Demonstrated ability to select, train, motivate and develop subordinates. Degree of sustained contribution from work group.		
8. Communication Expression of verbal or written ideas. Method and manner of speaking. Ability to observe and listen.		
9. Professional Development Commitment to professional growth through development of skills and knowledge.		
10. Adaptability Efficiency under stress. Receptiveness to change/new ideas. Poise and/or courtesy in tough situations.		
11. Attitude and Cooperation Degree to which employee is supportive of Company's directives, decisions and policies. Accepts and profits from criticism.		
Overall Rating When determining this rating, take into consideration the rating for major accomplishments		

- EMPLOYEE PERFORMANCE EVALUATION - Continued -

STRENGTHS:	AREAS FOR IMPROVEMENT:

EVALUATION SUMMARY:

Briefly summarize employee's performance:

FOR INTRODUCTORY PERIOD EMPLOYEES:	FOR REGULAR EMPLOYEES:
[ ] Satisfactory completion of introductory period	[ ] Satisfactory completion of employment year
[ ] Delay introductory period ReEval Date:	[ ] Delay continued regular status ReEval Date:
[ ] Less than satisfactory completion of evaluation Recommended Termination Effective:	[ ] Continued unsatisfactory performance Recommended Termination Effective:

SIGNATURES:

(The employee's signature means that the performance evaluation was reviewed with him or her. It does not necessarily indicate that the employee agrees with the evaluation.)

Employee:	Date Signed:
Direct Supervisor:	Date Signed:
General Manager:	Date Signed:
President:	Date Signed:

EMPLOYEE COMMENTS:

Write any comments you wish to make regarding your evaluation:

EMPLOYEE SELF-EVALUATION

EVALUATION CODE

E = Excellent	Performance consistently above standards with minimal supervision
C = Competent	Performance fully meets Company's standards
U = Unsatisfactory	Performance falls below minimum standard
NA = Not Applicable	

SUPERVISOR RATING OF EMPLOYEE

Rate the Following:	Eval. Code	Comments
1. Proficiency in Field / Specialty Degree of competence. Professional manner.		
2. Administrative Effectiveness Skill in planning, organization and implementing work assignments or projects.		
3. Leadership Skill in getting work done through formal or informal direction of others.		
4. Judgment / Decision Making Degree of analysis, objectivity and foresight used to make decisions.		
5. Relationships Ability to work effectively with subordinates, peers and superiors.		
6. Initiative and Resourcefulness Amount of drive and creativity. Ability to start and accomplish work. Degree of supervision needed.		
7. Supervisor Skill Demonstrated ability to select, train, motivate and develop subordinates. Degree of sustained contribution from work group.		
8. Communication Expression of verbal or written ideas. Method and manner of speaking. Ability to observe and listen.		
9. Professional Development Commitment to professional growth through development of skills and knowledge.		
10. Adaptability Efficiency under stress. Receptiveness to change/new ideas. Poise and/or courtesy in tough situations.		
11. Attitude and Cooperation Degree to which employee is supportive of Company's directives, decisions and policies. Accepts and profits from criticism.		
Overall Rating		

Comments:

EMPLOYEE SELF-EVALUATION -continued-

MAJOR ACCOMPLISHMENTS DURING EVALUATION PERIOD:

Employee: Briefly identify goals/projects or other accomplishments.	Eval Code:	Evaluator: Briefly summarize employee's performance.	Eval Code:

GOALS AND OBJECTIVES FOR NEXT EMPLOYMENT YEAR

List your goals and objectives. Your Manager may modify these during the review of your performance.

SIGNATURE

Employee:	Date Signed:

Return this completed form to your supervisor by the agreed upon date of_____

TIME SHEET

Recording Instructions: Round off all items to the nearest quarter hour. Use Military Time.
Example: 1:00 to 1:07 record as 1300; 1:08 to 1:15 record as 1315

Day	Date	Time In	Meal Break	Time Out	Time Out	Time In	Explanation of Hours Not Worked	ACCOUNTING ONLY Regular	Overtime
	01/16								
	02/17								
	03/18								
	04/19								
	05/20								
	06/21								
	07/22								
	08/23								
	09/24								
	10/25								
	11/26								
	12/27								
	01/28								
	02/29								
	03/30								
	04/31								

Codes		Military Time Conversion Chart			
		Hours		Minutes	
Sick	S				
Vacation	V				
Holiday	H	7:00 am	0700	15	.25
Dock	D	8:00 am	0800	30	.50
Sick/Vacation	S/V	9:00 am	0900	45	.75
Jury Duty	JD	10:00 am	1000		
Workers Comp	WC	11:00 am	1100		
State Disability	SDI	12:00 pm	1200		
		1:00 pm	1300		
		2:00 pm	1400		
		3:00 pm	1500		
		4:00 pm	1600		
		5:00 pm	1700		
		6:00 pm	1800		
		7:00 pm	1900		

Employee's Signature:	Date:
Supervisor's Signature	Date:

Routing Instructions: The immediate supervisor and employee must sign the time sheet prior to submitting to Accounting. Completed time sheets are due to Accounting on the 1st and 16th day of each month.

LEAVE REQUEST

Employee:	Position:
Department:	Location:
Date:	[ ] Full Time [ ] Part Time

TYPE OF LEAVE REQUESTED		
[ ] Vacation	[ ] Maternity	[ ] Military
[ ] Sick	[ ] Other	

First Day Off Work:	Return Date:	Number of Days Off:
Reason for Request:		
Employee's Signature:		

ELIGIBILITY
Number of Vacation Hours Accrued:
Amount of Sick Leave Available:

APPROVALS	
Personnel or Payroll:	Date:
Supervisor:	Date:
Owner / Manager:	Date:

EMPLOYEE CONFERENCE SUMMARY

To:	Date:
From:	
Subject:	

Issues Discussed:

Specific Examples:

Employee's Response:

Requirements Set and/or Actions Taken:

EMPLOYEE CONFERENCE SUMMARY -continued-

Time Lines and Specific Goals Set:

Plan for Follow Up:

SIGNATURES		
Employee:	Date:	
Supervisor:	Date:	
Owner / Manager (as necessary):	Date:	

TERMINATION NOTICE

Employee:	Position:
Address:	Department:
	Location:
	Phone:

Last Day of Work:
Reason for Termination:
I have received my final pay and vacation check in the amount of $
I have returned all items, equipment or documents with the exception of:
To be returned by:

I will receive any commissions due me at the time normally computed.

I have been informed of my right to continue any group health insurance I now have at my own expense. The employer has no other obligations to me, as I acknowledged at hire, that I accept that this employment is at the will of the employees and the employer and may be terminated at any time without cause.

Employee's Signature:	Date:

TO BE COMPLETED BY THE MANAGER

Employee's Name:		Position:		
Last Day of Work:	Type of Termination:	[ ] Voluntary	[ ] Discharge	[ ] Other
Reason:				

Company Property	Date Returned	Item	Date Returned
Car		Final Check	
Keys		Insurance Forms	
Credit Cards			
Uniform			
Company Manuals			
Employee Receivables			
Completed By:		Date:	

Return completed forms to Human Resources Department along with any employee-related materials.

TO BE COMPLETED BY HUMAN RESOURCES

Date Received:	LDW:	Effective Date of Term:

305

CHAPTER 10: Marketing

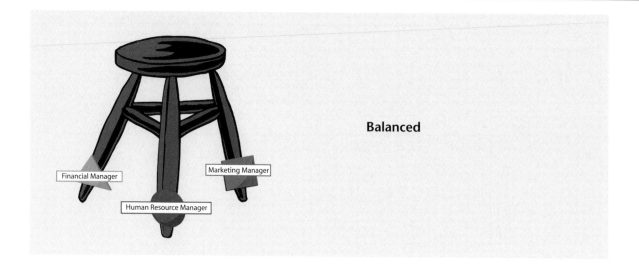

Balanced

Marketing is the third and final segment of the three main management areas that all companies have. Financial and human resources are the other two. Many business leaders will tell you that marketing is the lifeline to business success. We know for a fact that nothing happens until a sale is made.

As a small business today, you have lots of company and lots of competition. The Small Business Administration (SBA) estimates that there are over 5 million small businesses with fewer than 20 employees in America. Of these, between 6,000 and 7,000 are kitchen and bath businesses.

With this knowledge, we know that no sales will be made without customers. That is what marketing is all about—finding customers, enticing them to look at, and then to buy, your products and services.

- Marketing is the process through which you create and keep customers.

- Marketing is the matchmaker between what your business sells and what your customers buy.

- Marketing covers all of the steps that are involved to tailor your products, messages, distribution, customer service and all other business actions to meet the desires of your most important business asset—your customers.

- Marketing is a win-win partnership between your business and its market.

- Marketing is not about talking to your customers; it is about talking with your customers. Marketing relies on two-way communication between seller and buyer.

MARKETING AND SALES ARE NOT THE SAME

Too many people, including kitchen and bath owners, confuse the terms "marketing" and "sales." They believe that "marketing" is a high-powered or dressed-up way to say "sales." But, selling is not a substitute for marketing, even though the sales function is one of the ways to communicate your marketing message.

A sale is the point at which the product is offered, the case is made, the purchasing decision occurs, and the business-to-customer exchange takes place. Selling is an important part of the marketing process, but it is not, and never can be, a replacement for the marketing process.

SEVERAL PIECES TO THE MARKETING PUZZLE

- Requires a written plan and budget including co-op dollars
- Must be measurable and achievable
- Typically includes ads, promotions and public relations

LOOKING AT THE BIG PICTURE: THE MARKETING "WHEEL OF FORTUNE"

If you could get an aerial view of the marketing process, it would look like the graphic below. Every successful marketing program, whether it is for a billion-dollar company or a one-person operation, follows the same marketing cycle. Follow this "Wheel of Fortune" to go around the cycle, starting at the top and circling clockwise.

Marketing is a continuous cycle. It begins with customer knowledge and cycles around to customer service before it begins all over again. It is the strategic plan for your business.

It involves ...

- product
- development
- pricing
- packaging
- distribution
- communication ...

...of the marketing message, including the steps involved with making the sale. Unless you manufacture your own cabinets, countertops, etc., you will not be involved in every step in the cycle, but it takes all of these steps to complete the whole cycle.

As you loop around the marketing wheel, here are the steps you encounter:

- Get to know your target customer and your marketing environment.

- Tailor your product, pricing, packaging, and distribution strategies to meet the customer, market, and competitive realities of your business.

- Use your customer and product knowledge to create and project marketing messages that will grab attention, inspire interest, and move your customers into action.

- Go for the sale, but that is not all.

- Once the sale is made, marketing moves into the customer service phase, where your business works to ensure customer satisfaction so that you can convert the sale into an opportunity for repeat business and word-of-mouth advertising.

- After-sale, follow-up communication builds referrals of new potential customers.

In marketing, there are no shortcuts. To build a successful business, you cannot just jump to the sale, or even the advertising stage—you have to go through the entire marketing process.

To Fee or Not to Fee

In our industry, business people often limit marketing to communication, product selection and showroom development. However, the decision to include a design/retainer fee in your business strategy is also a part of marketing. An overview of the typical design fee/retainer systems used by professionals in the kitchen and bath industry follows.

"Do you charge a fee? What do you charge? Do you apply the entire amount towards the sale?" These are all great questions. In addition to these questions, professionals in our industry will have heated debates regarding just what is the "perfect" design-fee system.

The business model dramatically influences the type of fee best charged. Additionally, the experience base and reputation of the firm and/or individual designer have a significant impact on the ability of the organization and/or the person to charge a fee.

In addition, the first impression the firm and designer gives also influences how and when a fee is charged.

Most profitable firms do agree that some type of fee/retainer system is an important part of qualifying leads and effectively managing time. However, business leaders also are first to admit that, for many designers, it is hard to stand in front of a client and ask for a fee: there is a fear of losing a potentially large project because a client does not understand the fee schedule.

Oftentimes, you will hear designers talk about the one or two projects they lost (perhaps projects that would not have been profitable anyway) because of the client's reluctance to pay a retainer fee.

Experienced designers have found that, in reality, having an organized fee schedule properly presented to a qualified prospect means the client has a vested interest in buying from them; and, therefore, becomes a qualified lead.

For firms who always charge a fee, there seems to be a deep appreciation for the value of creativity. As one designer said, "Ideas are my 'stock in trade'. I am a design professional and it is my job to pull together a set of decisions that make sense functionally, economically and aesthetically. This planning is invaluable, and ought to be paid for."

Before discussing the various fees, here is a brief overview of typical fees charged by different business models.

A KITCHEN AND BATH DEALERSHIP REPRESENTING PROFITABLE PRODUCT SALES

Kitchen and bath dealerships make the majority of their profits from selling cabinets and countertops—installed. Other products might be added to this mix. For these types of firms, a flat design fee, or a percentage retainer fee determined by the estimated budget for the project, is typical. The copyright ownership of the plans remains with the design firm. The plans are not released to the client if a contract is not signed. These fees may, or may not, be applied to the project when orders for products are placed. These fees are normally paid with an initial deposit and a final retainer fee when the project documents are presented. The designer and company share the fees after all associated direct costs are paid.

A DESIGN/BUILD CONSTRUCTION FIRM

Charging for design and other pre-construction services is becoming common among major remodeling companies. Normally, a percentage fee (with a minimum fee established for smaller projects) is charged and billed in a three-tiered phase project. The plans remain with the design firm. They may or may not be released to the client if a contract is not signed to complete the work.

- A feasibility study that produces a master plan for the entire project, including drawings, written scope of work and construction estimate (guaranteed to be within a specified percentage of the actual cost to construct) begins the process.

- Design costs are then billed for the design process.

- A separate fee is charged for working drawings and all communication with staff architects during the project.

AN INDEPENDENT DESIGNER

Independent designers follow a business model much more closely aligned with interior designers: they are typically compensated for their planning services and the plans become the property of the client. They may or may not receive a commission or finder's fee for products specified or from firm's referred to. Professional ethics is at issue around these payments. The National Kitchen & Bath Association, the American Institute of Architects, and the American Society of Interior Designers, among others, have ethical standards that require the client be notified of any fees being paid to any design professionals collaborating on a project.

Independent designers may charge a flat fee for the conceptual planning part of the project, and then an hourly fee to create the project documents and assist in sourcing and/or shopping. In other scenarios, an hourly fee is charged throughout the entire process.

As you can see, there are specific types of fee structures that work well with specific business models. Following is a general review of the pros and cons of various design fee systems.

THE FLAT DESIGN FEE

A flat fee is charged to complete the conceptual design and preliminary budget. Fees range from $200 to $2,500 in the kitchen and bath industry. In some cases, plans are released to the consumer, for others they remain the property of the design firm. A simple design fee form is typically signed, with monies collected before the planning process begins or in a two-payment tiered system.

Note: Confer with your legal counsel when considering "selling plans." Much like an architect, you will need errors and omissions insurance if you are selling a design plan that may be construed as a document the consumer can build from. Your legal counsel may recommend you include a specific disclaimer on your plans.

- **Pros**

    A flat fee is easy for the client to understand. Consumers are typically more comfortable with this method than an hourly fee.

    The flat fee can be adjusted for different types of projects, or for different designers with varying skills.

    The flat fee can be easily combined with a "measure fee," which covers your first simple visit to the home.

    The flat fee is easier to divide between the design professional and the business owner.

- **Cons**

    The flat fee may not reflect the actual hours the professional needs to devote to the planning process. A way to avoid this is to list the number of times you will meet with a client, the number of solutions you will present, and the number of changes made to plans for the fee, with an hourly fee included in the contractual documents for work above and beyond the services included in the flat fee.

    Designers who are compensated with a percentage of a flat fee may focus too much attention on fees and not sales.

THE HOURLY DESIGN FEE

The second system is an hourly charge for design time and project documentation time. An hourly fee is charged for the designer of record's time and the back-up staff preparing drawings, researching product or writing specifications. Typically, hourly fees are used when no product is being sold.

A Comment From Ellen

For independent designers who expect their entire professional income to be generated from hourly fees, it is critical when building the business plan to understand the reasonable number of hours an individual can bill. There are approximately 235 productive days in one year after the elimination of Saturdays, Sundays, holidays, vacations and average sick leave. Translating productive days into hours, based on 7 hours per day, there are 1,645 potentially billable hours per employee. This should be further reduced by 5% for coffee breaks and such, leaving 1,563 hours. Experience suggests that the most efficient designers can expect to bill 75% of these productive hours, or approximately 1,200 hours. Therefore, an independent designer who has budgeted $5,000 per month for their overhead costs and expects to generate $75,000 in pre-tax income, needs to bill these 1,200 hours at $120 per hour to generate $150,000. ($15,000 safety net included.) Hourly charges range from a low of $35 to a high of $150 within the kitchen and bath and interior design industries.

- **Pros**

  Hourly charges insure the designer is compensated for all time devoted to a project.

  A well-organized designer can easily keep track of all hours devoted per project.

- **Cons**

  Consumers often feel they are billed too many hours.

  The designer who is billing by the hour only is not compensated for the years of experience that oftentimes results in an excellent—rather quick—solution. This is why a flat rate conceptual fee is charged first followed by an hourly fee for project documentation by many seasoned professionals.

  It takes very clear project documentation to track the hours charged to each job with an explanation of services provided.

A CONCEPTUAL DESIGN FEE COMBINED WITH AN HOURLY DOCUMENTATION FEE

This combination approach uses a flat fee or a percentage of the estimated budget as a conceptual design retainer, which is then followed by hourly fees for the designer of record and/or staff members to prepare the proper documentation.

- **Pros**

  This system allows the designer to be compensated for the great ideas offered during the initial phase of project development. A multi-tiered hourly charge for various members of the design team can then be costed to the client's account as work is performed.

  The design retainer contract can easily list a conceptual fee and the charges associated with the other designers.

- **Cons**

  Such a system requires very accurate budgeting skills "up front" to insure the client understands the costs associated with conceptual design solutions being presented.

The Retainer Fee

A retainer fee is a percentage of the preliminary budget estimate arrived at during the first visit to the client's home or upon plan review in the showroom. The fee ranges from 2% to 10% of the mid-range budget point. Therefore, on a project estimated at $40,000 to $60,000, the mid-range point is $50,000. A 5% retainer fee would be $2,500. Retainer fees do not typically include the plans becoming the property of the client: the copyright ownership remains with the firm. Typically, the retainer fee is applied to the contract when products are sold. The fees are collected in one payment at the beginning of the planning process, or as a two-phase payment system.

- **Pros**

  The fee varies based on the complexity of the project.

  This system works very well for seasoned designers with an outstanding reputation in their community.

- **Cons**

  Designers must be skilled in establishing accurate budget ranges at the jobsite and presenting potential solutions that intrigue the client.

  This system is difficult for a newcomer to institute because of the significant payment at the beginning of the design process.

Ellen recommends how to use this fee information:

"We have described the most typical fee structures used in the kitchen and bath industry. There are endless variations on these systems employed by successful members of our industry. Our goal has been to highlight the most successful systems for the new business owner and general managers/sales directors proposing a change in their companies' structure, and for existing business owners considering reformatting their fee-based compensation program."

MAKE THE TIME

How many times have we heard kitchen and bath owners say that they just do not have time to market? The answer to that is easy. Make the time.

Think of it this way. If marketing is the process through which a business creates and keeps customers, then marketing is the difference between "business" and "out of." When you look at it this way, marketing is the single most important process in any business, including yours.

Before You Go Much Further

In a recent article in *Remodeling* magazine (January, 2005), the authors identified that barely 29% of remodelers surveyed prepared a marketing plan and budget each year, and that 80% spent 3% or less of their annual revenues on marketing. What's holding them back? Nearly 20% said they have more leads than they can handle, 72% either said they cannot afford marketing or did not have the time to do it (or do not know how to do it).

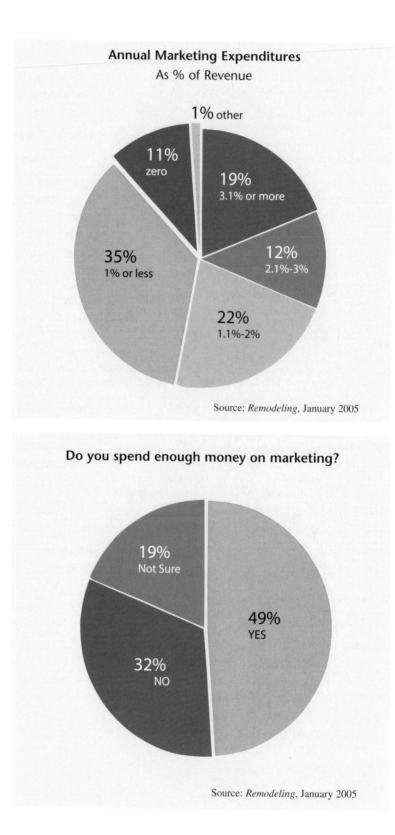

Annual Marketing Expenditures
As % of Revenue

1% other

11% zero

19% 3.1% or more

35% 1% or less

12% 2.1%-3%

22% 1.1%-2%

Source: *Remodeling*, January 2005

Do you spend enough money on marketing?

19% Not Sure

49% YES

32% NO

Source: *Remodeling*, January 2005

Measuring your Market Strength

To determine whether your marketing is strong, quickly rate yourself to see whether you think your business does well in the following areas:

	YES	NO
• You and those who help run your company have a complete understanding of the products and services that you offer.	❏	❏
• You have knowledge of the competition you face.	❏	❏
• You are aware of and responsive to the threats and opportunities that exist in your business world.	❏	❏
• You have a clear description of who your potential customer is and what it will take to make that person, who can choose not to buy, willing to buy from you.	❏	❏
• You think not in terms of making the sale, but, rather, in terms of developing mutually beneficial long-term relationships with your customers.	❏	❏

YOUR MARKETING PLAN AND BUDGET

Jim Krengel shares his view about how to go about developing the marketing plan later in this chapter. Len Casey presented an in-depth overview of the value of a strategic plan in Chapter 2. Both experts agree: a detailed marketing plan and budget are required to direct your business plan.

Part of developing a marketing plan is considering new opportunities. Be careful not to stray too far from your core competencies. If you do consider a new idea, treat it like a brand new business.

7 Steps in New Market Research
- Approach the new market as if you're starting a brand new company
- Learn everything there is to know
- Calculate your investment
- Research the profit margins
- Get your feet wet
- Consider hiring subcontractors
- Avoid putting your company's reputation at risk

Advice From an Expert

Marketing is such an important part of your business strategic plan that we have asked Jim Krengel, the author of an NKBA book, *Proven Promotions for Kitchen and Bathroom Businesses*, to share his thoughts and suggestions with us—based on 40+ years in the industry—on unique ways to market.

Do not try to rate the success of your marketing based on your sales figures alone. Sales may be strong in the short run, in spite of a weak marketing program, but it would be unusual for them to stay strong unless you "shore up" the marketing effort.

GETTING STARTED:
SETTING A MARKETING BUDGET

(Source: James Krengel, CMKBD and Lori Jo M. Krengel, CKD, CBD)

"Any business—big or small—should have an effective marketing plan and budget in place each year. The plan should include all marketing tactics for the year. Marketing specialists say that typical marketing budgets range from 1.5% to 3% of a business' annual sales volume. Kitchen and bath dealers, on average, invest 3% to 5% of their annual sales volume for their market budget."

"After identifying the budgeted marketing funds—make sure you include all available co-op funds. Prepare your plan by budgeting each marketing activity. Then, prioritize the marketing activities—in case you cannot fund the total aggressive plan."

When considering how to spend your marketing dollars, the Krengel's advice is to:

- Spend 10% of your marketing investment on the universe: everyone in your marketing area. This may be newspaper or radio advertising, for example.

- Invest 40% of your marketing investment on your targeted market.

- Spend 50% of your marketing investment on your repeat or referral client base. Expand the circle of people to include allied professionals, design/build remodelers or respected builders in your community who may become continuing clients.

"Create a promotional calendar for the year—plan each month graphing your expected sales compared to the marketing dollars expended. Big events such as kitchen tours, Street of Dreams, designer showhouses or October National Kitchen & Bath Month functions should be identified first. Community development activities are second. Traditional advertising budget is laid out last."

Timing is Everything

A recent study shows the first half of the year is the prime time in our industry—it is when consumers decide to do kitchen or bath remodels.

Kitchen & Bath Business (May, 2004) suggested that the decision timing for discretionary home improvements such as kitchen and bath remodels was probably impacted by anticipated bonuses and tax refunds. It is also possible that problems with existing kitchens and baths became all too clear during the holidays—creating a "never again" sense of determination. Additionally, there is the simple psychological impact of a brand new year—it is a goal-setting time of the year, people reflect on their lives, think about their jobs and decide what is important for the family.

Kitchen and bath businesses may find it extremely valuable to focus their marketing efforts on the first half of the year.

MARKETING BUDGETS

The most important commitment you can make to your marketing program is to stick to it. What does commitment mean?

- Establish a marketing budget.

- Spend the funds on the planned marketing programs.

- View the allocation as an important business investment.

- Manage the programs well.

How Much Should You Spend?

Use a percentage of your forecasted sales for the marketing budget. For retail-oriented businesses, like most kitchen and bath dealers, the percentage should be in the 3% to 7% range, which would include co-op dollars from vendors.

There are a number of other ways to budget.

- **The Arbitrary Method**: This is best-guess budgeting. The budget is between an intuition and experience, often using the numbers from the last year or two as the benchmark.

- **Competitive Parity**: This might be looked at as "keeping up with the Joneses." Your budget is based on awareness of how much your competitors are spending and how your business compares in terms of size and strength.

- **Goal-oriented Budgeting**: This is a "spend what is necessary" approach. It involves a serious look at what you expect your business to accomplish over the upcoming year and what level of marketing is necessary to accomplish the task.

What Percent is Right For You?

As you contemplate how much your business should allocate for marketing, consider the following:

- **The nature of your business and your market.** A business-to-consumer or business-to-contractor business requires more spending than business-to-business firms (attorneys and accountants, for example).

- **The size of your market area.** The bigger the area, the bigger the budget.

- **Your competition.** If you are the only game in town, that is one thing. If there are ten kitchen and bath dealers in town, that is another. Or, if you are currently the underdog and want to take on the leaders, you must spend accordingly.

- **Your objective and task.** The most important consideration in setting your budget is to understand what you want to accomplish with your marketing. Look at your sales and profit goals. The more aggressive they are, the more you will have to budget.

HOW TO BUILD A MARKETING PLAN

- State your business purpose
- Define your market situation
- Set goals and objectives
- Select a marketing strategy that appeals to your target audience
- Advance your position and brand strategy
- Establish your budget
- Blue print your action plan
- Start thinking long-term
- Use your plan

Partner With Your Supplier

Sit down with each of your major vendor partners prior to the start of a new year and review where you have been—and where you are—and where you want to go. Hold this meeting with the local rep and his/her boss (a decision maker). Instead of waiting for things to happen, be proactive and make things happen. By developing a plan together and knowing ahead of time where you want to go, you will have a much better chance of achieving your goals.

ANNUAL VENDOR MARKETING PLAN

COMPANY NAME:

I. Historical Data	
	A. Purchases (2 Yrs Ago):
	B. Purchases (1 Yr Ago):
	C. Purchases (This Yr):
	D. Gross Profit on Sales (2 Yrs Ago):
	E. Gross Profit On Sales (1 Year Ago):
	F. Gross Profit On Sales (This Yr):

II. New Year Projections	
	A. Projected Purchases Next Year
	B. Projected Gross Profit Next Year

III. Display Products	
	A. Changes This Year
	B. Changes Need To Be Made Next Year

IV. Ideas On How To Grow Sales and Margins in the Next Year	
	A.
	B.

ANNUAL VENDOR MARKETING PLAN - Continued -

V. Advertising, Promotion and PR Plan for Next Year		
What	When	How Much

VI. Problems / Issues to be Discussed

VII. Ideas On How To Strengthen the Partnership	
	A.
	B.

JIM KRENGEL TELLS US:
FOUND $: MAKING THE MOST OF CO-OP DOLLARS

You can dramatically stretch your advertising/promotional dollars by utilizing co-op funds. Surprisingly, statistics indicate that less than 50% of co-op funds are used throughout the course of a year. One reason this happens is that too few industry professionals clearly know what programs are available to them from their supplier partners. Secondly, many business owners do not take the time to clearly understand the guidelines/rules required by the supplier partner for co-op funding to apply.

Many distributors and manufacturers provide money for advertising/promotion if the activity or ad promotes their products with the product name and/or logo as part of the activity/ad. In addition to traditional advertising, some co-op funds will also cover photography, logo development, literature creation and other specialized promotional material.

When discussing the co-op program with your supplier partner, make sure you know the following:

- Who pays the initial cost?

- How is invoicing submitted?

- Is the message approved beforehand, or is a copy of the information submitted with the invoice?

- What identification requirements are in-place within the co-op program?

- What activities are covered, what activities are not?

Can You Afford Professional Help in Developing the Advertising Segment of Your Marketing Plan?

If you decide you just do not have the expertise to develop your advertising program, there certainly are many excellent agencies out there. Some create advertisements, logos, images, and do the entire placement. Others do all of this plus public relations (more on this later). None are inexpensive, but this could be an option for you.

What's the Plan? Creating and Tracking
Who creates your marketing materials?

- 24% Contracted Professional
- 28% Staff person, as part of another Job
- 6% Dedicated staff person
- 42% Other

Source: *Remodeling*, January 2005

HIRE AN ADVERTISING PROFESSIONAL

Being a successful kitchen/bath dealer or designer does not mean an individual is a gifted ad designer. Regardless of your location, there are usually one or two good design companies in the area. There are affordable national agencies that specialize in the kitchen and bath dealer business. Tell them about yourself and let them design your image or advertising campaign for you. Their creation might be something you had never thought of before.

These people are the professionals in their field. Let them produce the best ad for you and your budget. Give them enough insight and direction to get them started, then see what they develop. Having someone else's unbiased eyes is a great way to get feedback. Do not forget that the final decision will always be yours.

Once you have your plan in-place, monitor the leads generated.

SAMPLE BUDGET FORM FOR ADVERTISING

Year:			Total Promotional Budget:		$37,500
Sales from This Year:		$1,500,000	Percentage of Sales:		2.5%
Promotion Source	$ Spent	% of Budget	Leads	Sales Generated	$ of Sales
Yellow Pages	$6,750	18%	436	12	$336,000
Direct Mail	$3,000	8%	45	2	$57,000
Magazines	$3,750	10%	130	5	$78,000
Radio	$1,875	5%	27	0	0
Coupons	$1,500	4%	5	1	$33,000
Community Service	$3,375	9%	17	3	$67,000
Kitchen Tour	$8,625	23%	74	12	$395,000
Television Ads	$4,125	11%	36	3	$84,000
Goodwill (Service Calls, Referrals, Etc.)	$3,000	8%	17	11	$450,000
Additional Promotions	$1,500	4%	0	0	0

NOTE: These figures are for demonstration purposes only and are not an indication of how these mediums will work for you.

If your sales budget is $1,500,000 and you budget 5% for your marketing program, that is $75,000. You might figure 15–25% of this for outside professional help. The balance will be budgeted for other marketing initiatives planned by your firm and/or held in reserve for unexpected opportunities.

KNOWING WHO YOUR CUSTOMERS ARE

If you already know who your customers are, how they heard about you and why they bought from you, you are unique. In a recent *Remodeling* magazine survey only about one-half of the respondents differentiated between qualified and unqualified prospects, and only about one-half tracked their lead-to-sale ratio.

Most kitchen and bath owners know some of these answers, but unless they really collect hard data and do serious market research, there is a lot they do not know. Keep in mind, you, the business owner, may think you work for yourself, but you do not. You work for your customers.

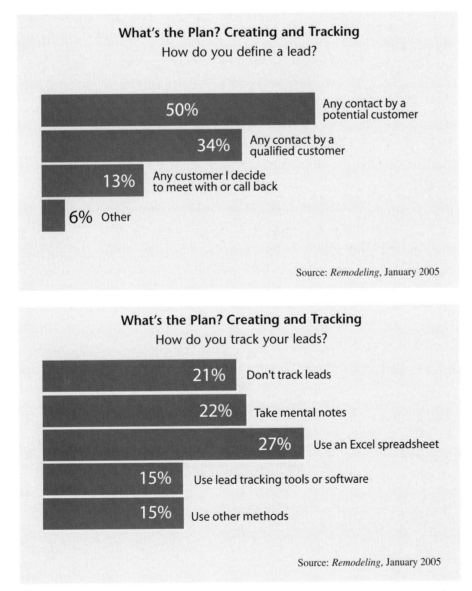

What's the Plan? Creating and Tracking
How do you define a lead?

- 50% — Any contact by a potential customer
- 34% — Any contact by a qualified customer
- 13% — Any customer I decide to meet with or call back
- 6% — Other

Source: *Remodeling*, January 2005

What's the Plan? Creating and Tracking
How do you track your leads?

- 21% — Don't track leads
- 22% — Take mental notes
- 27% — Use an Excel spreadsheet
- 15% — Use lead tracking tools or software
- 15% — Use other methods

Source: *Remodeling*, January 2005

Using NKBA's Business Management Form System

You should maintain an organized way to register leads visiting your organization. NKBA has a lead system that includes a registration card, record and register, as well as an analysis form. This is an excellent tool to use to track who comes to your firm and how they came to call on you.

Looking at the Anatomy of a Customer

An important part of knowing your customer is differentiating who is who among your clientele. It is called "market segmentation," and it is the process of breaking your customers down into segments that share distinct similarities. Here are some terms and what they mean:

- **Geographics:** Segmenting customers by regions, counties/municipalities, states/provinces, zip codes, etc.

- **Demographics:** Segmenting customers into groups based on such things as age, sex, ethnic background, education, marital status, income, household size, etc.

- **Psychographics:** Segmenting customers by lifestyle characteristics, behavioral patterns, beliefs, values, and attitudes about themselves, their families, and society.

- **Geodemographics:** Also called "cluster marketing" or "lifestyle marketing." Geodemographics is based on the age-old idea that birds of a feather flock together; people who live in the same area tend to have similar backgrounds and consuming patterns.

Collecting Information About your Customers

Target marketing starts with customer knowledge. Learn everything you possibly can about the person who currently buys from you; then you can direct your marketing efforts towards others who match the same profile.

DO-IT-YOURSELF FACT FINDING

You can get a good start on conducting customer research without ever walking out the front door of your business.

- Review addresses from invoices and group them into areas of concentration.

- Survey customers. Ask clients to sign a register when they come through the front door. Get names, addresses, etc., and ask "How did you hear about us?" Have salespeople ask the same thing. Keep track of the answers.

- Track responses to advertisements and direct mailers.

- Study web reports to learn about prospects who visit you on-line.

Who Are Your Customers?

If you are the typical kitchen and bath business, you deal in mid- to high-end products. So who are your customers?

- Identify the right client profile.

  1. Homeowners with combined incomes of $100,000 or more.

  2. Homeowners whose homes are 10 years or older.

  3. People aged 35 plus, especially the "Baby Boomer" segment.

  4. People who like to cook/entertain/enjoy their homes.

- Identify the right neighborhood.

  1. Homeowners of mid- to higher-priced homes.

  2. Homeowners building new mid- to high-priced homes.

  3. Homeowners remodeling either the kitchen or bath (home office, library, entertainment center, fireplace surrounds, etc., if you deal in those products).

  4. Homeowners with vacation/second homes.

- Identify key influences.

  1. New construction home builders (mid to high end).

  2. Remodel contractors who specialize in kitchen and baths.

  3. Interior design professionals who specialize in residential work.

There certainly are more criteria that make up your customer profile, but this covers a large part of it. Knowing this information, as well as the facts you will learn from your surveys, will tell you where to advertise, how to promote, and what kind of public relations to incorporate into your marketing plan.

ARE YOU OFFERING THE RIGHT PRODUCT/ SERVICE PACKAGE?

Did you know that the best products are not sold, they are bought? If you are a good marketer, when it comes time to purchase, you are not selling anyone anything. Instead, you are helping customers to select the products and services to solve their problems, address their needs, or fulfill their desires. You are helping them buy.

As a result, you devote the bulk of your marketing efforts to the steps that take place long before money changes hands.

These efforts involve ...

* targeting customers,

* designing the right product/service package, and

* communicating your offerings in terms that address your customers' wants and needs.

Then when the customer is ready to make the purchase, all you need do is facilitate a pleasant exchange and make sure that your customer feels good about trading his or her money for the right product/service.

Making Customer Service a Core Value

In small businesses, customers can get lost in the workload shuffle. They can be overlooked, treated like intrusions, asked to wait too long, and confronted with rules that send them right out the door. That should not happen—and it will not happen if you understand and apply the following basics of customer service.

* **"Services" and "service" are not the same thing.** Services are what you provide to customers as part of your total product offering. Service is how well you do what you do—how well you deliver what you are providing to the customer.

- **Service leads to customer loyalty.** Products lead to sales, but service hooks clients for life. To improve your service, consider the following:

  1. **Create a service guarantee.** Assure customers that you will meet or exceed promises. Make the guarantee straightforward and liberal (no small points), relevant and substantial (worth the effort it takes to request it), available immediately (no management approvals required), and easy to collect.

  2. **Listen for hints of dissatisfaction.** Compensate customers—on the spot—by offering upgrades, discounts or premiums when something goes wrong. Do not wait for a complaint.

  3. **Every month, spend time brainstorming on how to enhance your customer service.** Aim to create a service level that amazes customers and baffles your competitors.

- **Loyal customers are the best customers.** Loyal customers are the lowest-cost and highest-volume customers you will ever find. They reduce the cost side of your profit and loss statement. Loyal customers are new business ambassadors, spreading your message and serving as in-person advertising for your business.

- **Indifference sends clients away.** Many clients do not "fire" a business because of poor quality products, high pricing, or blatantly bad service—they leave because they felt they were treated with indifference—they were made to feel they were unimportant to the business. Fight indifference with an obsession for customer care and service.

- **Complaints are "springboards" to customer satisfaction.** Use customer complaints to lead your business to service improvements and satisfied clients. Follow these tips:

  1. Talk to your customers.

  2. Encourage complaints.

  3. When you receive a complaint, first fix the customer— and then fix the problem.

  4. Encourage customer "pickiness."

  5. Do a customer satisfaction survey on every job of $5,000 or more.

- **There is no such thing as "bad" customers.** There are good customers and non-customers.

- **Bad news travels faster than good news.** When you do a good job for a client, they may tell five people. However, when things go poorly, they are likely to tell 20 people. It is often not fair—but that is how it is.

- **It takes a great company to make a great customer.** If you want satisfied customers, make customer satisfaction a core value of your company. Insist on customer respect and courtesy. Empower your employees to do the right thing for your customers.

10 WAYS TO ENSURE CUSTOMER SATISFACTION

- Get to know your customers, recognize them as individuals, and treat them like friends, insiders and valued partners.

- Create a team of great service people within your business.

- Anticipate your client's needs.

- Communicate often.

- Thank customers for their business.

- Encourage customer requests and respond with tailor-made solutions.

- Bend your rules to keep loyal customers.

- Provide extra services and favors to high-volume and long-time customers.

- Make dealing with your business a highlight of your customer's day.

- Teach your customers to expect your company's customer service—and keep your standards so high that no other business can rise to the level you set.

How Would You Answer These Questions About Your Business?

- What does your product/service do for your customers? How does it make them feel?

- How is your offering different and better than your competitor's offering?

- How is it better than it was even a year ago?

- What do customers do if they are displeased or if something goes wrong?

- Are there any other products or services that you might offer that would make you even more "customer friendly?"

- What do you sell? How much? How many? What times of the year do they sell best?

The faster you can answer these questions, the better you will understand your business. And the better you understand your business, the more able you are to steer its future.

Analyze Your Mix

When is the last time you analyzed your product and services from a sales-profit point of view? Here is an example of how to do it:

ABC KITCHEN AND BATH PRODUCT/SERVICE ANALYSIS

Product/Service	Sales	GP%	GP $	% – Total GP $
Cabinets	$600,000	40%	$240,000	65.3
Countertops	$75,000	20%	$15,000	4.1
Plumbing	$50,000	25%	$12,500	3.4
Design Fees	$25,000	100%	$25,000	6.8
Installation	$250,000	30%	$75,000	20.4
Totals	$1,000,000	36.75%	$367,500	100

This analysis shows the obvious—cabinets are the big money makers.

But possibly less obvious, countertops are 7.5% of sales but only 4.1% of profit. By doing this, you can make decisions about adding products and services or possibly deleting some. A further breakdown would be to analyze the two to four (or six) cabinet companies you represent and see which names are the biggest contributors to gross margin. Of course, in order to do any of the above, you need to be tracking the information in the computer. An exercise like this, plus knowing your customers, will give you the information you need to put your marketing plan together.

Let the Cash Register and Market Knowledge Steer Your Business

- Sell what people want. More and more customers (especially those 75 million "Baby Boomers") are looking for one-stop shopping and turnkey jobs. Do you offer this? Should you?

- Promote the products your customers do not know you offer. Are your current sales 90% kitchens (like the majority of your peers)? Why not promote bathrooms, home offices, entertainment centers, and so on?

- Push your winners. Your product-revenue analysis exercise will tell you what they are.

- Bet on products and services with adequate growth potential. If you do not now offer installation as part of your package, should you? The right reasons would be that your customers want it and it would bring in added revenues.

KNOWING WHO YOUR COMPETITORS ARE

Every business has competition. Even if you are the only kitchen and bath business in town, you still have competition. Because kitchens are big-ticket sales, you are working with clients who may need a new kitchen, but they also need a new car and they want to take that trip of a lifetime. In this case, you are competing for the client's dollars. Competition is the heart of all sports, and it is also the core of the free enterprise system and business as we know it.

Competition is the contest between businesses for customers and sales. Competition is a good thing, and here is why:

- Competition promotes product upgrades and innovations.

- Competition leads to higher quality and lower prices.

- Competition enhances selection.

- Competition inspires business efficiencies.

Defining Your Direct Competition

On an annual or regular basis, ask yourself these questions:

- Who does our business really compete with? When your prospect starts to consider redoing their kitchen, what other businesses do they think of? Other kitchen dealers, the "big box," the local shop, a remodel contractor, or you?

- How does our business rate among all these other players? Create a list of all of your competitors, especially the main ones, and for each, assess the following three factors:

    1. What are this competitor's strengths when compared to your business?

    2. What are this competitor's weaknesses when compared to your business?

    3. What could your business do differently to draw this competitor's customers over to you?

"Mystery Shop" Your Competitors

Either you, or if that is not feasible, someone else should physically go and "shop" your competition. It is a terrific exercise and you will learn a lot. Following is a sample "shopping list" to use as a guide.

SHOPPING YOUR COMPETITION

Competitor Name:
Competitor Address:
Date of Survey:

Fill in the blank or rate each item 1 (low) to 5 (high):

Location and accessibility (easy to find, visibility, good location)	1	2	3	4	5	
Parking (closest to building, enough spaces, etc.)	1	2	3	4	5	
Overall appearance of building	1	2	3	4	5	
Outside Signage	1	2	3	4	5	
Front Window Displays	1	2	3	4	5	
Front of building and parking well lit	1	2	3	4	5	
Cleanliness of sidewalk and walk-up area	1	2	3	4	5	
Front Door (Signage, hours, etc.)	1	2	3	4	5	
First impression as you step through the door (open feeling, well lit, colors, displays, etc.)	1	2	3	4	5	
How quickly were you greeted?	1	2	3	4	5	
Did the initial contact try to qualify you?	1	2	3	4	5	
How well did they qualify you?	1	2	3	4	5	
Was the feeling of the showroom consistent with the price point of products? (High end, Medium, Low)	1	2	3	4	5	
Quality and cleanliness of the public restrooms	1	2	3	4	5	
Did the showroom layout flow?	[ ]Yes					[ ]No
Were the displays good looking and up-to-date?	[ ]Yes					[ ]No
Were there any "holes" in the displays?	[ ]Yes					[ ]No
Was the showroom clean?	[ ]Yes					[ ]No
Were salespeople work stations well located?	[ ]Yes					[ ]No
Were the desks and work areas neat?	[ ]Yes					[ ]No
Did display products have model numbers?	[ ]Yes					[ ]No
Did display products have prices?	[ ]Yes					[ ]No
Was there a kid's area?	[ ]Yes					[ ]No

What main products were displayed?

SHOPPING YOUR COMPETITION -continued-

Fill in the blank or rate each item 1 (low) to 5 (high):

Were there VCRs / DVDs and educational tapes	[ ]Yes	[ ]No
Did they offer product brochures?	[ ]Yes	[ ]No
How big was the showroom?	Sq. ft.	
How many sales consultants were there?		
Were the displays well lit?	[ ]Yes	[ ]No
Was their quote form customer-friendly?	[ ]Yes	[ ]No
Did they have a good mix and diversification of products?	[ ]Yes	[ ]No
Were the products on display current and up to date?	[ ]Yes	[ ]No
Did they offer coffee or refreshments?	[ ]Yes	[ ]No
If so, how were they served? (paper cups, china mugs, promotional mugs, etc.)		
Was there a closing area?	[ ]Yes	[ ]No
Were their quotes done by hand or computer?		
Based on the above answers:		
What is your overall rating of the showroom?	1 2 3 4 5	
What is your overall rating of the people?	1 2 3 4 5	

Other Comments:

BUSINESS IMAGE IS IMPORTANT

You have heard the saying a thousand times: "You only get one chance to make a good first impression." Most of the time, first impressions occur when you are not even around. It is in your advertisement, voice mail message, direct mail, business sign, employee, or maybe your logo on the back of a little league player's uniform. Most of the time, your marketing communications make your first impression for you.

Here is how one successful dealer developed an identifiable image.

Branding Your Business: A Case Study
Kimball Derrick, CKD: The Kitchen Design Studio

Realized his brand image had "grown"

Decided who he was, then created a unified image.

Brand Alignment

He made sure his staff could deliver on the
promise of the brand through proper training.

He then aligned the firm with organizations
(NKBA, AIA, ASID) and other companies who shared
his brand identity in terms of product quality.

All communications reflected his image,
allowing his firm to become a "branded" image.

Analyzing "Display Efficiencies": How Much and What Type of Sales Volume Should Each of Your Displays Generate?

Any visual merchandising book or college marketing course tells you that the efficiency of any retail sales environment is judged by comparing square footage to sales per display. This formula works well for high-volume retail organizations in the housewares arena—and even in fashion. In the kitchen and bath dealership environment it is a little different: successful firms often have several different types of displays.

- Displays that create a "statement" about who you are in the marketplace. These displays may feature the most expensive products in your mix and, therefore, may actually reflect a low percentage of your total volume.

- A second tier of displays represents the majority of your sales in style, finish and price range. It is an excellent idea to try to create a popular look in an entry level (affordable) price version as well as a similar look with add-on or step-up features.

- The third type of displays are smaller "vignettes". They typically demonstrate one center of activity in the kitchen, giving you a greater opportunity to show small areas of popular materials you sell, or emerging materials you would like to give a try. One note of caution: do not over-design these vignettes. Packing every possible detail into a small vignette can result in a display requiring an investment equal to a larger one that has more typical cabinets stretched between the highly designed, architecturally detailed elements.

Realize that displays are not a part of inventory. Plan to change displays on a regular basis. Change high-style displays and vignettes every two to three years. Change the hard-working "foundation" displays every three to five years.

Many successful managers have a five-year plan for their showroom, which includes display change-out schedules. Such planning is important to manage the expenses for this marketing endeavor and its impact on cash flow.

The Customer's First Impression of Your Showroom

Step back, if you can, and pretend that you are a customer. What would your first impression be of these areas?

- The company name?

- Company signage?

- The logo and colors?

- Your advertisements?

- Accessibility to the business?

- Customer parking?

- Front window displays?

- Signage on the front door?

- Is the walk-up to the front door clean?

- Immediate impression when entering your business?

- How are your employees dressed?

- Is your showroom well lit? Is it clean?

- How do you answer your phones?

- What is your voice-mail message?

- What impression does your website give?

- Are work stations neat?

Everything adds up to what image your business projects. And you have control over all of them.

Use the following sample survey to have a few friends rate their first impression of your business.

SHOWROOM PERSONNEL TELEPHONE / CUSTOMER SERVICE SURVEY

DOES HE OR SHE...	Always	Sometimes	Never	Don't Know
Answer the telephone in three rings or fewer?	4	3	2	1
Answer the telephone with a cordial salutation, company name and an offer of help? (For example, "Good afternoon, ABC Company, how may I help you?")	4	3	2	1
Avoid placing calls on hold for more than one minute?	4	3	2	1
Tell the caller they will be "connected" or "put through" rather than "transferred?"	4	3	2	1
Speak clearly on the telephone?	4	3	2	1
Thank customers for phoning?	4	3	2	1
Ask customers to phone again?	4	3	2	1
Allow callers to hang up the phone first?	4	3	2	1
Give customers full attention?	4	3	2	1
Exhibit a helping attitude toward "drop-ins?"	4	3	2	1
Offer visitors a chair or a place to sit?	4	3	2	1
Understand the importance of customer service?	4	3	2	1
Display a commitment to customer service?	4	3	2	1
Know that the job is a customer-service position and not just clerical?	4	3	2	1

SCORING: Add all the numbers you circled and compare your total with these scores:

51 – 56 Great! Very customer service-oriented.

41 – 50 Pretty good, with a little training.

31 – 40 Mediocre. Needs attention and guidance.

19 – 30 Time for a talk.

14 – 18 Needs to be replaced.

What Is It Like to Be a Customer of Your Business?

Pretend that you are a first-time customer and experiencing your business from a stranger's point of view. Or, ask an impartial person to do the "survey" for you. Have them call and visit the business, send an e-mail, look at your website, review advertisements—then have them give you all of their impressions.

Are You Consistent With Your Marketing Communications?

Pull samples of advertisements, signs, brochures, letterheads— everything with your name and logo—line them up and put them through this test:

- Does your business name and logo look the same every time so you make a consistent impression?

- Do you consistently use the same typestyle?

- Do your marketing materials present a consistent image, in terms of look, quality, and message?

If not, it may be time to make some changes. Does the image you are trying to project really reflect where your business is today? It is okay to change, in fact, "rolling-out" a new name and/or image could be both fun and rewarding.

ESTABLISHING YOUR BRAND

Perhaps you are thinking "we are just a small, ten-person kitchen and bath business, we hardly need a brand." Wrong. You do need a brand.

Do you market yourself as a business that sells cabinets, even more specifically brand X cabinets, or do you represent yourself as a design-build firm? There is a big difference.

Branding simply involves developing and consistently communicating a group of positive characteristics that consumers can identify with and relate to your business. If those characteristics happen to fill a meaningful and available position in their minds, a need they have been wanting and trying to fill, then you just scored a marketing homerun, and you are well on your way to meeting those sales projections.

The ABCs of Branding

Your name is your brand. When people hear your name, they conjure a set of impressions and characteristics that influence how they think and buy. Those thoughts define your brand. Everything you do contributes to your brand.

The Case For Branding

Branding makes selling easier. People want to buy from companies they know and like, and companies they trust will be there well into the future. A brand puts forth that promise.

With a well-managed brand, your company hardly needs to introduce itself. Within your target market, people will already know you, your business personality, and your promise based on what they have seen and heard through your marketing communicators.

Six Steps to Brand Management

1. **Define why you are in business.** Do you just sell cabinets or do you design and sell kitchens?

2. **Consider what you want people to think when they hear and see your name.** This includes current and prospective employees, customers, suppliers, competitors, and friends. You cannot be different things to different groups. You must have a brand that people know and trust.

3. **What words do you want people to use when defining your business**? Do you want them to say, "They sell cabinets" or "They design and sell dream kitchens?"

4. **Pinpoint the advantages you want people to associate with your business.** You design, sell, and install, i.e., you are "customer friendly" because you do it all.

5. **Define your brand.** Using steps 1 through 4, develop a statement about what you offer, your company values, your business personality, and the promise you convey to those who deal with your business.

Boil your findings down into one concept—one brand definition—that tells your story. Here are some examples:

Volvo is the safest car

CNN is the all-news channel

Disneyland is the happiest place on earth

Your brand could be: "We design and build dream kitchens and baths."

6. **Build your brand through every impression that you make.**
A well-managed brand creates a strong market impression, and a strong market impression fosters loyal customer behavior. Protect and project your brand through every representation of your business in the market place.

YOUR PROMOTIONAL PLAN

Establishing a Website

A major part of your budget is invested in advertising and promotion. In today's business world, having your efforts supported by a well-designed website is an important foundation of your plan.

Establishing a website as part of your branding activities may be high on your list of "things to do," says Steve Krengel, creator of Kitchens.com.

KEY CONSIDERATIONS FOR CREATING A SITE

A website is easier to update than printed material. If you print out 10,000 brochures and your area code changes, you suddenly have 10,000 pieces of outdated material. Changes to a website are much simpler and typically less expensive to make.

What should you include on the site? The same thing you would tell a potential client who walked in your store. What makes you better from the guy down the street? With that in mind, you may use the thoughts below to guide you in setting up a site.

- First, just as you check out your competition around town, do not forget to check them out online as well.

- Think about what your company does that satisfies your customers. Put this information on your website home page. As soon as a potential client visits any page on your site, they should understand immediately what you do, via the words and the pictures. If you are running a kitchen and bath showroom, do not put a picture of a frog on your home page.

- Even if you are not planning on a grandiose site, get started by securing your website address as soon as possible. (You can visit a domain site such as www.networksolutions.com.)

- Consumers who see your site address and a website that is kept current, view your company as up-to-date and on top of the latest trends and technology.

Knowing the difference between a "hit" and "user" will save you considerable time and money down the line, especially when you begin to be approached regarding placing advertising on other websites. A "user" is a visitor to your site. A "hit" is simply a graphic that has been downloaded. For example, let's say the site designer uses five graphics on the home page of your site. Each graphic count is a "hit." Additionally, you count one hit for each entire page that is downloaded. So, one user who visits your home page can create six hits just by visiting the first page of your website.

A Note from Karla:

"If you are unsure of the difference between "hits" and "users," please see Web Jargon ... Defined on page 352."

THE DOMAIN NAME GAME

Securing a domain name (i.e., www.Kitchens.com) for your company is of utmost importance. Do it today. If you are considering a website in the near future, you should have already secured your domain name.

When registering a domain, keep in mind the following:

- Ask your site design firm if they will register your domain name for you. Most firms offer this as part of their design package. Be sure to find out if there is an additional charge for securing a domain.

- When checking to see if a domain you want is available, do not include the www.

- If the .com version of your name is taken, try the .net or .biz. Visit www.networksolutions.com for further options of domain extensions. This list grows every couple of years.

- It does not matter if you use small letters or caps in your domain names. However, capitalizing the first letter of the words within the address makes the address easily recognizable when you use the website address in your printed materials.

- Do not shorten your name so that your domain is difficult to recognize. For example, do not shorten Designer Kitchens and Baths to www.DesKitBath.com. It is not an "attractive" domain, nor is it easy for people to remember. Your choice should be www.DesignerKitchens.com. If you cannot secure the name of your company, be creative. You can, instead, use www.Designer-Kitchens.com or www.DesignerKitchens-Co.com. It is extremely important to use key words (important words to your company) in your site address.

If you sign yourself up for a domain name, you must be able to host the site. A server is the computer hosting equipment that provides a foundation for your site to live on in cyberspace. If you do not have access to a server you can either pay an additional fee to the domain name registration company where you secure your website address or ask your website design firm to include the registration process as part of its service.

When another company secures your domain for you, insist that your domain name be billed and registered to your company. Listing you as the billing and main/registrant contact with the registering company does this. That way, you own your domain name, the company or person who registered the domain does not. This may prove especially helpful down the line in the event that you are not happy with that firm and want someone else to host/redesign your website.

REGISTERING A CANADIAN DOMAIN

In Canada, you may register a Federally Incorporated company or a corporation holding a Federally Registered Trademark. Or, you may register a provincial corporation, organization, partnership or proprietorship. The difference between the two is the way the website address will read. For example, www.Kitchens.on.ca would be the provincial subdomain (also called a third or fourth level domain) website address of a kitchen dealer in Ontario, Canada. (Most kitchen dealers would register their companies this way, using the provincial subdomain.) www.Kitchens.ca would be the website address if the company is Federally incorporated. Of course, Canadians or anyone may register a .com, .net or .org.

To register Canadian domains, begin by visiting www.CIRA.ca. The first step is assuring that your website address is actually available by visiting the Who Is section on the site. After that, you will choose from a list of CIRA Certified Registrars, who can register the name for you (each will charge a different fee). Domain names can be registered for 1 to 10 years. Registrars set their own timeline. Hence, if you want to register your domain name for a period of 10 years, make sure your registrar company of choice will, in fact, allow you to register your domain name for that amount of time.

RECOGNIZING AN E-MAIL ADDRESS

Whenever you see the "@" symbol, you are dealing with an e-mail address. If you see the www. AND the .com (or .net or .org, and so on), then it is a website address.

HOW TO WRITE YOUR WEBSITE ADDRESS

A written sample would be:

www.KitchensByKarla.com is a website address

Karla@Kitchens.com is an e-mail address

- It is not necessary to add the "http://" before your website address. The exception to this is when you are including your address "within" an e-mail. Adding the "http://" automatically creates a link from your e-mail address to that website. And that is a smart thing to do in the signature line of your e-mails. It then allows anyone reading your e-mail to link directly to your site.

- The "www." And the ".com" should always be in small letters. Anytime something is written in capital letters on line, in "netiquette," it is considered shouting.

- The verbiage between the "www." And the ".com" can be in either upper or lower case letters. Website addresses are normally case sensitive where the address goes beyond the .com. For example, if the website address was www.KitchensbyKarla.com/Wood-Mode.htm, the "Wood-Mode.htm" would have to be in the proper case.

LINKS

A link moves users from one location to another on the Internet. This could be from the top of a web page to the bottom of a web page, from one page within a site to another page within the same site or move the user from one site to a completely new site.

It is not a good idea to link from your website to another site. If you have gone to all the time, trouble and expense of creating a site for your company, do not send your visitors away to another site, especially one that could have the listing of your local competitors.

It is a good idea, though, to have links to your site. As soon as your site is established, you should send out an e-mail to all of the manufacturers you work with, associations you are a member of, local associations (i.e., Chamber of Commerce, the local BBB) and anyone else you can think of. Ask them to create links from their websites to yours. This will send potential clients to you from wonderful sources you are already associated with and can generate leads.

SEARCH ENGINES

Search engines are the equivalent to a online library. Web users insert keywords (i.e. kitchen designers) or information into databases (search engines) in order to find the sites that list information they are searching for.

Search engines are currently the number one way to find a website. The good news is you do not need to have your site registered with all of the hundreds of search engines out there. Focus on the following four top engines, which easily account for 95% of the search engine traffic.

| Google.com | Yahoo.com |
| AOL.com | MSN.com |

A Warning from Karla:

"It is important to stay on top of which search engines are "hot" and which are not. This changes over the years and if you are not listing your site on the top search engines, it will dramatically affect the traffic to your website. Talk to your IT (Information Technology) specialist and/or advertising/public relations account manager to learn what search engines are growing in importance."

If your site is not properly built from a technical standpoint, search engines will most likely not pick it up. It is just like being a professional kitchen designer: you can walk into any kitchen and tell whether it will function well, and you can see beyond the aesthetically pleasing aspect. It is the same thing with a website. It may look great, but will not function well, if it is not properly designed.

Building a site that it is easily found on search engines is called "Search Engine Optimization." There are ALT tags, META tags, key words, etc., which all work together behind the scenes to allow your website to be found. If the concept is difficult to grasp, image this: you are at a play. While you are paying attention to the actors on the stage (the photographs and words on a website), you realize that there are stagehands behind the scenes (ALT tags, META tags, key words, etc.) that are necessary to make that production work.

Also, in the event you are having a website built for your company, make sure the firm designing the site will also list your website with the search engines you have selected.

For the most valuable search engines, you can buy your position/listing. It can be expensive at times, as some search engines require that you pay a fee for each click through to your website!

MANUFACTURER WEBSITES

Not only is having your own website a great business tool, but using the websites of the manufacturers you work with, or want to find out more about, is helpful as well. The web offers a plethora of information. Incorporate using the web into your daily business routine. If you are not yet using the web, begin no later than tomorrow. For example, using the website of a manufacturer to look up product specs or to investigate a new cabinetry line saves you time. Not only is the information faster to access, it is also more likely to be timely. For example, if you pull out the spec book for a refrigerator, how long has that book been on your shelf? Are the specs still correct? The specs are much more likely to be up-to-date on the manufacturer's website.

WWW.NKBA.ORG

The NKBA's website has been recognized for its excellence on a regular basis. As a member of NKBA, you are welcome to use this website and information to your advantage. And, do not forget to check out NKBA's www.kbportal.com too. Everything from specs to new product information is found on this extensive site.

WEB JARGON ... DEFINED

- **Internet:** A network of computers around the world, including your own computer when you are online.

- **World Wide Web:** A collection of interlinked documents, such as a website.

- **AOL:** America Online

- **Browser:** Software on your computer that allows you to read web pages. Examples of web browsers are: AOL software, Internet Explorer and Netscape Navigator. If you are on the web, you are using a browser. Use of the browser comes free with most Internet Service Providers (ISP's) and new computers.

- **Domain Name:** Another name for your website address or URL (unified resource locator).

- **E-commerce:** Selling your products or services via the Internet.

- **Hits:** Occur every time a user "gets" something from a web page. For example, on a page that has 6 graphics, the user "gets" the 6 graphics, plus the actual page ... that's 7 hits. A hit will also be counted when you post something. For example, a post happens when a user fills out a form and submits it (such as the Order Literature Form on your vendors' websites).

- **ISP (Internet Service Provider):** Companies that sell the service that connects you to the Internet. An ISP usually costs around $20 per month. You do not need an ISP to have a website.

- **Link:** Like "magic," links automatically transport you from one location on the web to another (whether it be to another page or site).

- **Network Solutions:** A domain name registration company (there are 57 others).

- **Search Engines:** Online "libraries" that direct you to websites covering the subjects you are looking for.

- **Top-level Domains**

.com	commerce/company
.net	network
.biz	business
.info	information
.us	United States
.name	name
.org	organization
.mil	military
.gov	government

- **Users:** A user is one person. For example, if your website draws 500 users per month, you can approximate that just fewer than 500 people visited your site. The number is fewer than 500 because when users return to your site more than once because they have seen something they like, they most likely will be counted twice.

- **Web page:** An online "pamphlet" made up of one page only. (It is not a good idea to only have one page as your company website.)

- **Website:** An online "pamphlet" made up of multiple web pages.

A New Business Card Idea

A picture of your latest project is worth a thousand words, but a customized CD can provide much more to a prospective customer.

A NEW BUSINESS CARD IDEA

Create a CD as a marketing tool. It is possible to include music, video clips showing your crew at work, a voice-over describing the type of work your firm does, and/or still photographs. A link to your company's website is possible as well. Such a CD is a great tool to leave with the consumer, rather than a printed brochure. It is also much easier to update.

Advertising

The opportunities to spend money on advertising are unlimited. Some are good, and some are not so good. Your job, and not an easy one, is to identify the advertising media that will help you accomplish your overall marketing strategy goal. What media will your clients be looking at and listening to? If your clients are at the higher end, the look of the *Penny-Saver* flyer is not right for you. But the upscale home and garden magazine in your area might be. Here are just some of the media available:

- Yellow Pages

- Newspaper

- Radio

- Television

- Regional magazines

- Trade magazines

- E-mail

- Website

- Direct mail

- Door hangers

- Billboards

You will probably decide on a combination of several of these. Do devise some way of tracking the results of your different advertising activities so you can determine which paid off. Possibly offer a gift, special, or some other incentive for responding to an advertisement. At the very least, have your designers/salespeople ask, "How did you hear about us?"

Match your advertising vehicle and P.R. efforts with the publications your clients read.

DEVELOP AN ADVERTISING CAMPAIGN

Do not plan your advertising campaign by the seat of your pants, or simply react to media salespeople dropping in. Have a plan and schedule. For example:

	Month		
Type of Advertising	Jan	Feb	Mar
Home magazine	x		x
Newspaper		x	
Direct mail	x	x	x
Radio		x	x
Television		x	x
Billboard	x	x	x

PROTECT YOUR REFERRAL BUSINESS

Jim Krengel, CMKBD, shares great ideas ...

- First, stay in touch with your clients between the contract signing date and the installation start date.

- After the sale, do not let clients just walk out the door and not talk to them for the next four to eight weeks.

- Call them to let them know the status of items or send postcards and notes to keep them informed.

- Let them know what is going on behind the scenes to prepare their project. If you do not, they may think their project is not a priority.

- When the delivery date for the cabinets is set, call and let them know when an exact starting date is scheduled, and send them a notice informing them when your craftspeople will come and what to expect.

- Let them know about the preparation work that will be happening, what they should expect and what is expected of them, like emptying cabinets and removing valuables and mementos from the work area.

NEXT, LET THE NEIGHBORS KNOW YOU WILL BE WORKING IN THE AREA.

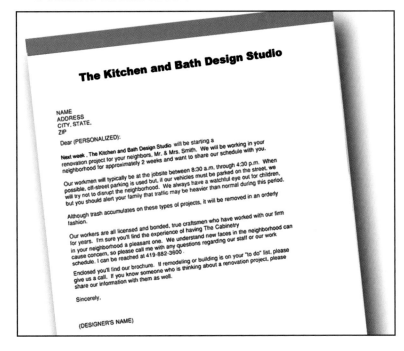

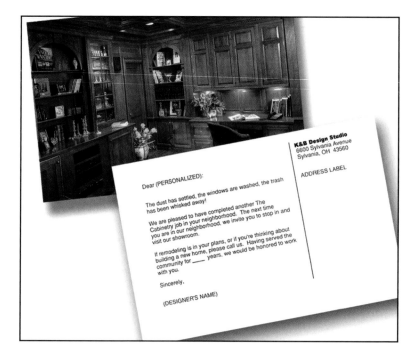

Public Relations

PR (as it is often referred to) is a terrific means to help get your "word" out. PR is the art of keeping your name before the public in a positive way other than through paid advertising. Good PR is always the best and most economical way to let the people know who you are and what you do. PR is an article about you, your company, your employees, projects you have done, awards you have won, new products and just about anything that a magazine, newspaper, radio or television station thinks might make good reading, listening, or watching. Free publicity can expand awareness of you and your business. The public (your clients) puts more credence in this type of "advertising" because they know a third party printed it; it was not paid for.

PR resources are usually free. The trick is to get the attention of editors, writers, and reporters. Indeed, just about everyone else in the business world is trying to do the same thing.

Good PR very rarely just happens. You have to make it happen. Either you or a paid professional PR person has to schmooze the above-mentioned sources, and you have to present them with something that, in their opinion, their readers, listeners, and watchers will be interested in. Sure, it takes time, effort and creativity, but the results can be very beneficial.

Here are successful PR activities which should be in your plan every year:

- Enter design competitions.

- Schedule professional photography of your better projects.

- Maintain a list of editorial contacts (regional and national).

- Submit your work to regional and national publications.

- Participate in high-profile charitable events.

- Network with your client base and allied professionals.

Promotions

There are probably even more opportunities to spend money on promotions. Once again, your challenge is to make decisions on where you will get the biggest bang for your buck. Here is a short list of some promotion ideas:

- Home and Trade Shows

- Open House in Your Showroom

- Sales

- Educational Seminars Hosted in Your Showroom

- "Lunch and Learn" Programs for ASID, AIA, etc.

- Host Trade Association Meetings

- Cooking Demonstrations

- Charity Functions

- Parade of Homes/Street of Dreams Participation

- Kitchen Tour Sponsorships

- Designer Showhouse Participation

- Celebrity Chef Book Signing in the Showroom

GETTING YOUR
WORK PUBLISHED

You have successfully marketed, sold and produced another quality project. A project that you are proud to have your name on, one you want to share with others. You take some snapshots to pass around to friends and family. You gather people at your office for "show and tell." And that's about it.

Occasionally, though, a project comes along that has a special quality that screams to be published. Perhaps your design focused on an architectural detail, such as a barrel ceiling. Or, it is an historic landmark in your city. Most likely, it is just a beautiful project with extraordinary attention to the many details. Or, it may be the emphasis on universal design, the environment or another specific issue. The project is right for publication. The question is, how to do it.

While the major consumer publications may seem too formidable to undertake on your first attempt, there is really nothing mysterious about working with local media for some profitable publicity.

Taking the Mystery Out of Local Publicity

When it comes to getting kitchen and bathroom projects published, the principles involved are:

- Clarity of the materials you send to editors.

- Persistence in contacting the right people.

- A spirit of helpfulness when you are working with editors.

Working with Editors

All three of these principles have one item in common—working with editors.

The most important aspect regarding media relations is cultivating relationships with local editors. To do this successfully, make an effort to understand the editors' news needs and frequently send them the right kind of information in the right format. They will appreciate your efforts and, in turn, they will keep you in mind when they have a need for specific information. It may not happen overnight, but, like any good investment, it will pay dividends over time.

The following tips are offered to assist you in cultivating editor relationships:

1. Understand that publicity differs fundamentally from advertising in that it is not something that you pay for outright. Editors are under no obligation to use your material. They may use part of it, or change it, or add other material to it.

2. Submit material in an easy-to-understand format. News releases should be printed, double-spaced, and only as long as is absolutely necessary. Answer the questions who, what, when, where, why and how, as far up in the release as possible.

3. Remember to be persistent in a friendly and helpful way with editors, offering them material that presents interesting information to readers. If you have doubts about the appropriateness of your news, give the editor a call before writing it up and sending it.

4. Call editors a few days after the material is sent to find out if the information was received and considered. Ask what type of information the editor would like to see in the future.

5. Offer to serve as a source of information for future articles on kitchen/bathroom trends, design and related topics.

6. Time your material appropriately. Work with editors to find out when they need material on remodeling, an interview about kitchen and bathroom design trends and so on.

Occasionally, designers will get lucky, and an editor will make the first contact. It is likely that those who live in larger cities have been approached by an editor of a local newspaper or magazine. Most city magazines feature home and design sections three to four times per year. The editors are always looking for projects with an interesting story.

Always respond to requests for material from major magazines. Also, keep any letters they may send to you in your magazine reference file for future inquiries. When you feel you have material they will be interested in, you will have the name of the editor to contact.

If you aren't on their contact list, write or call the home editor, offering to write an article or propose an idea for a future story.

Become a Local "Expert"

If you have built up a reputation with local editors, and they turn to you for information regarding kitchen and bathroom design, approach them with the idea of an "Ask the Expert" column or writing or developing a rough draft of a small article on a weekly or monthly basis. The editors may appreciate having the so-called "expert" appear in their papers and, in return, you will receive great publicity for your firm.

Readers could be invited to write in with their remodeling questions or problems; your answers would display your expertise and knowledge. Or, just create articles using general concepts such as trends, remodeling expectations, working with a pro, universal design, environmental issues, etc.

The syndicated column "Ask the Builder" featuring Tim Carter of Cincinnati started out in just this fashion. He became the local expert by asking and answering some of his own questions, and readers soon responded. As the column became successful, he was eventually syndicated in 100 cities. He is now not only known as the local expert, but as a national expert as well and has definitely carved a niche for himself and his company.

Going National

As stated earlier, it may seem like an impossible task to get your work published in a national publication. This is not necessarily true. Large national magazines employ a network of editorial scouts, sometimes known in journalism as stringers. In each major metropolitan area, there is someone who is regularly contacting designers, architects and builders on behalf of the magazines, looking for projects and story ideas. These scouts will ask to see photos (it is a plus if you have "befores" as well as "afters") and plans of installations you have done. When they find a project they like, the scouts will want the address of the location. Next, they will take their own scouting shots to submit to the magazine's editors. When this happens, ask if you can assist by driving the scout to the location. This gives you the opportunity to tell the scout more about your company as well as an opportunity to "sell" your project. Point out details the scout might otherwise miss, or explain why something was done the way it was.

The scout will shoot the photographs and submit them. If the editor decides to do the story about your design, the magazine will probably arrange for additional professional photography suitable for their publication.

Submitting Projects

If your geographic location is not large enough to merit a scout in the area, you can write or submit projects to the magazines yourself. When submitting projects, there are several points to remember. Begin with what makes a project publishable from an editor's standpoint. The following list was compiled by NKBA with the help of national design editors.

1. Projects must be well designed (meaning they meet or come close to meeting NKBA's Kitchen and Bathroom Planning Guidelines).

2. Simple and charming are appealing. So are elegant and classic.

3. Huge projects can become unphotographable because the room cannot be fully captured in one or two photos.

4. Big, expensive rooms that are too extravagant or ostentatious are not favorable.

5. Very small rooms may not offer enough visual interest or may be difficult to photograph.

6. Warmth is important. Cold, stark rooms have little photographic appeal.

7. Very dark woods are difficult to light and photograph because details and highlights get lost.

8. High-gloss cabinets are hard to photograph, making certain projects less publishable.

9. Some bathrooms can become "mirror nightmares." Too many mirrors and reflections cause problems with lighting for photography and make it difficult to position camera equipment.

10. Rooms decorated with busy wallpapers or fabrics are less likely to be chosen.

It is important to note that these are not hard and fast rules; rather, they are guidelines that will help you determine which projects have the best chance of being selected for publication.

Once you do choose a project, submission is easy. Editors want to see:

- **Floor Plans.** It is not necessary to redraw plans; make copies of the ones you shared with clients.

- **Perspective Renderings.** Again, simply make copies of the ones you shared with clients.

- **Photographs.** Professional photographs are not required for major national publications and for many regional or city publications. Scouting snapshots are fine, and then the magazine will arrange for its photographers to shoot the project if it is accepted.

    Nevertheless, there are good reasons to invest in professional photography of your projects to best portray your work in your portfolio, brochures, ads, on your website, and for any other marketing activities. In addition most trade magazines and many smaller consumer magazines do use professional photography supplied by designers.

    Either way, in addition to shots of the finished project, it is also sometimes helpful to submit your own "before" photos, as well.

    When submitting photos or plans, never send originals. Editors are conscientious about returning material they receive if you enclose a stamped, self-addressed envelope, but there is always the chance that your materials will not be sent back. In such a case, your previous transparencies (and a lot of effort) would be lost.

- **Design Statements.** Take the time to write some notes about the project. Catch the editor's interest with a brief summary of the design concept, the problems you encountered and how you solved them. For a consumer magazine, this should be explained in terms of how the project meets the homeowner's needs.

For a professional or trade magazine, you might describe any technical, architectural or installation problems you solved. The summary should be as brief as possible, and the most impressive details should be the first words after the greeting.

Pick only one or two magazines to send the material. Try to establish a rapport with the editors. Be aware of which magazines seem to feature the kind of projects you do.

Two of the best resources that NKBA members have for getting their work published are the Associaton's official consumer publication and the Association's annual professional design competition. In addition, NKBA works closely with other publications providing a vehicle for members to reach consumers on a national level. The NKBA Communications Department has formed strong partnerships with all of these publications, and can help direct you in your efforts. This is a wonderful opportunity for NKBA members to get their foot in the publishing door.

As a professional courtesy, do not submit the same project to more than one magazine at a time. Send it to one publication and wait for the editor's response. Give the editor at least six weeks to get back to you; travel and press deadlines often keep them from responding as quickly as they would like to. If the first magazine you approach chooses not to publish your project, send it to another. If you do send a project to more than one magazine at the same time, tell each editor that other magazines have received the same material.

If your material is returned "Thanks, but no thanks," do not be discouraged. Many times, the editor has just seen four white kitchens and you have sent in the fifth. To keep readers turning the pages, editors look for variety and a change of pace.

Editors also consider other factors when choosing projects, some logistical and some technical. If they do their own photography, they need more than one project in the same area to make the expense of flying in a photographer worthwhile. You might work with others in your area to give the editor and photographer several projects to consider. This will increase your chances. However, whenever you finish an outstanding project, submit it right away. The editor may have photography scheduled in a neighboring state/province, and it will be easy to work you in.

Sometimes, a project is turned down because it appears to be too difficult to photograph, even though the design has merit. As mentioned earlier, it takes special skill in lighting to photograph high-gloss cabinets or very dark woods, and some rooms that are "mirror nightmares."

Keep in mind that just because an editor says no the first time does not mean he or she won't consider another project from you. If the editor takes the time to explain the reasons for rejecting your first submission, take it as a good sign. Look for another project and send it. In the cover letter, mention any previous publicity the project has received—a local newspaper story or even your own local advertising.

When the Editor Calls

Much of the discussion thus far has focused on what to do if a project is not accepted for publication. If an editor receives material on a well-designed project that meets the needs of the magazine, chances are good that it will be selected for publication. The editor will contact you to inform you that the project has been selected. A professional photo session will be arranged, and additional information will be secured from the designer as well as the client. It is for this reason that it is essential to get permission for publication from the client before you go to the trouble of querying an editor about a project. If the clients have had a good experience with you, chances are they will want you to get this recognition; most feel honored to have their homes featured in local or national magazines. But clients should be warned that professional photography could take a full day and maybe longer. In addition, they will be expected to sign a release form giving the publication permission to take and use photos in a number of ways, not necessarily limited to a single feature.

The magazine's editorial staff should inform you of when the project will be published. If they are unable to provide an exact date at the time the photography and interviews take place, they will contact you later to give a publication date.

Exposure in a consumer magazine—national, regional or local—can do a great deal for your business. Acknowledge that fact and formally thank the editor and the magazine for the opportunity. Follow up is not only good for increasing your chances of repeat business from customers, it also increases your chances of getting future exposure in the same magazine.

Remember, you have to promote your own company because no one else will.

8 Tips for Preparing a Press Release

- Make sure it's newsworthy
- Write it well
- Use a style guide
- Develop a great lead
- Use inverted pyramid structure
- End with a boilerplate
- Send photos
- Proof carefully

Meet the Press: Tips for Preparing a Press Release

(Reprinted Courtesy of *Remodeling* magazine, January 2005, by Stephen Wilson, Biz-comm Inc.)

There is a general assumption that getting your company mentioned in the local paper is free publicity. Yes, it is publicity—but it is not free. In fact, if done poorly, it can be a most costly experience in futility.

The vehicle for most public relations efforts is the tried and true press release. Press releases do work. The *Columbia Journalism Review* found that a single issue of the Wall Street Journal had 111 stories taken from press releases word-for-word and only 30% of these stories had additional facts collected by reporters. More to the point, an estimated 80% of all published newspaper and magazine stories began as a press release to promote a service or product and build image.

A press release is a written document with a clear headline, quotes and facts with attribution to support a news story, background on the featured company, release date, and basic contact information for follow-up.

Can the average remodeler write a press release? Most remodelers have no experience and lack the necessary writing skills, making the result less than satisfactory.

Here are eight tips to help you prepare your next press release and increase your chance of seeing it in print.

1. Make sure it is newsworthy. Avoid blatant, self-serving "puffery." That helps you lose credibility with an editor.

2. Write it so it does not have to be rewritten. Save the editor time. Make it stand on its own.

3. Use a style guide. Most newspapers use the *Associated Press Stylebook*.

4. Develop a great lead. Make the editor want to read further.

5. Use an inverted pyramid writing structure. This means the most important information is up top; the least important, at the bottom. Editors are forced to select articles that fit the column inches available. With the inverted pyramid approach, the editor can cut off as much as they need to make it fit without diluting the message.

6. End with a boilerplate paragraph about your company—who you are, what you do, and contact information.

7. If photos are available, include them either attached to an e-mail, on a disc, or in the form of prints.

8. Proof carefully. Then proof again.

If this is all more than you bargained for, there are good reasons to hire an agency. An agency provides experience; it can prepare the press release in a manner recognized by an editor as professional; it is seen as a third-party submission; it may have already established a relationship with several editors and maintain a media list; the cost of a professionally prepared press release (not an in-depth article) is small compared to the level of effort for an internal job; and, most important, an agency typically employs professional writers.

SALES AND SELLING

As mentioned earlier, some people believe marketing and sales are one and the same. They are not. Marketing is that whole broad picture. Selling is part of marketing, the most important part, because with no sales there will be no marketing. A formal definition might be: sales is a component of the marketing process whereby your company, either directly or indirectly, contacts, convinces, and contracts with customers to purchase your products and services.

Almost everyone in the kitchen and bath business works hard at learning design skills, but few put any resources into selling skills. Remember—"Nothing happens until a sale is made." Without sales, you will be out of business. Shouldn't you make sales training every bit as important as design training?

There are numerous books, tapes, CDs and seminars (including NKBA sponsored) on selling skills. As the selling skills of your sales team improve, their productivity will increase and the company will make more money. Plus, and maybe the biggest plus, you will have happier, more satisfied, clients (and more of them).

Selling can be broken down into seven easy steps:

- Prospecting for Clients

- The Initial Contact

- Qualifying the Client

- Presentation of Products and Services

- Meeting Objections and Concerns

- Closing the Sale

- Getting Referrals

It is important that sales staff use an organized way to gather information about the client's project. The NKBA Business Management Form System, available to members, includes an excellent survey form for both kitchen and bath projects, and should be the "roadmap" when gathering information from the client before the planning process begins.

The Seven-step Selling Cycle

Following is a brief description of what is involved with each of the seven steps in the selling cycle. If you can memorize a seven-digit telephone number, you can memorize these. It is important that you go through the selling process one step at a time—doing a good job with each step. Skipping a step or not doing a thorough job with each diminishes your chances of getting that all-important order.

- **Step No. 1** – Prospecting for Clients. Finding potential buyers for the products and services you sell. Many—perhaps even the majority—of your prospects are referrals from happy clients. In addition, all your marketing efforts (advertising, promotions and public relations) are geared to "drive" clients into your business. Without prospects—you will not need the next six steps!

- **Step No. 2** – The Initial Contact. This can be a satisfied client telling another person about you. It can be someone seeing one of your advertisements, or it can be the initial telephone call to your business. Once they know your name, where you are located and a little bit about you, potential clients may drive to your store to look. All of the above, plus the prospect's initial impression of the drive-up, your store front, the first step through the door and how they are greeted—are part of the initial contact. You only get one chance to make a good impression, so make sure everything you do up-front will make the client want to stay and hear your whole story.

- **Step No. 3** – Qualify the Client. Next to writing the order, this is the most important step in the selling cycle. Within the first ten minutes of face-to-face conversation, the salesperson needs to determine if spending more time with the prospective client is worthwhile for both you and the prospect. This is where you have to ask a number of open-ended questions, encouraging the client to open up and tell you why they drove to your store in the first place. Questions such as:

  1. Who are you?

  2. Have you visited our store before?

  3. What is your project?

  4. What is your timeframe?

  5. Do you have a designer?

  6. Do you have a builder?

  7. Have you been shopping other places?

  8. Where is the project?

  9. What is your budget?

Ask additional questions if you require more information to determine if it will be worth your time and the client's time to continue. Only proceed to Step 4 if you believe it will be beneficial to both of you.

- **Step No. 4** – Presentation of Products and Services. This is where you start selling yourself, your company and your products—and in that order. Each of the above has a "value-added" package, things that are valuable to the prospect; things such as being a CKD/CBD or CMKBD or your years of experience, length of time the company has been in business, if the company offers one-stop shopping (i.e., all the products and services required to do a "turnkey" job). This is where you also demonstrate products, talk features and benefits, and sell "value" over "price." When you add value—price becomes less important.

- **Step No. 5** – Meeting Objections and Concerns. Yes, every client will have some concerns—even objections. Your job is to determine what they are—answer them—and make them go away. Do this by asking the right questions and being a great listener. You should be listening at least two-thirds of the time during the selling process. Remember, you have two ears and one mouth—use them in proportion.

- **Step No. 6** – Closing the Sale. This is why you spend all that money to drive clients into your dealership—and—why you go through Steps 1 through 5. Writing the order/closing the sale is what it is all about. If you do a good job in Steps 1 through 5, closing the sale should be almost a "given." But—and do not forget this—you have to ask for the order. There is a number of ways to do this, and you will know when it is time.

- **Step No. 7** – Getting Referrals. This is the lifeblood of the business. Happy clients tell other folks what a terrific job you did. You need to learn how to "work" your referrals to your advantage. Do not just "love 'em and leave 'em." Make them clients for life. This all leads right back to prospecting the client (Step 1) and the cycle begins all over again.

Yes, there is more to it, but learning sales skills is easier and quicker than earning a CKD certification. Make this an important part of your overall marketing plan.

Another important part of marketing and selling is to identify the various features and benefits of each salesperson, the company, your services, and your products. Then, learn how to market and articulate them to your clients. When you do this, you are marketing and selling value, and when you sell value, you make price become less important.

After the Sale, Follow Through

If you have done a terrific job with the completed project and you have a happy client, there are several things you can do to make them a "client for life" and utilize them for future client referrals. You should work as hard with past clients as you do looking for new clients. Word-of-mouth can be your best (also your worst) form of advertising and public relations.

Here are several suggestions for what happens after the sale is completed.

- Telephone the client. "Did the project turn out as well as you hoped it might?" "Are you completely happy with the end results?" "Is there anything else we can do?" "Thank you, again, for the opportunity of working with you."

- Send a Thank You note ... personalized and handwritten.

- Make a personal visit to the job after the client has "settled in."

- Get a testimonial letter for your scrapbook.

- Ask your client if they would distribute several "referral" cards to their friends, family and neighbors. Reward them with a small gift for each referral card brought to the showroom. Give them a larger reward if the new prospect buys.

- Make a follow-up telephone call three months, six months and one year after the job has been completed. "Is there anything we can do?" (Touch-up, adjust a hinge, straighten a door, etc.)

- Make them feel like they received a "warranty for life."

- Build a past client database and communicate with them on a regular basis using newsletters, e-mails, special announcements, etc. They bought a kitchen this year ... maybe they will buy a bathroom or entertainment center next year.

Keep those happy clients working for you.

SHOWROOM CUSTOMER SERVICE SATISFACTION SURVEY

Customer Name:
Address:
Phone:

We have recently completed a design project with you. We appreciate your business and thank you for the opportunity to serve you.

In order to help us continually do a better job in our showroom operation we are asking our clients to complete the below Customer Service Satisfaction survey. We have enclosed a self-addressed stamped envelope for your convenience.

Fill in the blank or rate each item 1 (low) to 5 (high):

My overall impression of your showroom	1	2	3	4	5
The selection of products on display	1	2	3	4	5
Being waited on in a timely manner	1	2	3	4	5
My salesperson was friendly and accommodating	1	2	3	4	5
My salesperson was knowledgeable and helpful	1	2	3	4	5
My quote was completed in a timely manner	1	2	3	4	5
My quote was complete and accurate	1	2	3	4	5
Your prices were competitive	1	2	3	4	5
My products were delivered on time	1	2	3	4	5
The delivery process was easy	1	2	3	4	5
Your invoicing was timely and accurate	1	2	3	4	5
My overall evaluation of my salesperson	1	2	3	4	5
My overall evaluation of your showroom	1	2	3	4	5

General Comments:

DESIGN PROJECT CLIENT SURVEY

1. What would you consider to be our greatest asset?

   Design ❑   Service ❑   Installation ❑   Product ❑   Other _____

   Comments: _____

   _____

2. What would you consider to be our greatest weakness? _____

   _____

3. Were your communications with us handled satisfactorily?   Yes ❑   No ❑

   Comments: _____

   _____

4. Do you feel the design service retainer was a benefit for you?   Yes ❑   No ❑

   Comments: _____

   _____

5. Was the designer available when needed?   Yes ❑   No ❑

   Comments: _____

   _____

6. Was your kitchen or bath ordered, delivered and completed in a timely and satisfactory manner?
   Yes ❑   No ❑

   Comments: _____

   _____

7. What could we have done to make your project better? _____

   _____

8. Do you have any suggestions regarding the design process that could help us serve our clients better?
   Yes ❑   No ❑

   Comments: _____

   _____

   _____

DESIGN PROJECT CLIENT SURVEY -Continued-

9. Do you have any suggestions for our installers that could help serve our clients better?

   Comments: _____

   _____

10. Do you feel our service/warranty work is:

   Below Average ❑   Average ❑   Above Average ❑   Not Required ❑

11. Would you do business with us again?   Yes ❑   No ❑

   Why? _____

   _____

12. Is there anything you would recommend to others who are considering a project like yours?

   _____

   _____

13. How did you find [Firm's Name]?
   Advertising ❑   Yellow Pages ❑   Building Sign ❑   Other _____
   Referral – Name: _____

14. What was the deciding factor for you, in selecting [Firm's Name]? _____

   _____

15. If you were the owner of [Firm's Name], what would you do to make us a better company?

   _____

   _____

16. May we place your name on our customer referral list?   Yes ❑   No ❑

17. Any other comments? _____

   _____

   _____

We certainly appreciate you taking time in helping us with this survey, so we may give the very best service.

Name (Optional): _____
Address: _____
Phone: _____

STAYING IN TOUCH WITH CLIENTS ON A REGULAR BASIS

- **Holiday Cards.** These are a common tool used by hundreds in the industry.

  The most popular times for sending out holiday cards are during December. But how many cards do you receive to celebrate St. Patrick's Day, Groundhog Day, St. Valentine's Day or Halloween? Here are some ideas for customized cards you can create.

Halloween: "Remodeling your kitchen or bath is a tricky business, but working with you is a real treat."

St. Valentine's Day: "We love our customers! Thank you for helping make us such a success!"

St. Patrick's Day: "Faith and Begorrah! Happy St. Patrick's Day to all our friends. The luck of the Irish was upon us when you chose us as your designer. Thanks!"

Birthday cards are an extra special way of recognizing your customers.

- **Newsletters.** Newsletters are an excellent tool for keeping in touch with your clients. Attractive, lively newsletters can communicate valuable information in an interesting, easy-to-read format. They position your company as an expert and as one that has personality. Costs can vary, depending upon whether you produce it yourself or have it professionally prepared.

  To create a high-impact, user-friendly newsletter:

  1. Keep the stories short and easy to read. People are too busy to read long stories.

  2. Two sides of an 8.5" x 11" sheet are all you really need. Do not make the newsletter longer than four pages.

  3. Include stories about your company, such as awards that have been won, certificates earned, new staff, profits, special charity projects in which you're involved, etc.

  4. Design the newsletter to be a self-mailer. Do not staple or tape it. It discourages the reader.

5. Use the newsletter to inform past and potential clients about promotions, sales, new products and services.

- Call clients of completed projects occasionally to see how things are and if there is anything you can do. The perception will be that you really care. Take pictures of the finished projects for your scrapbook.

- Throw neighborhood "parties" at a client's home after the project is completed. You sponsor the refreshments, the client sponsors potential prospects.

ASK FOR REFERRALS

- Those who refer are very special supporters of your company. They need to know that you value their support.

REWARD REFERRALS

(Source: Keith Rosen, *Innovative Selling and Time Management for Sales Professionals*, June, 2004 *Qualified Remodeler* magazine)

The biggest blunder people make is, once they start getting referrals, they forget to thank the person who provided them.

1. **Recognize the referral.** Call or send a thank you card letting your past client know you appreciate them thinking of you—and taking time out of their busy day to send you a referral.

2. **Keep in touch with the past client.** Send a card when the project sells as a thank you.

3. **Thank them again.** As the new project is underway, call the referral and thank them in person. There may be a new project in the works for you.

- Develop a Thank You gift program to give the client at the end of the job.

A gift lets the customer know that you value the business they have given to your company.

The gift does not have to be large or too expensive—but, instead, show sincere thanks.

Hint: When purchasing a gift, be sure to buy something that will be around the house for a considerable time. Wine, cheese, candy and flowers are not recommended, since they disappear shortly after the customer receives them.

Some examples of appropriate gifts:

A. A nicely organized binder full of project information, such as the warranties, paint color reference numbers, pertinent telephone numbers, etc. Add a "before" and "after" photo to top it off.

B. An attractively framed, professional photo of the finished project. Not only will they appreciate the effort you took, the neighbors will see it when it is hung on the wall.

C. A magazine subscription will keep coming and coming and coming. A dozen times a year, your customer will be reminded of your great service.

D. A pen and ink sketch of the home, matted and framed.

E. Something fitting with a hobby or personal interest of the customer.

F. A coordinating silk or dried flower arrangement.

G. An attractive brass or ceramic planter with a healthy houseplant.

H. A fruit or ornamental tree for the yard.

I. A cutting board with your name on it.

J. Send clients a customer satisfaction survey. Keep it short and simple. Offer a small incentive for completing it ($10.00 gift certificate to Starbucks or Ben and Jerry's). Make it easy by including a stamped self-addressed envelope.

Great Promotional Ideas from Jim Krengel, CMKBD

Here are some more noteworthy tips to boost your exposure to new clients.

- Present slide shows using a continuous loop in a showroom display of your work. Add music, make it lively!

- Offer cooking schools to demonstrate how well-designed products and kitchens make cooking easier.

- Write an article for a newspaper or offer to produce a column called "Ask the Expert."

- Have a large photo album available in your showroom with before and after photographs of your projects (8" x 10" photos make the greatest impact).

- Display magazines in your showroom with "Design and Installed by ..." tabs indicating your published projects.

- Create a book with testimonial letters from past customers.

- Use your own printed graph paper for layout and design.

- Offer your customers a "Remodeling Survival Kit," consisting of a picnic basket, microwave entrees, gift certificates and coupons for meals out, etc.

- When there is a problem and it is the company's fault, fix it and give the clients something for their inconvenience— a cutting board, a dinner out, a gift basket.

SUMMARY OF HOW TO BUILD A MARKETING PLAN

- **State your business purpose.** One (to the point, clear, concise) sentence on the purpose of your plan.

- **Define your market situation.** Describe the changes, problems, and opportunities that you will face over the coming marketing plan for:

  1. Your customers

  2. Your competitors

  3. Your products and services

  4. The marketing environment

- **Set goals and objectives.** What do you want your marketing plan to achieve?

  1. Grow sales

  2. Sales the same but margin up

  3. Fewer (or more) products/services

  4. Larger, expanded target audience

- **Select a marketing strategy that appeals to your targeted consumer.** Outline your tactics. Go into detail on any strategy changes. If you decide to add installation to your package, you will need to list all the things you will need to do to make this happen (both the internal and external issues).

- **Advance your position and brand strategy.**

  1. Position – Your business niche—only your business can fill.

  2. Brand – The characteristics, attributes, and implied promises that people know to be true about your business.

- **Establish your budget.** Do not use last year's budget. Establish by total dollars to be spent. Start with zero-based costs and build the budget, one step at a time.

- **Blue print your action plan.** Describe in four columns the action, the budget for the action, the deadline, and the responsible party for each step along the way.

- **Start thinking long-term.** This is where you begin looking ahead. Start by making a list of the market development opportunities you will research over the coming year for possible action in future marketing plan periods. Here are some examples:

  1. New or expanded business locations to serve more customers.

  2. New geographic market areas outside your current market area.

  3. New customers, different from those represented by your current customer profile.

  4. New products or product packages that will inspire additional purchases.

  5. New customer service programs.

NEW-MARKET CHECKLIST

(Reprinted Courtesy of *Remodeling* magazine, January 2005, by Stephen Wilson)

Stephen Wilson, owner of Biz-comm, Reston, Virginia, offers these eight tips for taking on a new market.

1. Learn everything there is to know about the new market.

2. Calculate your investment in terms of equipment, personnel, training, and systems management.

3. Research the profit margins to make sure they're attractive enough to you.

4. Approach the new market as if you're starting a brand new company. Develop a stand-alone business and marketing plan, and make sure your core business is healthy enough to support the start-up until it becomes profitable.

5. Get your feet wet. Perform some of the work as a test project before proceeding full-speed.

6. To decrease your risk, consider hiring subcontractors before committing to employees.

7. Avoid putting your company's reputation at risk. Market the new entity separately until you're sure of its success.

8. Use your plan. This is the easiest and most important step. Share it with others. Use it to help others (advertisement agency) help you. Use it to keep yourself on-track as you manage your business to marketing success.

IN CLOSING...

To begin doing a better job of marketing yourself and your firm, you should, at a minimum:

- Go back to your past customers for new business and new business leads. Stay in touch with customers.

- Develop your brand.

- Follow up on leads immediately; they grow stale quickly.

- Use low or no cost awards to recognize sales improvement ideas and high performance frequently. Have your salespeople compare and swap effective selling techniques frequently.

- Use public relations to maximum advantage. Target public activities that will be visible to your potential customers.

- Assess the competition; know your competitors' products, sales techniques and current pricing.

- Seek and fully utilize co-op advertising dollars.

- Keep your advertising message simple, memorable and reflective of your unique selling value. Build an advertising program with a consistent message—and stick to it.

- Profile your customers. Use advertising vehicles targeted to their income, lifestyle, reading and listening habits.

- Analyze the most profitable product and service sales. Concentrate sales and marketing efforts on those products and services.

- Make sure your company vehicles, showroom and storefront are neat and clean, and completely identify and positively advertise your firm.

- Respond to all callbacks promptly. Use them as a potential source of new business.

CHAPTER 11: Professional and Profitable Project Management

The design responsibility and project management accountability are areas that most individuals in the kitchen and bath industry undertake regularly and feel quite competent in. However, within the industry, this is a place where money is lost day in and day out. Once the job begins, profit erosion can eat away at what you net from each project.

To manage a job successfully, professionally and profitably, protect profits once the kitchen/bath or other fitted furniture is sold. Do this by designing better projects. Not bigger, fancier, or more elaborate but projects that are better because they are backed by detail. This includes drawings, careful jobsite dimensions, accurate estimating, a proactive customer management program, an organized method of communication on the jobsite - and a well-structured cost accounting system.

> An Industry Historical Perspective by Ellen
>
> *"As a design professional within our industry since 1972, I have had a varied set of experiences. First as the owner of a multi-branch design firm in Sacramento, California, that catered to an upscale clientele. Then part of my career was spent with cabinet manufacturers. As a training consultant and a writer, I have shared ideas with designers throughout North American, the Pacific Rim and Europe. I have seen how some firms suffer from consistent profit erosion once the job begins, while others carefully protect every penny.*

PROFIT EROSION

In the kitchen and bath industry some type of margin reduction will probably take place, particularly with full-service "design/build" undertakings on most projects. Given the reality of the industry that some margin loss is to be anticipated, this section will focus on the key elements of minimizing this erosion while doing the best job possible to manage the project, as well as job accounting.

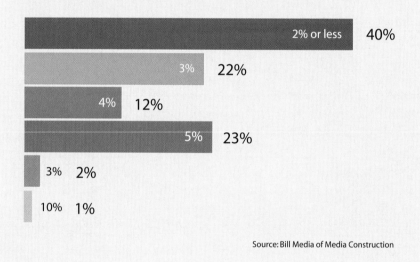

Assuming zero slippage is the goal ...
Some slippage is inevitable, what % is tolerable?

2% or less — 40%
3% — 22%
4% — 12%
5% — 23%
3% — 2%
10% — 1%

Source: Bill Media of Media Construction

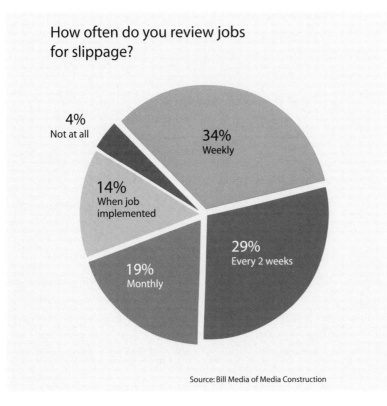

How often do you review jobs for slippage?

4%
Not at all

34%
Weekly

14%
When job implemented

29%
Every 2 weeks

19%
Monthly

Source: Bill Media of Media Construction

MANAGING THE PROJECT

To Minimize Profit Draining Mistakes: Get it Right the First Time

The profits resulting from your design will only be as good as the initial jobsite survey and measurements taken. Minimize measuring mistakes. Successful firms often share the responsibility of returning to the jobsite after the contract is signed to double-check measurements, and take a "committee" approach to reviewing the cabinet order acknowledgements or other purchase orders.

The second most important element in profitable projects is a clear set of project documents. The National Kitchen & Bath Association asserts that there is no substitute for the following set of documents:

- A "before" floor plan, with electrical notations. Digital photography in the project package helps as well.

- An "after" floor plan that includes all cabinet nomenclature in a clear and easy to read format. On the floor plan, list cutout and overall dimensions for appliances; draw the countertops' actual depth, and draw appliance doors open.

- Dimensioned elevations that match the floor plan perfectly. Too often, changes are made in the floor plan and, because of a time crunch, those changes are never translated to the elevation.

- An electrical plan, with construction details for a simple project. A separate construction plan may be required for more complex projects.

- Copies of all the appliance or equipment spec sheets (pull these off the Internet, not from outdated catalogs).

- A completed contractual document spelling out all of the products supplied and work completed.

- A system to document changes made during the project.

The NKBA Business Management Forms System, available to members, contains a complete set of project documents useful for a new firm and worth review for a seasoned professional. Use this type of an organized approach to manage each project. Such a tracking system for the details protects your profits and minimizes any "slippage" while the job is underway.

To Keep Profits You Need to Know Who Your Client is Before You Settle on the Markup Percentage (Sometimes Called a Factor).

- **Type of project.** All jobs are not the same and so need to be marked up differently.

  A large job that is located one hour away from your showroom with a great deal of construction coupled with low- to medium-priced products requiring extensive jobsite assembly is quite different from a job with the same selling price that is a few minutes away from your office and that requires little cabinet construction. Factor in the jobsite location, type of project and type of client and change the markup accordingly.

- **Is the job a collaborative effort or are you completely in charge?** A major question arises in new construction where you may be working with a builder or other contractor and dependent on his/her measurements. Successful individuals in our industry either insist on delivering and installing the products, maintaining control from start-to-finish, or charge for several jobsite visits to verify the construction (window and door placement) and the mechanicals (electrical and plumbing) to make sure the room reflects the plan.

- **How many influencers are involved in the project?** If there is an interior designer or a general contractor involved, you need a clear method of communicating with these individuals. Make sure the drawings you are working from reflect any changes. Be sure everyone is working off the latest, correct drawings.

Maintain a Clear Purchase Tracking System

In addition to good plans and a clear understanding of the type of project and client you are working with, the firm needs to have an effective purchase order system.

- If your firm is large enough, the advantages of a single purchasing agent are evident:

  1. Quantity Buying

  2. Multiple Orders

  3. Volume Freight Discounts

- Whether large or small—the purchase order is an important part of job costing, and needs to flow through from estimating sheet to accounting. This allows you to match up the purchase order amount with the actual invoice amount. Oftentimes, a four-part purchase order works well.

  1. One copy is sent to your receiving department or to the subcontractor involved in the project.

  2. One copy remains in the client's file.

  3. One copy goes to accounting.

  4. One is sent to the supplier partner file (this is the one used to match invoices).

Maintain a Staging Area to Keep Track of All Parts and Pieces for the Project

You need a staging area. Whether you have a warehouse or not, you need some organized way to gather products for a job before it begins, as well as to receive those "odds and ends" that come in as you complete the job. Without some type of staging area, time is wasted. And that translates into money lost. Do not start a job until you have everything on hand.

Hold a Pre-Installation Jobsite Conference

To Get the Installation Experts Briefed: Hold a Pre-Construction Conference

Hold a pre-construction meeting at the jobsite with the homeowners and all subcontractors. Explain in detail who, what, when and how the work will be completed.

When the Project is Ready to Start: Pass the Baton

Efficiently moving contract details, including plans and specs and all pertinent data—from sales and design to production—can pose immense challenges. As one remodeler said,

> *"It seems I'm always pushing out last minute drawings, product selections, permits or signed contracts ... This upsets my lead carpenters because they'd like a week or so to review the job: in many cases, they want to visit the job ahead of its start date with me. I really struggle with this."*

In 2005, *Remodeling* magazine surveyed a series of remodelers who talked about the importance of delivering a complete package to production so you do not lose any profits because of a lack of information.

Although there is no perfect solution, the firms interviewed offered these suggestions:

- **Transfer of Project Information.** Issues are more likely to occur if the sales department is involved in production, because salespeople often retain details in their heads. The company may find it useful to have a production manager—or even the owner—review the project information to make sure the design, product and construction details are clear as well as complete.

- **A standard document package takes weeks, not days, to put together.** Job size and client indecision increase the time required. Give yourself enough time to get the document package pulled together.

- **Make sure there is one format for the project document package and complete each book.** Profits will suffer if the installation team tries to work with a jobsite book that is missing some information.

Hand Off an Organized Job Site "Bible"

Key items should be in the jobsite "bible" or workbook, which is used for the pre-installation conference, given to the lead installer and then remains in one specified place on the job for the duration of the project:

CONSTRUCTION SITE BOOK CONTENTS

(Source: "Pass the Baton," June, 2004 *Remodeling* magazine)

- Map and written directions to jobsite. Access information.

- Contract scope, with no financial details.

- Construction calendar.

- Homeowner target dates for open selections.

- Salvage report listing what to keep and where to put it.

- Subcontractor list, with contact information and job scope details.

- Cut sheet of materials, specifications, install sheets, product warranties.

- Salesperson and homeowner's contact information, with e-mail addresses and 24-hour emergency contact information.

- Plans and elevations.

- Permit and inspection reports.

- Miscellaneous, such as receipts for homeowners.

- Change order request forms.

- Place for checks from homeowner.

While the Installation is Going On, Start the Punch List

Another big profit drainer occurs when a project is not completed or "closed out" efficiently. Whether they are called "call backs," or "service calls," repeated call backs to finish the project and collect your money are a waste of everyone's time and efforts. If the designer has done his or her job, the punch list will be constantly under review at the jobsite. It consists of a list of items to be touched up, adjusted or replaced. The list is agreed to between the firm and the client.

The client must understand the punch list will not be completed until all the parts are in. Towards the end of the project, too often, the punch list becomes an "evolving" document. It keeps changing, which makes it hard to manage. Schedule a meeting with the client, review every inch of the project, identify what needs to be done. Better to get it written down once and then work feverishly to get the job closed out so you can collect your money and leave.

MANAGING THE CLIENT

Ask any seasoned kitchen and bath pro about client complaints—and they typically fall into several categories. Have you heard any of these?

- "A recurring complaint we hear is that the project took longer than the homeowner anticipated. The client thought someone would be working on his/her project every day—and felt there could have been better communication. We have added an in-house expeditor to work as a liaison between the field crew and the homeowner." Jim Klappa, J Builders—Greenfield, Wisconsin

- "When we do receive a complaint it usually has to do with communication. We deal with this first by attempting to find out what are the clients priorities for our performance—once we've agreed on expectations, we then keep lines of communications open." Ronald G. Iossi, United Services by RG Iossi—Davenport, Iowa

- "We often get 'so-so' marks for our subcontractors. We found that when a homeowner asks a subcontractor a question—as they walk in the door—the sub may not answer correctly because he is not up-to-speed on the project. But the homeowner misinterprets this: they think the sub does not know what they are doing. To handle this, we make sure the lead carpenter greets the subs and introduces them to the client, which keeps us in charge." Christopher Repp, Repp Construction—Orchard Park, New York

- "One of the big things I hear is the need for dust control and surface protection—notably, among my high-end clientele. We curtain everything off, use fiberboards, dust cloths and plastic to keep dust and damage to a minimum. We also use scaffolds rather than ladders so nothing is leaning against any surfaces." Bill Carter, William Carter Company—Sacramento, California

- "The most consistent complaint is the length of time it takes to complete a project. We've overcome this by providing the homeowner with a written schedule before the job begins and then give them weekly updates. We use Microsoft Project to schedule jobs and to keep track of 'lost days' so we can show the client why there is not someone on their project every day." Michael High, Casa Linda Remodeling—San Antonio, Texas

- "The biggest complaint that we occasionally get is dissatisfaction with subcontractors. Either the sub's personality ruffles feathers or they're not as accommodating as our crew is. We handle this on a case-by-case basis. I do try to match personalities of clients with the lead carpenters and the subs I assign each job. I also try to 'fill in' the subs and employees with the 'flavor' of the job—things like the clients' personalities and the name of the pets." Myron "Butch" Ledworowski, Little American Builders—Middleton, Wisconsin

If these types of consumer complaints sound familiar, try refreshing your project management process to manage the client, as well as the project.

Keeping Customers Satisfied During Installation

You've just signed a contract to do a $50,000 kitchen remodel and the job will start in 8 to 12 weeks. You know what to expect during the waiting period and once the job starts—you do it all the time. But your client may only remodel or build once or twice in a lifetime. You have the responsibility of not only doing a quality job, but of keeping the client happy during the complete renovation.

Communicate. Communicate. Communicate. There is no substitute for doing a first-class job in this all-important area.

MANAGING THE CLIENT:
UNDERSTANDING REMODELING FEVER

Remember, a kitchen/bathroom project is a big-ticket item and, as such, it is very emotional for both the customer and the installer. In fact, the term "remodeling fever" describes the natural pattern of customer emotions during a typical remodeling project. The graph below shows this pattern.

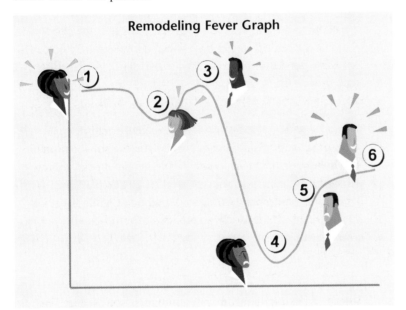

Remodeling Fever Graph

The steps are:

1. The sales contract is signed, and the customer feels that a dream is about to be realized. This is the highest degree of happiness, optimism and satisfaction.

2. Production begins. Demolition, storage of materials in the customer's space, the need for a telephone, key and bathroom bring the realization to customers that they will be under siege for a period of time.

3. Watching rough carpentry shape the space so quickly raises the customer's expectations; the job seems to be going so well that, undoubtedly, it will be finished before the completion date.

4. The natural slow pace of electrical and mechanical rough-ins, inspections and drywall, with numerous workers of various levels of thoughtfulness roaming the house, unexplained delays, work done and redone, begin to take their toll on the customer. At drywall, they hit bottom.

The space makes almost no visible progress over the span of a few days, the drywallers may arrive at odd hours to do what appears to be invisible work, and then the ultimate blow of drywall sanding assures the most even-tempered of homeowners that they have made a terrible mistake in undertaking their kitchen or bathroom remodeling project.

5. The trim-out stage, which appears so simple to the layperson's eye, moves ever so slowly. A day's work makes almost no visible difference to the customers. At this stage, the customers feel that the job will never be finished. However, they do begin to have a good overall view of what the space will look like and how it will "live."

6. Completion marks an improvement of outlook and a relief that the space will be the customer's to use and live in. In many jobs, much goodwill is lost by the slowness with which the punch list is handled. Workers dribble in and out and mess up what was completed by the last worker. Painters touch up and leave drips on the newly finished wood floor, while the floor finishers scratch the newly painted base trim when they return to remove the drips.

The homeowner's life returns to sanity. They move back into the kitchen or bathroom and begin to enjoy the new space. Their appreciation of the installer begins to return and grow as time goes on. However, there was a long downslide during production, and it is a long time, if ever, before the client's satisfaction returns to the original level.

Knowing this natural pattern will motivate the dealer/designer to create a system to help the client live through this process.

EXPLAIN THE "REAL WORLD" INSTALLATION SCHEDULE

The installation is the worst part of the project for clients. It disrupts their life, is inconvenient and messy. It can also be stressful because clients fear that, once the project starts, the contractor (you) and subs won't be around to work or answer questions.

Be aware: Many television shows today are creating unrealistic installation timeline expectations for the consumer. By providing work schedules, introducing clients to your reliable subcontractors, and helping them to prepare for the construction phase, you will protect yourself from such misconceptions.

THE PROJECT TIMELINE

Develop a detailed schedule or timeline for the complete project and share it with your client. Show time frames for demolition, framing, building inspection, rough work, cabinet and appliance installations, finish work and completion. Indicate when subcontractors will be there and who they are. Allow extra time for scheduling delays, hidden conditions, custom work, add-ons or more elaborate plans.

No two jobs are the same, but here is a rough timeline of tasks for a basic kitchen and bath project:

- One to five days to tear out existing fixtures, walls, floors and appliances

- One day to change electrical wiring and plumbing

- Two to five days for framing

- Four days to install new drywall and tape the joints

- One to two days to install a new kitchen floor if resilient and four to eight days for tile/granite/wood

- Three to five days to install new cabinets

- One to two days for new fixtures and appliances

- One to two days for new granite countertops or four days for limestone. (Note the down time from the demolition date to the installation date for stone countertops.)

- Two to seven days for light fixtures, wall papering and painting

Note days when no one will be on the job. Your clients will expect something to happen every day, and will get nervous when nobody shows up and nothing is happening. If there is a schedule change or delay, be sure to let them know right away, and modify the project timeline.

Make Sure Everyone Makes a Good Impression

Most important—be sure your subcontractors are dependable, clean and do quality work. You may be great, but if they aren't, it reflects poorly on you. Make sure they leave the home and work area as clean as possible each day.

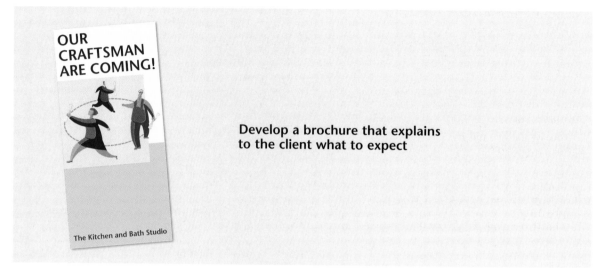

**Develop a brochure that explains
to the client what to expect**

The Remodeling Process

It is also a good idea to provide clients with brochures on what to expect during the remodeling process. It is important for the homeowner to realize that remodeling is not an exact science and that constant communication is vital. The introduction meeting and brochures are a good start, but there are a number of other issues to address with the homeowners before the project begins.

Consider using a tri-fold brochure titled, "Our Craftsmen are Coming," to help prepare the homeowner about what will happen when the workers arrive. This brochure also alerts the client to what their responsibilities will be. Jim Krengel's firm, Kitchens by Krengel, Inc., in St. Paul, Minnesota, has been using this brochure for nearly 30 years. It is sent out prior to the start of remodeling. He states that this brochure has eliminated any number of problems before they begin. A copy of the brochure follows.

Our Craftsmen are Coming ...

Thank you for your recent order. We appreciate the opportunity to serve you. We would like to take a few moments to tell you what to expect and what you can do to help make your project a pleasant experience.

WHAT TO EXPECT

Designing a new project is great fun. And most people manage to focus on the future while they endure the actual remodeling. But no one said it was easy!

The Job is Starting!

You are excited and enthusiastic, but are you ready to deal with the disruptions to your home and your routine? If your project is extensive, you might consider moving out temporarily, or at least plan a vacation for part of the time. If you are going to stay home, here are some strategies to help you through.

• After the materials are ordered, your designer will schedule a pre-construction meeting at the jobsite with you and our project manager. Here, such items as where to place the lock box, store materials for the project and exchange messages will be discussed.

• Good communication prevents most problems, so make sure you agree on a system for staying in touch. Oftentimes, the lead installer and project coordinator are the best contact people. Share your concerns as they arise. A minor adjustment early on might avoid a major expense later.

Do Not Panic!

If you discover a problem, get all the facts, then call your designer or project coordinator. Questions that do not need an immediate response can be left in the project binder. We understand that problems are an inherent part of the remodeling process and will work with you to alleviate your concerns and solve them as soon as possible.

Expect the project to feel like it is taking too long. There will be times—usually three to four weeks into a project—when it seems like not much is happening. During the first few weeks, there is a flurry of excitement following the demolition of your existing project and the creation of a new space. However, as we approach the fine details of the project, it is the quality of the work—not the speed—that will distinguish a [company's name] project.

SCHEDULING

About one month before delivery, our production manager will call to say which WEEK you can expect delivery. Our production manager will call again to confirm the DAY of delivery.

Cabinets and other materials will be delivered by van or semi-truck to your home. You must provide a storage area for them until installation begins. Be sure to inform your insurance company (homeowner's policy) of this storage.

On the first day of installation, we will bring all the tools and materials that we will need for the work. Our production manager will contact you if there is any delay.

A "TYPICAL" project will take approximately eight to ten weeks from the time we arrive to start the work to substantial completion. Small detail items may take longer. This period can obviously vary depending on the scope and complexity of the project. Please be aware, there will be days when no one is working at your jobsite. We will review the overall project schedule with you so you are familiar with our plans. Our men arrive at approximately 7:30 AM and depart at 4:00 PM.

BEFORE OUR CRAFTSMEN ARRIVE ...

• Preparation Work. Did you decide to do some of the preparation work yourself, such as removing old cabinets or flooring? Please check your contract, if any of this work is your responsibility, please have it completed before our installers arrive. This will avoid delays and/or extra labor charges.

• Clearing the Decks. If we are removing the existing kitchen, please remove everything you want to keep. Clear off the countertops and empty the cabinets. Even if you are only having new countertops installed, you should empty your cabinets—the work creates a lot of dust. Empty closets, too, if we have work to do in them.

• Protect Your Valuables. Paintings, hanging plants, knick-knacks, anything on your walls and adjacent walls,

should be moved to another room. Valuable antiques are irreplaceable and often fragile, we do not like to move them. Please give them the care they deserve by making arrangements to have them moved in advance.

• Debris. Since all new cabinets have a protective wrapping, there will be an accumulation of cardboard, paper, etc. Old appliances and countertops may also be thrown away. More than likely, there will be a dumpster placed on your property and our production manager will determine with you where the best location for this is.

• Safety. We'll appreciate your cooperation in keeping everyone, including pets, out of the room being remodeled. Some of the adhesives are toxic when wet, some cannot be

removed from clothing, and power equipment and sharp tools are always dangerous when children are around. In addition, some products break easily when they are partially cut and fit. You will receive a better installation when all of the installers' attention can be concentrated on the work.

• Contact Availability. While it is not necessary for an adult to be present while work is in progress, we ask that you please place a permanent note beside your telephone where you can be reached. If an emergency occurs, we'll need to know how to reach you quickly. Lock boxes will be provided, if needed, so that our installers are able to enter your home if no one is present.

BEFORE OUR CRAFTSMEN ARRIVE ... –continued–

• Dust Covers. Sanding, sawing and other preparation work does make dust. You may wish to cover furniture and other objects in rooms adjacent to the work area to protect them. Old sheets and inexpensive drop cloths are ideal.

• New Construction. New construction may leave plaster or drywall joint cement droppings on the floor. If your drywall or plaster contractor didn't clean up when

he finished, please arrange to have it done before we begin.

• The Installers. Our installers are experienced and have received specialized training. Our product manager has reviewed your order for accuracy, has discussed it with the installers and will have covered the details on your particular design. The installers are professionals and take pride in their knowledge and craftsmanship.

• Leftovers. On some products, we send a greater quantity to the jobsite for our convenience than what we've estimated for the job. The installers will return this excess to the warehouse. Normally, our installers remove all waste and debris for disposal. Please tell them if you want the waste pieces.

THINGS TO EXPECT

• Most kitchen remodeling jobs require that water be cut off in part of the house during installation. Remember, dishes can be washed in the bathroom or laundry sink, though the use of paper plates tends to be the most "hassle-free." There are also hot plates that are available to you that are convenient to use when your cooktop or range is out of working order. A little advanced planning makes the inconvenience more tolerable.

• Our cabinets are of high quality construction, but doors, drawers, etc. are not given final adjustment at the factory. When our installer starts installing cabinets, you may notice some doors and drawers do not line up correctly. This is normal. However, he is trained and knows how to adjust these situations. When installation is complete, he will ask you to inspect the job and he will be happy to adjust any doors and drawers to your satisfaction. If a door or drawer is damaged in shipment and cannot be repaired on the job, we will gladly reorder the same item from the factory. This is your uniquely designed project and we want you to be pleased with it.

• Some scratches and splintering may occur if doors are shortened. Baseboards are vulnerable to damage when materials are fit to them. Our

installers exercise the utmost caution, but some damage is inevitable. These chips, splinters and scratches are not covered by your contract or warranty. Since they are usually of a very minor nature, most homeowners either touch them up or leave the marks until the next time the room is painted. We can recommend painters when you decide to repaint.

• Change Orders. During the remodeling process, you may decide to add a few additional items for our installation crew to complete. It is the perfect time with our people already on site and your lives already disrupted. Please be sure to have our lead installer prepare a change order for this work and note that it will add additional time to the completion of the project.

Water Leaks ...

On most jobs, plumbing is disconnected, moved and reconnected. Please check for water leaks several times following hook-up. Sometimes a leak is so slow that it may not be apparent until the following day. Your alertness will prevent water damage due to a sustained leak. If you discover a leak, place a pan or bucket to catch the drip while you wait for the plumber. Please be sure that it is a leak, not just condensation, before calling.

AFTER THE INSTALLATION

• Protect your investment. Use the cleaning materials and methods recommended by the cabinet, counter, floor, appliance and fixture manufacturers.

• Appliance Literature. All of the "use and care" booklets and warranties packed with your new appliances will be left inside the appliances by the installer. Read them carefully and file for future reference. If you need service on any appliance, please call our office for the name and phone number of the factory authorized service company.

• Moving Appliances and Furniture. BE CAREFUL! Do not damage your new floor when moving objects over it. It is of utmost importance that heavy furniture or appliances not be dragged across floors. Heavy objects tend to settle into the floor somewhat and when you pull or push them, they are actually pushing against the slight dip of the top surface, which may be damaged.

While we have certainly not touched on every item or obstacle that you will encounter during your project, we have tried to give you an overview of what to expect. Be patient and have faith in our crew to complete your project. The finished project will be worth the wait and serve you with years of enjoyment and beauty.

Again, thank you for your order and we look forward to working with you on your project in the future.

American Kitchen & Bath Shop

Dear [Personalized]:

Thank you for your [kitchen/bath] order. Our suppliers advise us that all materials will be ready to start your project approximately [date]. We will verify the exact starting day several days in advance. We have found neighbors like to know when construction work is going to start; therefore, we will be sending everyone on your block the attached letter.

Unless unforeseen delays develop, we expect to take [number] working days (Saturday and Sunday not included) to have the contract substantially complete.

Please assist us in proceeding with your installation without delay by doing the following:

- Unload all wall and base cabinets, clear all countertops and walls, and remove all of these items from the kitchen area before the day we start.
- Help us protect your children by keeping them away from dangerous power tools.
- Secure any pets away from access areas such as halls, basements, utility rooms, etc.
- Review the plans and specifications. The work will be done exactly as outlined in the plans and specifications.
- Authorize an adult to be on the premises while the job is in progress and/or make a key available for access to the premises. We will need a security code if the alarm system will be activated.
- Review your contract for the payment schedule. We have enclosed a pre-addressed envelope for your convenience.

As we begin the project, I hope you will call me for assistance if there are any questions, at any time: [office/cell/e-mail information].

Our clients are our most valuable asset. We appreciate your business and look forward to serving you.

Very truly yours,

FINISHING UP THE JOB: WHAT WARRANTY ARE YOU OFFERING?

Interpreting the U.S. Magnusen-Moss Warranty Act

In the United States, the Magnusen-Moss Warranty Act is a comprehensive procedure dictating how warranties can be offered to consumers.

For Canadian dealers, there is no equivalent of the Magnusen-Moss Warranty Act governing the content of manufacturers' warranties (except for specific product categories, such as motor vehicles). All dealers in the United States and Canada should take the time to read and understand suppliers' warranties to be aware of what you may be required to do.

Review manufacturers' warranties and the warranty you plan to offer with your legal counsel.

Definitions

- **Full Warranty:** These are summaries of the federal minimum standards which permit a written warranty to be designated as a "full" warranty:

    1. The warrantor must remedy the problem without charge in a reasonable time to conform with the terms of the written warranty.

    2. A warrantor may not impose any limitations on the duration of any implied warranty on the product.

    3. A warrantor may not exclude or limit the damages for breach of the warranty unless the exclusion of limitation conspicuously appears on the warranty.

    4. After a reasonable number of attempts by the warrantor to remedy defects or malfunctions in the product, the consumer is allowed to elect either a refund or replacement without charge for the product. If the warrantor replaces a component part of a product, the replacement includes installing the part without charge.

- **Limited Warranty:** Any warranty failing to meet any of the four previously listed standards must be classified as a "limited warranty." The Act does permit the Federal Trade Commission to develop rules for extending a warranty when the consumer has been denied the full service of the product.

- **Implied Warranty:** Created by law in all 50 states, it means a product will do what it is supposed to do. (In all but seven states, a seller may negate the implied warranty by declaring in writing that a product is sold "as is" with no warranty.)

PARTNERING WITH YOUR MANUFACTURER'S REPRESENTATIVE

It is customary in our industry to ask a manufacturer's representative to visit a jobsite. At times, this visit allows the dealer/designer to show the rep an innovative and beautiful project.

More often, a visit is a result of unresolved matters involving the clarification—and differentiation—between product quality, specifications and warranty replacement work. Additionally, from time to time, a dealer will request a field inspection by a rep to help find a solution to a product a consumer feels needs replacement and the dealer knows is within acceptable industry standards.

Unresolved matters involving quality issues and other concerns precipitate the need of a field inspection by the rep. The dealer and designers are responsible for in-depth product knowledge and for presenting the product accurately. The dealer or client's agent is also responsible for insuring the products were installed according to the manufacturer's recommendation and the standards of the industry. The manufacturer's rep should resolve only quality issues directly attributable to product.

The Goal of the Field Inspection is to End Up With a Completed Job and a Happy Customer

Have clear agreement about the roles the dealer principal/designer and manufacturer's rep will each play during such a call. This helps reach the desired result.

First, fully inform your rep of the situation. Give him or her as many details as possible before visiting the jobsite. Tell the rep everything—from how the customers were to work with to how much money they still owe you. For example, as John K. Morgan reported in a *Kitchen & Bath Design News* article in October, 2002:

> *"If one of my customers tells me that the drawers are binding when opened and closed, as a rep, I know to check out the drawer issue with the factory prior to the visit. If the drawers are binding, chances are that when I call into the plant they will already have seen a similar occurrence and have a ready solution. If it is a new issue, it gives the manufacturer time to research it and advise me as to what path we need to follow to try to find a solution. It is important to show up prepared."*

Either the design firm's representative or the manufacturer's rep should arrive at the jobsite early.

- **Tenet No. 1:** The manufacturer's rep should never visit the jobsite without the dealer representative. You—the dealer— need to see and hear everything discussed.

  This tenet includes not just jobsite visits—but telephone calls, e-mails and other types of communication. You, the dealer, should be included in all forms of communication about the issue.

- **Tenet No. 2:** The manufacturer's rep is just that—a manufacturer's representative. His or her focus is on the product and whether or not it conforms to the manufacturer's standards and was installed according to manufacturer guidelines. John Morgan, again, gives us an excellent example:

"If a customer is concerned about warped doors, I show up with a level. I look for shims to see if they were installed properly. If the complaint is cabinets are out-of-square, I walk into the door with a square in hand. I am prepared to find and report quality issues that are genuinely attributable to the manufacturer."

"The client that has not been managed well by the dealer and has unrealistic quality expectations around a product should be immediately referred back to the dealer. The rep's sole focus is to report issues that concern his/her product, complaints based on other products or poor installation are not the manufacturer representative's responsibility."

- **Tenet No. 3:** The manufacturer's rep is not carrying "a checkbook." Be aware it is not uncommon for the consumer to assume that there is a "deal" (discount, rebate, free product) to be had. As leverage, this type of consumer may start out by pointing out every conceivable imperfection. Or, may ask for a resolution one issue at a time.

A good rep first records everything he or she observes, as well as all issues raised by the client. The rep never addresses them one by one! Why is this so important? If at all possible, a product replacement or repair—not money—should be the solution. It is much more beneficial to the manufacturer to have a satisfied customer than it is to have the customer live with a cabinet he or she is not happy with—but has received a credit for.

- **Tenet No. 4:** The manufacturer's rep, the dealer and the installer are all teammates. A conference should be held before the visit, and discussions held away from the jobsite if there is an issue of shared responsibility for the quality issue raised by the client.

THE IMPORTANCE
OF JOB COSTING

Scrutinizing job costs can lead to business changes that result in increased profits. (See page 161 for a cost discrepancy form.)

THE IMPORTANCE OF JOB COSTING

(Source: *33 Ways to Boost Cash Flow in Your Kitchen and Bathroom Business, The Great Cash Hunt*, by Stephen P. Vlachos, CKD, CBD, and Leslie L. Vlachos, M.Ed)

Not too many years ago, job costing was a daunting task. Matching up invoices, purchase orders and sale slips was all done by hand and involved piles of paper. Today, there are a number of software programs that make our lives easier. However, it is amazing how many kitchen and bathroom dealers do not bother to job cost. It is like walking a tightrope without a net!

Job costing is critical to a successful business.

- It is identifying every cost related to a job and comparing it to the estimate so you can determine exactly what the total job cost is and, therefore, what your profit is.

- Remember, relying solely on your monthly P&L to tell you whether or not you've made money only masks where the problems are that are limiting your profit.

- One of the most overlooked items in any job costing is the time factor. Maintaining daily time records is critical so you know how much time you've spent on that project from a planning and estimating stage. For any hourly employee, it is equally important that their time be posted to the job.

- Job comparative costs should be posted as invoices are received, with an explanation requested if the actual invoice differs from the estimate by an agreed-to percentage factor.

- Job costs should be scrutinized on a monthly basis to look for areas where money is being lost.

COST DISCREPANCY REPORT

Job Name:	Date:
Item in Question:	
Item Cost on Purchase Order:	
Item Cost on Vendor Invoice:	
Difference Between Anticipated Cost and Amount Invoiced:	
Explanation / Action to be Taken:	
Signature:	

COST DISCREPANCY REPORT

Job Name:	Date:
Item in Question:	
Item Cost on Purchase Order:	
Item Cost on Vendor Invoice:	
Difference Between Anticipated Cost and Amount Invoiced:	
Explanation / Action to be Taken:	
Signature:	

David Newton, a respected industry leader and key educator affiliated with NKBA, translated the concept of total quality management to the kitchen and bath business in an NKBA publication some time ago. He shares a story of how a kitchen dealer can employ the principles of process improvement.

THE STORY

Three years ago, Helen and Beth formed Unique Kitchens, Inc., a small kitchen and bath design/sales firm. They have an excellent relationship with several local high-end cabinet, appliance and plumbing distributors. A draftsperson (Judith) and a delivery man (Larry) round out the staff of four. Two subcontractors provide installation.

Last month Helen and Beth's accountant noticed that the profit on one high-end cabinet line was below the standard markup that Unique Kitchens, Inc. needed to remain profitable. The team met with the accountant, a representative from Martin Distributing (the supplier of the high-end cabinet line) and the installers.

The accountant identified several small entries on the ledger for Martin Distributing Company. Ray, Martin's representative, produced the invoices for the first quarter. Many of the invoices were for only a minor amount, but when totaled, added up to approximately 6% to 7% of the total sales. The minor invoices were typically for items that needed to be field-installed, such as finished end panels, molding, toe base, hardware and some accessories. The installers admitted that they had called on several occasions to add items missing from the cabinet orders, but present on the installation drawings.

Larry, the deliveryman, talked with the installers, then called Ray to order the missing parts. Ray, understanding the urgency, asked for next day delivery from the manufacturer. The next day, UPS would deliver the missing parts to Unique Kitchens, Inc. Larry then would deliver the parts to the jobsite.

THE LOST PROFITS

> Any one job would create the following additional charges:
>
> - Missing Parts (which appear on invoices)
> - UPS Next Day Air Charges (which appear on invoices)
> - Larry's Extra Trip*
> - Installers Extra Charges*
>
> (*Do not appear on cost recap but reduces profits.)

Fortunately, the client was never aware of the delay and was not inconvenienced. But we cannot always be this lucky.

The team meeting was not used to place blame, but rather to identify and solve this continuous problem. First, the team identified the problem.

THE ANALYSIS

Now it was critical to find a way to prevent the problem from reappearing. Based on the facts presented, the following was determined:

- Larry, empowered to solve delivery problems, acted correctly to prevent inconvenience to the client.

- The installers charged a reasonable price for their additional time, and completed the job to meet the client's expectations.

- Ray was quick in responding to Larry's request for additional product. And Ray was correct in charging for the missing product.

THE PROBLEM

So, what happened? Judith, the draftsperson, did an excellent job in producing elegant drawings. Her drawings, however, did not indicate finished end panels where applicable. And her molding was stacked using three pieces of molding, but it appeared as only two pieces. The cutlery divider, cutting board and bread box were also missing from the original order, and were part of the special rush order along with the end panels and extra molding. Through a team effort, the problems were identified and actions were suggested to prevent the problem from recurring.

- The missing accessories were not ordered because a standard 3-DB-18 was ordered instead of a 3-DB-18-S, which included the accessories. Action Taken: The team suggested that each order be cross-checked in the future.

- The finished end panels for this cabinet line are now an additional cost and must be ordered separately. This was a recent change from the manufacturer, and notification was sent through a Product Information Bulletin (PIB) about three weeks ago. Action Taken: Beth will be in charge of posting all PIBs for a six-month period of time. All team members will read and check off on the PIB.

- The drawing showing the molding was not clear. Action Taken: The additional drawing of molding detail should be included on all plans in the future. It was suggested that a scale of 1 inch equals 1 foot be used for clarity whenever possible.

During the problem identification phase for Unique Kitchens, Inc., a cabinet flow chart was used to identify the normal flow for the cabinet order process. A second chart highlights the additional procedures needed when a problem develops combined with the typical flow chart.

Normal Cabinet Flow Chart

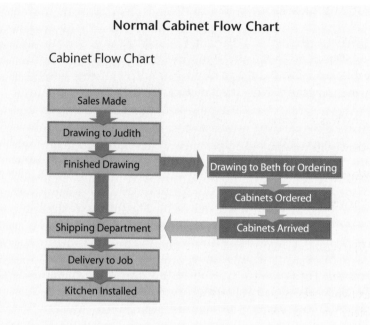

Cabinet Flow Chart

Cabinet Flow Chart with Additional Procedures Required

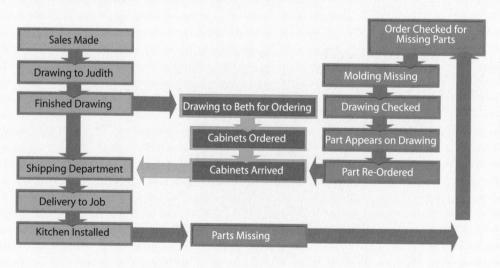

Cabinet Flow Chart

THE CAUSE OF THE PROBLEM

By visually illustrating the additional time spent to order the needed material, we see where elimination of problems can save Unique Kitchens, Inc. a great deal of time and money. Another tool used by the company was the process of asking at least five questions.

1. Why was the molding missing from the order?

   Answer: It was not ordered.

2. Why was the molding not ordered?

   Answer: It did not appear on the drawing when Beth made out the order.

3. Why did it not appear on the drawing by Judith?

   Answer: The drawing was a perspective view, and it appeared as two pieces of molding, rather than the three, so the third piece was not ordered.

4. How can we illustrate this better to prevent a reoccurrence of this problem?

   Answer: A profile drawing in a scale of 1 inch equals 1 foot would make the drawing clear and better identify the three pieces needed for the molding. Alternatively, a full set of project elevations should accompany the floor plan and perspective.

5. What action will we take immediately?

   Answer: Effective today, Judith will add an enlarged view to all drawings involving molding or any special details whenever possible, using a scale of 1 inch equals 1 foot. Effective today, all floor plans will be accompanied by scaled, accurate elevations.

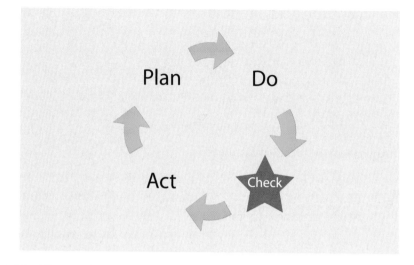

Take Time to Solve Problems

A good manager schedules time to tackle problems.

A good manager also is aware of other problem-solving roadblocks, and works hard to make sure they do not "derail" his or her efforts to eliminate profit draining problems from the installation.

WHAT CAN DERAIL PROBLEM-SOLVING EFFORTS?

Not devoting enough time to:

- Get the team "on board"
- Hold team meetings
- Listen
- Allow everyone to respond

WHAT ARE OTHER PROBLEM-SOLVING PITFALLS?

- Failing to publicize early successes; regardless of size
- Manager's reluctance to empower employees
- Lack of finances or resource commitment
- Teams not working together/not reaching a consensus
- Individual needs taking precedence over the team or company needs
- Management disagreements (owners disagreements/family differences)
- Lack of understanding the task at hand/the definition of quality

CLIENT EVALUATION

Sometimes you just cannot seem to satisfy the client once the job starts. Next time, look for signs of trouble during the planning process.

In a speech he delivered during the Remodeling Show in October, 2004, Case Design/Remodeling president Mark Richardson outlined "criteria" that remodelers should follow in order to find clients who will allow their companies to "maximize profit and reduce risk." Here are some highlights from the session. (Excerpted from *Remodeling* magazine, January, 2005)

- **Does the client have past remodeling experience?** Those who do usually have a more realistic perspective. Those who do not will require more education about the remodeling process.

- **Is the client honest?** If a homeowner balks at pulling a permit, walk away.

- **Will the client let your company control the job?** Without that control, "chances are you'll never be able to make money," Richardson warns.

- **How do they communicate?** If spouses disagree about a project's direction, "you can get caught in that valley."

- **Is the client emotionally stable?** Richardson says remodelers need to be particularly wary of homeowners with unpredictable mood swings.

"The issue is not to blackball people," Richardson says. "But you need to get a 'yes' to all of these criteria. If you get 'no' or 'maybe,' you need to fix it or walk away."

Richardson notes that remodelers should be honest with themselves, too, and not get pushed into projects that fall outside the scope of the work they typically handle (for example, a suburban-focus remodeler taking on an urban project) or are larger than their operations can manage.

Richardson is a big believer in following policies and processes to ensure consistent profit. "The more you can get into a formula and process, the better."

411

CHAPTER 12: The Future of Your Business

Congratulations—your small business is running very nicely. You have incorporated many of the activities suggested to help make your business stronger financially, better managed in all aspects, and, most importantly, you are having more fun. Perhaps you are working fewer hours and earning more dollars. Your people are the best and you are on "cruise control."

This is all good, but you cannot rest on your laurels—you cannot afford to stay the same. Most experts say that your business is either growing, moving ahead and getting stronger, or it is starting to slip. It cannot stay the same. Therefore, now the challenge is to continue to grow and strengthen your business. Start thinking about an exit strategy. After investing so much money, time and talent into the business, you do not want to watch it slip backwards.

GROWTH AND CONTINUITY

Business Style

You have picked your niche—middle to higher-end kitchen and bath products. Your customer base is a healthy split between homeowners, custom home builders and high-end remodel contractors. You have grown sales revenues to almost $3 million, and your margin has been over 40% for the past several years. Your "team" is stronger. They are talented, loyal, hard-working, productive and, consequently, are well compensated. Your "brand" is that of a design/build firm. So, where can you go from here?

Controlled Growth

One option is to open a second store on the other side of town (where there is a lot of new growth) or in a town 35 miles away where the only other kitchen and bath dealer is not very strong. You know what it takes to be successful, so you can replicate it in a new area.

A second choice is to add more products or services to your present offering. Why not try to become a true one-stop shopping store? You have enough property (yes, you own the property) that you could add another 2,000 or 3,000 square feet. You could add lighting, tile, appliances, flooring, doors and windows and door hardware. This would mean that your clients do not need to go anywhere else—you would show, and sell, it all. You already have the infrastructure in-place with systems, policies and procedures. Learning these new products would not be all that tough and, by adding just a couple more employees, you could truly become unique. Your forecasts suggest you can grow revenues by one-third while maintaining 40% + gross profit margins.

Third, add new services to your organization. Rather than subcontracting exterior addition work, you may expand your installation team to be able to handle this type of work.

Planning for Growth

Approach your controlled growth following the exact pattern you have already developed. Prepare a detailed three- to five-year business plan, including all the sections discussed previously. After the financial, cash flow and people projections, complete your market research, timeline and financing requirements.

Truth be told, you have done such a good job reinventing your present business, you are just a tad bored and are ready for an exciting new challenge. You know any one of the above growth projects would be a three- to five-year process and, by then, you will be giving serious thought to your personal exit strategy. And the good news is—you will have added to the net worth/value of your business.

PLANNING YOUR EXIT STRATEGY

Almost every good business advisor will tell you to start planning your exit strategy the day you start or take over your business. Thinking about how you will leave the business starts on day one! Of course, very few kitchen and bath owners ever give any thought to this unless, of course, they just had a string of unbelievably bad days and they never want to hear of or see the business again.

So, just how do you start to plan your exit from the business?

Succession Planning

No one likes to think about their death or that they might become incapacitated in some way. But, should this happen to you—without a plan—what would happen to your business, to your family? Succession planning is your way to ensure the continued viability of your vision and, therefore, should be part of any small business plan. You need not only to create a succession plan for your own sake, but it is something you owe your employees, vendors, family and/or investors. They all depend on your business, to some extent, for their livelihood.

Succession planning is the process whereby replacements are identified and groomed, not only for the "top spot," but for other key positions as well.

As you start to create a succession plan, you will need to answer these three questions:

- First, what is your vision for the future of the business in your absence?

- Second, who can best implement that vision?

- Finally, what plan can you create to see that the vision is carried out?

Whatever plan you create needs to be memorialized in two places: it should become part of the operating agreement of the business; and, if ownership shares are being transferred, it must be detailed in your Will or Living Trust.

If continuing the business is appropriate, you need to decide who is capable of replacing the person in question, be it yourself or someone else. You and your team have duties. Who can best handle these duties? Do not try to clone yourself—just try to identify someone who can step in and lead. Examine skills, personality, leadership ability, work ethic and intelligence.

Once you have identified the person who you think would be the best candidate to fill the position—speak with him or her about this and get their perspective. Find out if the person really wants to take over the position. If the answer is yes—start immediately coaching and mentoring him or her in everything they will need to know.

And, last—but not least—put your succession plan in writing so that there will be no mistake regarding what you want.

The Exit Strategy
- Independent home-based business—close business, retire to second career.
- The practice. Sell business to senior sales associate, work as contributing designer and landlord.
- Sell business and property to new owner with staff in place. Retire to yacht.

Selling Your Business

Maybe you have decided to sell the business. You were unable to locate a suitable successor, or you want to reap the benefits of your hard labor, or it is simply time for you to move on. A business sale requires forethought because it is a complicated, time-consuming transaction. Finding qualified buyers, going through your books and inspections, transferring real estate and closing the deal can take a long time, perhaps a year or more. So, to make sure you actually are able to find a viable buyer and close in a reasonable amount of time—a few tips are in order.

- **Get your ducks in row.** Like the sale of a home, the sale of a business requires that you increase the curb appeal, among other things. Do everything possible to make the business show well.

- **Get a business valuation.** Too many kitchen and bath dealers over-estimate the value of the business, especially the good will, thinking it is worth more than it is. It is wise, then, to pay for a professional business valuation early in the process so that you know what to expect and will be able to honestly evaluate any offers you may receive. The value of your business is based upon its profitability, goodwill, assets and liabilities.

- **Get your books in order.** One reason buyers purchase existing businesses is because they want to reduce their risk, and the only way they can see whether your business is "risky" or "safe" is by looking at your books. All records—profit and loss statements, balance sheets, tax returns, contracts, permits, leases—everything—need to be in order.

- **Boost your profits.** People buy existing businesses because they are profitable. It follows, then, that one of the best things you can do to ensure a lucrative sale is to increase sales and profits—to the extent possible. Many small business owners work hard to show the smallest possible profit before tax so that their tax consequences are minimized. If you are contemplating the sale of your business, you need to maximize the profit before taxes—for at least three years—so you can maximize the selling price.

- **Speak with your advisors.** Your attorney and accountant should have some good advice about the sale of your business—they may even know of some potential buyers. In any case, use these professionals throughout the selling process.

- **Use a business broker.** You have decided to sell. You have spruced up the business. The books are in good order. Earnings have been good. Now, where do you find a buyer? You can run ads in the classified section of newspapers and magazines, or you can utilize the Internet. But finding a buyer and having help through the selling process are two different things. Business brokers are like real estate agents—they find buyers, and they help you through the whole process. They are not cheap (since they are usually paid a percentage of the sales price), but they can provide an invaluable service in helping make a sale happen.

- **Determine the price.** How much should you expect to get for your business? When it comes to price, there are four questions to answer:

  1. **What does the business own?** A business with assets is obviously more valuable than a business without.

  2. **What does the business owe?** The value of your business is offset by its liabilities. Less is more, of course.

  3. **What is the business' profitability?** Again, the same principle applies; bigger profit equals bigger price.

  4. **What about the intangibles?** What makes the business unique? Do you have a great location, favorable lease, or experienced, talented employees? These all make a difference.

These four items determine the value of your business. There are several methods of doing this. Seek professional help in this area.

Mergers and Acquisition

When selling your business—do not ignore the possibility of merging with or selling to a competitor. What your business might bring to another business could be the "perfect fit." The two merged businesses just might compliment each other beautifully in products, services and people. The 1980s and 1990s saw more business mergers than anytime in United States history.

So, you can see that having a well-planned and timed exit strategy is very important—to you, your family, your employees, your vendor partners and, of course, your clientele. Do not wait—start now.

WHAT DOES THE FUTURE HOLD?

This is probably the hardest question of all. Nobody can foretell the future.

Suffice it to say, people will always need kitchens and baths. Most likely, they will continue to be two of the most important rooms in the home. All projections indicate that luxury products (i.e., the nicer things) will continue to be in demand for many years to come.

Certainly styles, colors, finishes and layouts will change and evolve—but kitchens and baths are personal spaces. And they are high-ticket items. People want to see and touch the products they will be buying. They will continue to need the personal attention that today's kitchen and bath businesses are able to render. It follows that there will always be a niche for the small, local entrepreneurial kitchen and bath dealership.

- Clients may eventually force dealers to offer one-stop shopping and one-stop services. It will be those kitchen and bath dealers who respond the fastest and best to the demand that will be the winners.

- There is no question that technology will continue to grow, expand and change. Will there be virtual reality showrooms? Maybe, but clients will still want the personalized services that our industry offers.

- The opportunity for the smaller, service-minded kitchen and bath dealer to win a fair share of the market will continue to be there.

One of the most exciting communications, information transfer and business developments in recent memory is the Internet. For a small business, the Internet can be one of the most effective innovations to come along in years. Why? The Internet can give your small business access to a "worldwide" marketplace.

Customers of today (and tomorrow) are using the Internet to learn all they can about products they will be using in kitchen and bath projects. They probably go to the Internet before the Yellow Pages to research what businesses are out there, where they are located and what products and services they offer. So, we strongly believe that you need a professionally designed, all-inclusive website that describes—in detail (and with pictures)—exactly what your business offers. Clients are not buying kitchens and baths on the Internet—yet, but it is only a matter of time before virtual showroom tours and whole packages can be handled on line. Be a leader and be proactive in this important area.

The future is in your hands. If you want to survive and thrive you will have to become complete business managers. Hopefully this book has helped you to become just that.

The National Kitchen & Bath Association has recently updated its extensive Business Management Forms System, available to its members. Representative samples of the forms are shown here and on the next page.

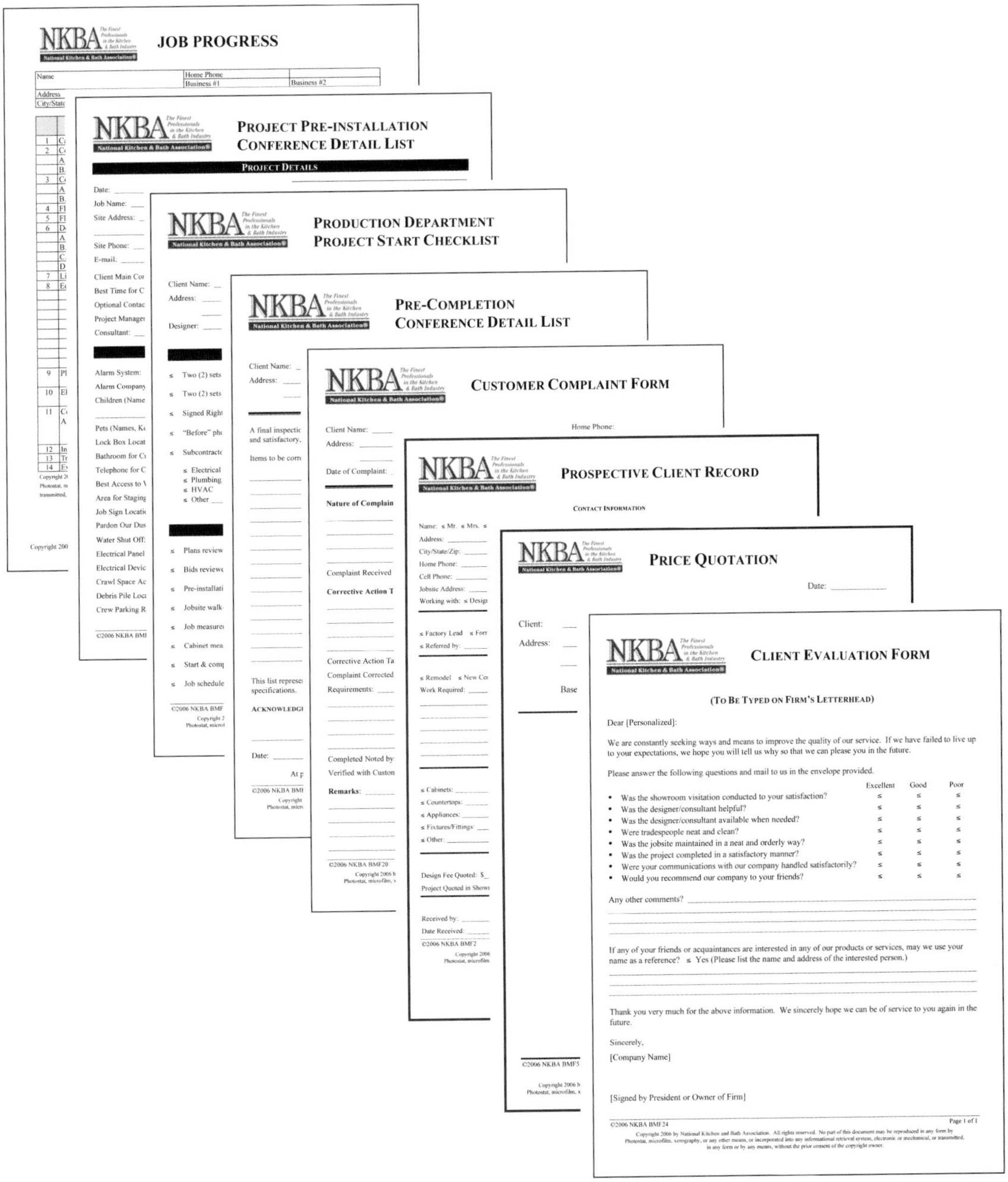

These forms provide systems for lead tracking, quotations, estimates, surveys, specifications, contracts, change orders, plus job progress, service, completion and follow-up. For more information on the NKBA Business Management Forms System, contact NKBA at 800-843-6522.

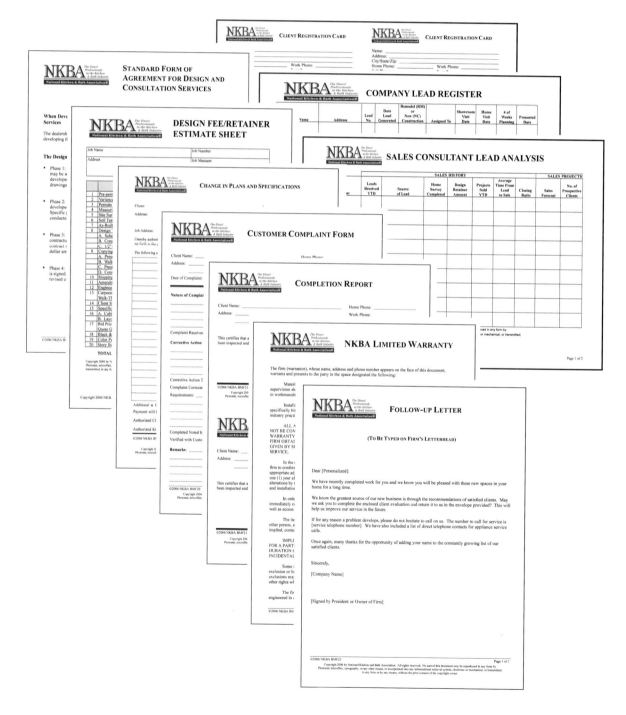